OXFORD WORLD'S CLASSICS

THE POETIC EDDA

THE collection of Norse–Icelandic mythological and heroic poetry known as the *Poetic Edda* contains the great narratives of the creation of the world and the coming of Ragnarok, the Doom of the Gods. The mythological poems explore the wisdom of the gods and giants and narrate the adventures of the god Thor against the hostile giants and the gods' rivalries amongst themselves. The heroic poems trace the exploits of the hero Helgi and his valkyrie bride, the tragic tale of Sigurd and Brynhild's doomed love, and the terrible drama of Gudrun, daughter of Giuki, Sigurd's widow, and her children. Most of the poems exist in a single manuscript written in Iceland around 1270, but many of them pre-date the conversion of Scandinavia to Christianity and allow us to glimpse the pagan beliefs of the North.

CAROLYNE LARRINGTON is a Fellow and Tutor in medieval English at St John's College, Oxford. She co-edited *The Poetic Edda: Essays on the Mythological Poetry* (2002) with Professor Paul Acker of the University of St Louis, and now the follow-up volume *Revisiting the Poetic Edda: Essays on Old Norse Heroic Legend* (2013). She is the author of more than twenty articles on Old Norse literature, a book: *A Store of Common Sense: Gnomic Themes and Styles in Old Icelandic and Old English Wisdom Poetry* (1993), and she also co-edited the neo-eddic poem *Sólarljóð* for the Skaldic Poetry of the Scandinavian Middle Ages series. With Judy Quinn she founded the Eddic Research Network and is a member of its Steering Group.

OXFORD WORLD'S CLASSICS

*For over 100 years Oxford World's Classics have brought
readers closer to the world's great literature. Now with over 700
titles—from the 4,000-year-old myths of Mesopotamia to the
twentieth century's greatest novels—the series makes available
lesser-known as well as celebrated writing.*

*The pocket-sized hardbacks of the early years contained
introductions by Virginia Woolf, T. S. Eliot, Graham Greene,
and other literary figures which enriched the experience of reading.
Today the series is recognized for its fine scholarship and
reliability in texts that span world literature, drama and poetry,
religion, philosophy, and politics. Each edition includes perceptive
commentary and essential background information to meet the
changing needs of readers.*

OXFORD WORLD'S CLASSICS

The Poetic Edda

Translated with an Introduction and Notes by
CAROLYNE LARRINGTON

REVISED EDITION

OXFORD
UNIVERSITY PRESS

OXFORD
UNIVERSITY PRESS

Great Clarendon Street, Oxford, OX2 6DP,
United Kingdom

Oxford University Press is a department of the University of Oxford.
It furthers the University's objective of excellence in research, scholarship,
and education by publishing worldwide. Oxford is a registered trade mark of
Oxford University Press in the UK and in certain other countries

© Carolyne Larrington 1996, 2014

The moral rights of the author have been asserted

First published as a World's Classics paperback 1996
Reissued as an Oxford World's Classics paperback 1999, 2008
Revised edition 2014
Impression: 1

Published in the United States of America by Oxford University Press
198 Madison Avenue, New York, NY 10016, United States of America

British Library Cataloguing in Publication Data

Data available

Library of Congress Control Number: 2013956086

ISBN 978–0–19–967534–0

Printed in Great Britain by
Clays Ltd, St Ives plc

ACKNOWLEDGEMENTS

My first debt of gratitude is owed to the late Ursula Dronke, an inspirational teacher and scholar who first taught me Old Norse and introduced me to the poetry of the *Edda*; her own edition of the *Poetic Edda* is inspirational. Every scholar of the *Edda* owes a great debt to Anthony Faulkes, whose model translation of the *Snorra Edda* has been constantly at my elbow. Margaret Clunies Ross, Britt-Mari Näsström, Matthew Driscoll, Andrew Wawn, Paul Acker, Judy Quinn, and Beatrice La Farge all contributed in one way or another to the interpretations in the original volume.

In the almost twenty years since the first edition of this translation was published, eddic scholarship has blossomed. Klaus von See, Beatrice La Farge, Katja Schulz, and their colleagues at the Johann-Wolfgang-Goethe University in Frankfurt-am-Main are bringing to completion the multi-volume *Kommentar zu den Liedern der Edda*, a series which has shed new light on the history and complexity of eddic poetry, and which has been invaluable in my work on this new edition. Special thanks must go to Beatrice La Farge for sharing still unpublished material with me and to Peter Robinson who kindly supplied me with a PDF of his *Svipdagsmál* edition. Hannah Burrows (and the General Editors of the Skaldic Poetry of the Middle Ages) generously gave permission to use Hannah's edition of *The Waking of Angantyr*. All the scholars mentioned above have of course continued to shape my thinking about eddic poetry; to them should be added a lively and inspiring younger generation of Norse scholars: David Clark, Brittany Schorn, Jóhanna Katrín Friðriksdóttir, Hannah Burrows, Tom Birkett, and Michael Hart. Judith Jesch and Heather O'Donoghue have, as ever, offered encouragement. The Stofnun Árna Magnússonar in Iceland welcomed me to work on the final stages of this revision; and I owe colleagues and friends there, in particular its director Guðrún Nordal, a longstanding debt of thanks. And grateful thanks go to Ragnheiður Mósesdóttir and Matthew Driscoll for their hospitality in Reykjavik.

With Judy Quinn in particular, co-founder of the Eddic Network, I have shared eddic conversation for many years, and I owe more than I can express to her readiness to talk about eddic interests, and to her friendship.

FOR JOHN, AGAIN

CONTENTS

INTRODUCTION

THE old, one-eyed god Odin hangs nine days and nights on the windswept ash-tree Yggdrasill, sacrificing himself to himself; the red-bearded Thor swings his powerful hammer against the giant enemy; the ravening wolf Fenrir leaps forward to seize the Father of the Gods in his slavering jaws; the terrible passion of Brynhild for the dragon-slayer hero Sigurd culminates in her implacable demand for his murder—all these famous scenes from Old Norse myth and legend are vividly staged in the *Poetic Edda*. From the creation of the world out of the yawning void of Ginnungagap to the destruction of the gods in the mighty conflagration of Ragnarok, the poetry of the *Edda* gives some of the best evidence for the religious beliefs and the heroic ethics of the pagan North before its conversion to Christianity around the year 1000. Its stories are the interpretative key to modern depictions of northern myth and legend, in painting, sculpture, literature, film, computer games, and the operas of Richard Wagner, to list only a few of the *Edda*'s modern reflexes. These stories also formed the bedrock from which the complex and highly sophisticated court poetry of medieval Scandinavia sprang, composed in a poetic style which employs mythological and legendary material in its rhetoric of allusion.

The *Poetic Edda* is distinct from the famous Icelandic sagas, such as *Njals saga*, since these are written in prose and tell the stories of historical persons; however, some of its heroic themes are played out in works such as *Laxdæla saga* and *Gisla saga*. In an earlier form, the *Poetic Edda* is a major source for Snorri Sturluson's great mythographic treatise, the *Prose* or *Younger Edda*. As a body of heroic and mythological poetry, the *Poetic Edda* is comparable in scope to such great masterpieces of world literature as the Finnish *Kalevala*, Ovid's *Metamorphoses*, Hesiod's *Theogony*, or the *Mahabharata*; yet the *Edda*'s generic range, incorporating as it does comedy, satire, didactic verse, tragedy, high drama, and profoundly moving lament, surpasses all these. Despite this, the poetry is not difficult to understand: its language is neither obscure nor complex, but often strikingly simple and direct. Since the rediscovery of the *Poetic Edda* in the late seventeenth century, its themes have captured the imaginations of many artists: Thomas Gray, William Morris, W. H. Auden in Britain, Richard Wagner, August Strindberg, and Carl Larsson in Europe; the great Argentinian author, Jorge Luis Borges, was also inspired by eddic poetry. Fantasy writers, such as J. R. R. Tolkien, C. S. Lewis, and Alan Garner, have incorporated its themes and motifs into the worlds about which they write; the wolves and winter of Lewis's Narnia, Tolkien's dwarfs and dragons, and even the Weirdstone of Brisingamen owe their genesis to the poems in this collection.

The Codex Regius, the manuscript in which the *Poetic Edda* is preserved, is an unprepossessing-looking codex the size of a fat paperback, bound in brown with brownish vellum pages; it is in the care of the Arnamagnæan Institute in Reykjavik, and was, until recently, on display in the manuscript exhibition in the Culture House in Reykjavik. Most of the mythological and heroic poems it contains survive only in this single manuscript, abbreviated in what follows as manuscript R. In the 1270s, somewhere in Iceland, an unknown writer copied these poems, preserving them as a major source of information about Old Norse myth and legend, and as a majestic body of poetry. Six of the mythological poems are found wholly or in part in two other manuscripts, one of which is AM 748 4to (hereafter A). A good number of other poems in the eddic style are recorded elsewhere, very often inserted into prose narratives dealing with the exploits of legendary heroes. One of these poems, the *Waking of Angantyr*, has been added to this volume. During the *Poetic Edda*'s history, poems in eddic metre contained in other manuscripts have made their appearance in the canon. The mythological poems *Baldr's Dreams*, the *List of Rig*, the *Song of Hyndla*, and the broadly heroic *Song of Grotti*, are included here. Also added to this revised volume are two poems which may be characterized as neo-eddic: *Groa's Chant* and the *Sayings of Fjolsvinn*. These two poems are probably fourteenth century in origin; they imitate the style of earlier eddic verse and indicate the continuing importance of composition in the eddic style well after the introduction of Christian doctrine and Latin learning to Iceland. The *Waking of Angantyr*, an eddic poem preserved in *Hervarar saga ok Heidreks* (the *Saga of Hervor and Heidrek*), one which has fascinated poets and audiences from the eighteenth century onwards, and a second later version of the *Seeress's Prophecy* conclude the book.

Although the majority of the poems were recorded in the late thirteenth century, it is thought that most of the mythological verse and a few of the heroic poems pre-date the conversion of Scandinavia to Christianity in the late tenth century. No satisfactory method has yet been found to date the poems relative to one another, nor has it proved possible to localize them to Norway or Iceland. It has been argued that the description of the end of the world (Ragnarok) in the *Seeress's Prophecy* is reminiscent of volcanic eruption and hence may be Icelandic in origin, while the absence of wolves or bears in Iceland may point to a Norwegian homeland for poems in which these are mentioned, such as the *Sayings of the High One*, but even if Icelanders did not encounter wolves every day, they knew quite well what they were. In general, the mythological poems are thought to pre-date most of the heroic poems, though some of the latter, the *Lay of Hamdir* and the *Poem of Atli* in particular, are believed to be among the earliest eddic poems.

Why the name 'Edda'? Snorri Sturluson, an Icelandic author and historian who lived between 1179 and 1241, wrote a treatise on Norse poetry which he called an *edda*, a word whose etymology is uncertain but which clearly means 'poetics' where it occurs in fourteenth-century Icelandic. When Bishop Brynjolf Sveinsson presented a manuscript which had come into his possession to the Danish king in 1662—hence the name Codex Regius—he was well aware of its importance, for he had believed that the mythological poems which Snorri quoted from extensively in his *Edda* had been utterly lost. Thus Bishop Brynjolf connected his collection with the name 'Edda' found in Snorri, and assumed that the poems constituted part of that 'great body of human wisdom which Sæmund the Wise collected', as he wrote to a friend at the time. The famous Icelandic scholar Sæmund the Wise (1056–1133) had studied at Paris and was a byword for learning. Thus the contents of the Codex Regius came to be known, erroneously, as the *Sæmundar Edda*, or the *Elder Edda*, while Snorri's treatise (written before the Codex Regius was compiled) is known as the *Snorra Edda*, the *Prose Edda*, or the *Younger Edda*. The Codex Regius remained in Copenhagen until the principal Icelandic manuscripts began to be returned to Iceland in the early 1970s to be preserved in the Arnamagnæan Institute. Too precious to be risked in an aircraft at that time, the manuscript travelled back on a ship with a military escort, to be welcomed by crowds and public acclaim at the Reykjavik docks.

Snorri's Edda *and other related works*

In order to explain the many mythological and heroic allusions in Norse poetry Snorri set out, in a more or less systematic way, the main myths and heroic legends of the Scandinavians. His selection was no doubt affected by his primary purpose of clarifying poetic allusions but he was also concerned to provide an explanation for the Norse gods that fell in line with Christian orthodoxy. His *Prologue* thus explains the gods as refugees from Troy, able to dominate the inhabitants of Scandinavia through their superior wisdom, and if he knew the story of Odin's self-sacrifice from *Sayings of the High One*, with its disturbing parallels to the Crucifixion, he omitted it from his account.

It is probable, as Anthony Faulkes suggests, that the pagan religion was never systematically understood by those who practised it. Different areas of Scandinavia worshipped different gods at different times in the pre-Christian era; the localized nature of cults and rituals produced neither dogma nor sacred texts, as far as we know. Rather pre-Christian religion was 'a disorganized body of conflicting traditions that was probably never reduced in heathen times to a consistent orthodoxy such as Snorri attempts to present'.[1] Nevertheless, Snorri's *Edda* is the only near-contemporary account of Norse myth and legend beyond the *Poetic Edda*, and, as such, frequent reference will be made to it in this volume to throw light upon the allusions and obscurities in our poems. Two other texts will be referred to frequently in the Notes. One is *Ynglinga saga*, one of the constituent sagas in Snorri's great history of the kings of Norway, *Heimskringla* (*Circle of the World*). *Ynglinga saga* is the first saga in *Heimskringla* and thus contains much legendary and semi-mythological material. The other text is *Volsunga saga*, probably composed in the mid-thirteenth century, thus at much the same time as Snorri was writing and the Codex Regius was being compiled. *Volsunga saga* tells the full story of Sigurd the Dragon-slayer, and that of his ancestors and descendants. In part it is based on eddic poems, but here and there it has new information, and is invaluable for filling in the great gap in the *Poetic Edda* caused by some missing leaves between the *Lay of Sigrdrifa* and the *Fragment of a Poem about Sigurd*. Details of these, and other relevant texts, are given in the Select Bibliography.

[1] Snorri Sturluson, *Edda: Prologue and Gylfaginning*, ed. A. Faulkes (London, 988), p. xxvii.

The Old Norse cosmos

In explaining the mythological background of the eddic poetry the modern scholar faces the same difficulties which Snorri Sturluson had to try to overcome in his *Edda*. A body of myths, often contradictory, incomplete, or obscure, has to be synthesized into a logical system. Just as Snorri could not help but be influenced by his Christian beliefs in his account—to the extent of providing an analogue to Noah's Flood in his version of the early history of the world—so we cannot now read the *Poetic Edda* without using Snorri to clarify and explain. In what follows, I offer a synthesis of Snorri, eddic poetry, and certain skaldic verse which makes use of mythological motifs. The picture given is misleading in its coherence and clarity, yet essential for the understanding of the poems.

In the beginning there was only a chaos of unformed matter. In some poems the world is formed out of the body of Ymir, the primeval being, who is dismembered by the gods; in others the gods raise the earth out of the sea. The gods are descended from the giants: Odin and his mysterious brothers, Vili and Ve, are the sons of Bor, grandsons of Buri, who, according to Snorri, was licked out of the primeval ice by the cow Audhumla. The sun and moon are placed in the sky and time begins. The gods construct the home of the gods (Asgard) and a world for men (Midgard), and then they create the dwarfs who live in the earth and work in metal, followed by humankind. The first man and woman are created from driftwood found on the shore. Hereafter, unlike in Greek myth for example, humanity plays little part in the gods' adventures. Now divine history begins. The main tribe of gods, the Æsir, is visited by a female figure, Gullveig, probably a type of the goddess Freyia, who practises *seid*, a disreputable kind of shape-changing magic. The Æsir burn Gullveig three times but she is always reborn, and goes about among humans teaching them her magic. Possibly as a result of their mistreatment of Gullveig, the Æsir are challenged by another tribe, the Vanir, who demand a share of the sacrifices made to the gods and war breaks out. The Vanir seem to be undefeatable, and so peace is negotiated and hostages are exchanged: the fertility deities, Freyr, Freyia, and their father, the sea-god Niord, come to live among the Æsir permanently. To the Vanir are sent Hænir and Mimir. Hænir annoys the Vanir by refusing to participate in discussion and by constantly asking Mimir for his opinion, so the Vanir cut off Mimir's head, preserve it, and send it with Hænir back to the Æsir (*Ynglinga saga*, ch. 4).

In the centre of the universe is Yggdrasill, the World-Ash whose roots go far down below the earth. At their tips are the worlds of the dead, the hall of Hel, and the domain of the frost-giants. Beneath the tree are sacred wells which impart wisdom; these are presided over by the fates and can be reached by the rainbow bridge, Bifrost. Circling the world is the Ocean in which lurks the Midgard-serpent, a monstrous serpent which will attack the gods at the end of the world (Ragnarok). The gods possess many palaces (catalogued in *Grimnir's Sayings*); an important building in Asgard is Valhall (Valhalla) where Odin assembles dead heroes in preparation for the final battle at Ragnarok.

Gods and goddesses

The Æsir are: Odin, the chief of the gods, deity of war, poetry, trickery, and wisdom. In the *Poetic Edda* Odin is to be found as a wanderer, disguised as a one-eyed old man obsessively seeking out wisdom, challenging it in others, or verifying the inescapable events of Ragnarok. Odin appears occasionally in the heroic poetry as a patron of human heroes, watching their progress and sizing them up for a place in Valhalla. Odin's red-bearded son Thor is patron of farmers and sailors. Armed with his mighty hammer, Miollnir, he fights against the giants; though strong, he is sometimes foolish. Tyr is the god of justice; he is one-handed because he placed his hand in the jaws of the wolf Fenrir, as a pledge of good faith when the gods were trying to bind the monster with a deceptively weak-looking magic fetter. Scenting treachery, Fenrir only agreed on condition that one of the gods place his hand in his mouth, and when the magic bonds tightened on Fenrir, Tyr's hand was snapped off.[2] Loki is a strangely ambivalent figure, son of a giant and foster-brother of Odin. His loyalties lie sometimes with the gods, sometimes with the giants. In certain myths he does his best to get the gods out of trouble—trouble he often got them into in the first place—but in the story of the death of Baldr and the events which follow, his sympathies are clearly aligned with the giants and at Ragnarok he will fight on their side. Loki is

---

[2] Snorri Sturluson, *Edda*, trans. A. Faulkes (London, 1987), 28.

capable of shape-changing and fathered monsters on the giantess Angrboda. These are Fenrir the wolf, the Midgard-serpent, and Hel, goddess of death, who, according to Snorri, is half corpse-blue, half human pink.

Baldr, son of Odin and Frigg, is the most beautiful and most beloved of the gods. Through the machinations of Loki he is killed by his blind brother, Hod, with a mistletoe dart, and goes down to Hel. He will return after Ragnarok. Vali is born to avenge Baldr, while Vidar, another son of Odin, exists to avenge his father at Ragnarok by killing Fenrir. Other Æsir include Bragi, god of poetry, and Heimdall, watchman of the gods, who will blow his mighty Giallar-horn at the coming of Ragnarok, and whose hearing is lodged in the well of Mimir under Yggdrasill. Ull is patron of hunting, and shoots with a bow. More obscure figures, Vili and Ve, brothers of Odin whom Frigg takes as husbands when Odin is away, and Lodur, a god who seems to play some part in the creation of humanity, as well as Hænir, whose adventures among the Vanir are mentioned above, scarcely figure in the extant stories.

The goddesses (Asynior) are less prominent in the Norse myths than in some other European mythologies. Frigg is the chief female deity of the Æsir, married to Odin, and mainly figured as the suffering mother of Baldr. Gefion is a patroness of human kings; she created the Danish island of Sjælland by ploughing out Swedish land, leaving the lake which is now Lake Mälar in central Sweden whose outline matches the shape of Sjælland. Snorri lists many other goddesses, some of whom are simply personifications of abstract qualities, such as Var, goddess of pledges, who is invoked in a marriage ceremony in *Thrym's Poem*. Nanna is the virtuous wife of Baldr. Golden-haired Sif is married to Thor. Idunn possesses the apples of youthfulness which keep the gods from ageing.

The Vanir are Niord, a sea-god, and his children, Freyr and Freyia. Both these last are associated with fertility. Certain giant women are connected with the gods: Skadi, daughter of the giant Thiazi, comes to Asgard seeking compensation for her father's death. She agrees to make peace if she can conclude a marriage with one of the Æsir. Skadi hopes to marry Baldr, but she is tricked into marrying Niord. The marriage is not a success, and the two separate. Gerd, daughter of the giant Gymir, is wooed by Freyr's servant Skirnir on Freyr's behalf in the poem *Skirnir's Journey*. Although it is not clear in that poem that a marriage is contracted, Snorri tells us in his history of the kings of Norway, *Heimskringla*, that the couple had a child, Fiolnir. Freyia is married to Od, an obscure figure who may be a doublet of Odin. She is said to have many other lovers, including her own brother, Freyr.

Giants and other beings

The giants are the oldest inhabitants of the universe and thus possess much ancient wisdom which the gods covet. They live in the mountains to the east and are imagined both as hostile and bestial, particularly the frost-giants, and conversely as civil and cultivated, like the giant Ægir who feasts the gods in his hall. Giantesses especially may be hideous and haglike, little distinguished from troll-women, or radiantly lovely, like Freyr's beloved, Gerd. The gods are intermittently threatened by the giants, who use cunning to try to obtain various treasures or women from the gods. The gods in return often raid Giant-land to recover their stolen women and possessions; sometimes they win giant women or such valuable cultural property as the mead of poetry, a story to which Odin alludes in *Sayings of the High One*.

Other beings who inhabit the mythic world are elves, who are very little mentioned; they have been interpreted as the spirits of dead male ancestors, the counterparts of the *dísir*. These may be female ancestors or fertility spirits, and are often inimical to humans. Dwarfs are solely masculine and share some qualities with the giants. They work at smithing and produce ingenious treasures for the gods. Norns are figures of fate who may be present at a child's birth, prophesying his future, as in the *First Poem of Helgi Hundingsbani*. As determiners of fate, the norns are sometimes blamed when events go against human heroes or other mortal beings. Trolls and troll-women, monstrous, wicked, and often stupid creatures of folklore, live in the rocks. Valkyries have a double identity. In some poems they are envisaged as divine figures, women who serve mead to the dead warriors in Valhall, and who fulfil the will of Odin in overseeing battle and making sure that victory is awarded to the right man. Elsewhere some valkyries are clearly human in origin. When they fall in love with a hero they ensure victory for him, and eventually marry him. Tensions between the valkyrie bride's family or her defeated suitor and the chosen hero mean that their union is shortlived, despite the strength of their love. Shield-maidens are human girls who, scorning domesticity and female tasks, take up the warrior life; as such they overlap with valkyries. Swan-maidens apparently share some shield-maiden characteristics; they have swan cloaks which enable them to transform themselves into birds, as in Tchaikovsky's ballet *Swan Lake*. Swan-maidens are common in Northern European folklore and they appear fleetingly in the *Poem of Volund*.

Mythic history

Our main eddic source for the history of the gods is the poem the *Seeress's Prophecy* (*Voluspa*), a systematized and allusive account of the events which concern the gods. After the war between the Æsir and the Vanir the wall of Asgard is broken, and a wandering master-builder offers to repair it in a very short space of time, in exchange for the sun, the moon, and Freyia. If he takes any longer, he will forfeit his reward. The gods are confident that the task is impossible, but the smith has an unnaturally clever stallion to assist him and by the first day of winter it is clear that he will fulfil the contract. Loki is blamed for advising in favour of the bargain and so he changes himself into a mare and entices the stallion away. The smith loses his temper, revealing his giant nature; Thor strikes him down with his hammer, breaking the promises the gods had made to him. Within the text this breach of faith on the part of the gods seems to be the first step in a moral decline. The binding of Fenrir, with the attendant broken promise which causes Tyr to forfeit his hand, the death of Baldr, and the binding of Loki with the guts of his own son portend the destruction of the gods at Ragnarok (literally: the Doom of the Gods, though the word *rök* 'doom' is sometimes confused with *røkkr* 'twilight', most notably by Snorri, hence the alternative term 'Twilight of the Gods' or 'Götterdämmerung'). When the end comes, summer will disappear, winter will be vicious and constant. Then Yggdrasill will tremble, the fire- and frost-giants, with Loki at their head, will attack the gods. The first generation of gods will be destroyed and the earth collapse into the sea. However, the earth will rise again, and the younger generation of gods, and humans who have survived the catastrophe by hiding in Yggdrasill, will populate the world anew. Whether a new Golden Age returns, or whether the new world is much like the old, with a balance of good and evil, depends on how one reads the final verses of the *Seeress's Prophecy*.

Within the framework provided by the creation and Ragnarok, those adventures of the gods retold in the mythological poems occur. An exact chronology cannot be determined for them, but since Loki will free himself from his bonds at the onset of the catastrophe, those poems in which he actively assists the gods, such as *Thrym's Poem*, or *Loki's Quarrel*, in which he provokes them apparently beyond endurance, can be ordered in respect to one another in mythic time. Odin journeys through the worlds for varying purposes: he gathers and imparts human knowledge in *Sayings of the High One*, he contends in wisdom and confirms his apprehension of Ragnarok in *Vafthrudnir's Sayings*, and acts to overthrow King Geirrod in *Grimnir's Sayings*. Skirnir's wooing of Gerd for his master Freyr precedes the god's fight with the giant Beli, in which, lacking his sword, he kills his opponent with a deer-antler. Tyr and Thor bring Hymir's kettle back from Giant-land before Ægir's feast, during which Loki assails his fellow deities. The confrontation between Harbard (the disguised Odin) and Thor at the ferry, in which Harbard trounces his son in argument, and the failed attempt of the dwarf Alviss (All-wise) to marry Thor's daughter complete the mythological section of the Codex Regius.

Heroes

Forming a transition between the mythic and heroic poems is the story of Volund, the abused smith who takes a hideous revenge on his oppressor. Volund is known in Anglo-Saxon England as Wayland the smith; the Old English poem *Deor* alludes to some of the incidents recounted in the *Poem of Volund* and scenes from the tale are also illustrated on the eighth-century whalebone box known as the Franks Casket, preserved in the British Museum and in the Bargello in Florence.

The heroic poems of the *Edda* must originally have consisted of several different cycles about the individual heroes Helgi, Sigurd, Gunnar, and Hamdir. However, before the Codex Regius was compiled, much of the heroic poetry had already been loosely joined together in the story of the Volsungs: *Volsunga saga*, a prose version of these events containing some stanzas of eddic poetry, was probably compiled around 1250. Both in this text and in the Codex Regius sequence, Helgi remains a separate figure, scarcely integrated into the Volsung clan. He is a hero whose fate is determined by his involvement with Sigrun, a valkyrie who helps him to victory over his enemies, then marries him. Her choice of a husband embroils Helgi in family conflict and he has to fight off Sigrun's suitor to win her. Helgi dies as a result of his alliance with the valkyrie. Two different versions of the story of Helgi, slayer of Hunding, appear in the *Poetic Edda*: in the first, the poem concludes with Helgi's winning Sigrun's hand; in the second, Helgi is killed after the marriage by Sigrun's brother in revenge for Helgi's slaying of their father. In a variant of this pattern, equally embroiled in inter-generational feud, Helgi Hiorvardsson avenges the death of his maternal grandfather on King Hrodmar, a thwarted suitor of Helgi's mother. Helgi falls in battle against Hrodmar's son, having first bequeathed his valkyrie bride Svava to his brother. The name 'Helgi' means 'sacred' and at the end of *A Second Poem of Helgi Hundingsbani* the compiler tells us that Helgi and his lover were reborn as another couple, Helgi and Kara, whose story has not survived. There is little evidence for belief in reincarnation in what we know of Norse religion, but it seems clear that the role of Helgi, lover of the valkyrie, can be filled by different heroes whose history offers a variation on the basic narrative pattern.

The poems which follow the three Helgi poems trace the history of Sigurd, son of Sigmund, slayer of the dragon Fafnir, and possessor of the treasure-hoard which was later to become known as the Rhinegold. After various adventures, including betrothing himself to a valkyrie, Sigrdrifa, Sigurd arrives at the court of the Giukungs, where he marries Gudrun. Sigurd assists Gudrun's brother Gunnar to win the hand of Brynhild, another valkyrie, who at some stage has become identified with Sigurd's earlier fiancée. Brynhild has sworn only to marry the man who knows no fear; this is Sigurd, but he is now already bound to Gudrun. Sigurd magically exchanges appearances with Gunnar and rides through a wall of flame to Brynhild's side. The two sleep together for three nights, with a drawn sword between them to safeguard Brynhild's honour. Brynhild marries Gunnar, believing him to be the man who crossed the flame-wall. At some point (presumably in the poems contained in the missing leaves of the manuscript) Brynhild discovers the truth and incites Gunnar and his brother Hogni to kill Sigurd, claiming that he had in fact been her lover, despite the oaths he had sworn to Gunnar. After his death she commits suicide. Neither the compiler of the Codex Regius nor the author of *Volsunga saga* entirely succeeds in rationalizing the Sigurd material. In the *Edda* Sigurd becomes involved with one valkyrie, Sigrdrifa, whom he meets on the mountain Hindarfiall and who is never mentioned again; in *Volsunga saga* the author replaces Sigrdrifa with Brynhild, only to have Sigurd encounter her a second time at her foster-father's house. Thus Sigurd betroths himself twice to Brynhild before he meets Gudrun. The complications can only be resolved through the introduction of a magic potion, which causes Sigurd to forget his prior commitments to Brynhild entirely until he has won her for Gunnar.

Gudrun provides the link to the next instalment of the saga. Atli, originally the fourth-century leader Attila the Hun, is imagined to have been Brynhild's brother. After Sigurd's death Gudrun is unwillingly married to Atli, and so the new cycle begins. When he lures her brothers to his court and kills them for the treasure they had inherited from Sigurd, Gudrun murders him and her own sons by him in revenge. In the late poem *Oddrun's Lament*, yet another sibling is grafted onto the Brynhild–Atli family: Oddrun, who becomes Gunnar's lover after Brynhild's death. Atli's discovery of the affair here motivates Gunnar's murder: a motive found only in this poem and in *A Short Poem about Sigurd*, probably dependent on *Oddrun's Lament*. Gudrun contracts a third marriage, bringing to it her daughter by Sigurd, Svanhild, and producing further sons, Hamdir and Sorli. Svanhild is sent in marriage to the tyrant Iormunrekk. He has her trampled to death by horses when he believes her to be unfaithful to him with his son, Randver. In the last poems of the *Poetic Edda*, Gudrun dispatches her remaining sons on a doomed quest for revenge on Iormunrekk.

The figures in the Volsung poems belong partly in history, like Attila the Hun and Gunnar, king of the Burgundians, and partly in legend. There is probably influence from southern German texts, particularly in the poems' setting, but the story of Sigurd, Gudrun, Brynhild, and Gunnar is quite distinct from the plot of the Middle High German epic, the *Nibelungenlied*, which uses the same characters. Here Gudrun metamorphoses into the monstrous Kriemhilt, bent on killing her brothers in revenge for Siegfried (Sigurd), and Etzel (Atli) is the well-meaning dupe of his terrifying wife. Richard Wagner made use of *Volsunga saga*, written down around 1300, as the main source for his Ring Cycle, though he employs the *Poetic Edda*, known to him both from the works of Jakob and Wilhelm Grimm and from Karl Simrock's 1851 edition of the *Poetic Edda*, for the main ideas of *Das Rheingold* and *Götterdämmerung*.

Other eddic poems

The last seven poems in this volume are recognizably eddic though they are not preserved in the Codex Regius, but in manuscripts of Snorri's *Edda* or other late thirteenth-century codices. Some are mythological in content: the *List of Rig*, though incomplete, tells how human society gains a class system and how the institution of kingship begins. In *Baldr's Dreams* a dead seeress prophesies the death of Baldr to Odin. Another seeress is questioned by Freyia in the *Song of Hyndla* about the genealogy of her protégé Ottar, who needs to know his lineage in order to lay claim to his inheritance. The *Song of Grotti* is sung by two giantesses who are forced to labour for King Frodi, a semi-legendary Danish king, whose kingdom will be destroyed as a result of his mistreatment of them. *Groa's Chant* and the *Sayings of Fiolsvinn* (together known as *Svipdagsmal*) recount the story of Svipdag. Forced to set out on an impossible bridal-quest by his wicked stepmother, Svipdag solicits advice from his dead mother, and then debates with the giant Fiolsvinn about his chances of being admitted to the presence of the lovely Menglod. The Appendix contains a second version of the *Seeress's Prophecy*. This rather different version from the Codex Regius text is preserved between a discussion about how to deal with excommunicated men and a history of Troy in Hauksbók, a manuscript compendium dating from around 1300.

Reception

The Codex Regius was sent to Copenhagen in 1662; in 1665 Peder Hans Resen published an edition of the *Seeress's Prophecy* and *Sayings of the High One*, providing them with a Latin translation. With the addition of a text of Snorri's *Edda*, the Resen volume introduced Norse mythology to the wider world. A copy was given to the Bodleian Library in Oxford in the early 1670s; and the writer Robert Sheringham was able to draw on it for his study of the origins of the English published in 1670. A Swiss–French diplomat, Paul Mallet, wrote a two-volume account of early Scandinavian beliefs and history in 1755 and 1766 entitled *Introduction à l'histoire de Dannemarc* and *Monumens de la mythologie et de la poésie des Celtes*. Like many of his contemporaries, Mallet believed that the northern races were Celtic in origin, hence his title. In his work Mallet summarized parts of the *Seeress's Prophecy* and quoted from the *Sayings of the High One* in French translation, and also reproduced the first few verses of *Baldr's Dreams* which had been published by the Dane Bartholin in 1689. Mallet's book was translated by Thomas Percy under the title *Northern Antiquities* in 1770. Thus it was primarily from Percy that English Romantic writers learned about Norse myth and heroic legend, plundering *Northern Antiquities* for 'Gothick' detail, valkyries, vikings, shield-maids, and drinking out of enemy skulls (a fallacy based on a mistranslation). They also made 'versions' of the Norse heroic poems they found in Percy. Most notable was Thomas Gray's *The Descent of Odin*, expanding upon Mallet's excerpts from *Baldr's Dreams*, in his *Norse Odes* of 1768. In 1787 the Arnamagnæan Commission in Copenhagen began to publish a fully edited text of the Codex Regius and other eddic poems, at last permitting proper scholarly study and translation of the contents. By 1797 Amos Cottle had produced a rhymed English translation of the first volume of the Copenhagen edition, based on the Latin translation. Cottle's level of understanding may be gauged by the fact that in *Thrym's Poem* he depicts Freyia as consenting to go to Giant-land to marry Thrym, thus making a nonsense of everything which comes afterwards in the poem.[3] For a direct and scholarly translation from Norse into English, the British public had to wait for Benjamin Thorpe's 1866 *Sæmundar Edda*. The final volume of the Copenhagen edition, containing the heroic poetry, did not appear until 1828. By this time the 'Gothick' enthusiasms of English poets were beginning to wane, just as such ghoulishly dramatic stories as the night spent by Sigrun with the dead Helgi and Gudrun's murder of her sons were becoming available to them.

More to Victorian taste were the Icelandic family sagas with their stories of grim courage, stark choices, and manly heroes. Victorian scholars and amateurs of Old Icelandic translated the sagas of

[3] I discuss the history of English translations of the *Poetic Edda* in my essay in *Old Norse Made New* (see Select Bibliography).

Burnt-Njal and Grettir, and *Laxdæla saga* and *Eyrbyggja saga* among others. Though investigation of Norse myth revived, with the beginnings of the study of comparative mythology later in the century, Snorri's *Edda* proved a more manageable source of information than the *Poetic Edda*. William Morris and Eirikur Magnusson drew on some of the Sigurd poems, in addition to *Volsunga saga*, for their version of the Sigurd story, *The Story of Sigurd the Volsung and the Fall of the Niblungs* (1870), but it remains true that the first flush of interest in 'Eddick' verse in the late eighteenth century has never been surpassed. In the 1960s, following late on his pre-war journey to Iceland with Louis MacNeice, W. H. Auden (with P. B. Taylor) produced versions of the *Edda* poems; Taylor reissued the selection with twenty-three further poems in 1981 after Auden's death. Although these scarcely give an accurate impression of the structure or sense of the poetry, they convey Auden's personal vision of the North with memorable phrases and striking simplicity. Nevertheless, in the twentieth century Snorri's *Edda* with its rationalized and systematic account of myth and the Norse heroes has been regarded as more straightforward than the difficult and allusive poetry of the *Poetic Edda* for English readers; retellings of the tales of Norse gods and heroes have remained perennially popular as children's literature. In Europe the reinterpretation of eddic themes and the Sigurd story by Wagner, and their subsequent association with Nazi propaganda, proved hard to shake off in the immediate post-war period.

Rehabilitation of Norse myth in Britain came with J. R. R. Tolkien, and, to a more limited extent, his friend C. S. Lewis. *The Hobbit*, *The Lord of the Rings*, and the Narnia series drew strongly on eddic mythology. Tolkien reworked the eddic wisdom-contest form in Bilbo's riddle-exchange with Gollum; the hobbit wins the duel with a variant of Odin's last question to Vafthrudnir. The dwarfs of *The Hobbit*, and indeed Gandalf himself, draw their names from the *Dvergatal* or Tally of Dwarfs in the *Seeress's Prophecy*. Bilbo's conversation with Smaug the Dragon echoes the *Lay of Fafnir*, not to mention of course the prominence of the accursed ring like Andvari's Jewel in *The Lord of the Rings*. In 2009, Tolkien's version of some of the heroic poems, *The Legend of Sigurd and Gudrún*, was published for the first time. Lewis was introduced to what he called 'Pure Northernness' by Arthur Rackham's illustrations for the libretto of *Götterdämmerung*, yet the importance of snow, wolves, and giants in his heterogeneously imagined world of Narnia testifies to his eddic reading. Alan Garner, in *The Weirdstone of Brisingamen*, which takes its name from Freyia's splendid necklace, Diana Wynne Jones, Kevin Crossley-Holland, and Joanne Harris have all deployed themes from the *Poetic Edda* in their writing for children and young adults. Neil Gaiman's *American Gods* (2001) centres on Odinic myth transposed to modern America. A. S. Byatt's recent *Ragnarok* (2011), though drawing in part on a nineteenth-century German retelling of the myths, and in part on Snorri, traces the creation and final destruction of the world, and regards Loki as the intellectual's god, wondering, speculating, thinking, endlessly poking at that wonderful universe created through Ymir's murder, just to see what will happen.

Eddic stories have inspired Hollywood treatments: the 1994 film *The Mask* starred Jim Carrey as a mild-mannered bank clerk transformed into a manic superhero when he puts on a mask belonging to Loki. The more recent film *Thor* (2011) saw the title hero in exile from Asgard for disobedience to Odin; as in *Thrym's Poem* he is once again in search of his lost hammer. Thor's moral growth during his stay on earth allows him to baffle Loki's plan to turn Asgard over to the frost-giants and to save Odin and the other Æsir. Thor and Loki reappear in *Avengers* (2012). Popular television series such as HBO's *Game of Thrones*, based on George R. R. Martin's series *A Song of Ice and Fire*, explore Ragnarok's precursor, the unending winter, and feature dragons, shield-maids, wolves, and giants. Video and online games also use eddic names, concepts, and geography, while the myths are foundational in the music of viking metal bands; their eddic-related names include *Ásmegin* (Power of the God), *Einherjer*, *Týr*, and *Månegarm* (Moon-Garm).

Finally, the poems of the Edda have been a crucial source of inspiration for modern revivals of Germanic paganism in Scandinavia, Germany, and the English-speaking world. The *Sayings of the High One* and other eddic wisdom poems offer common-sense principles for living; while the gods do not necessarily provide inspiring role-models at all times, the courage and self-reliance shown by eddic heroes, the emphasis on the keeping of oaths, and the importance of hospitality are foregrounded in the ethics espoused by followers of the Asatru, and in many other neo-pagan belief systems.

Critical interpretation

The poems of the *Edda* were used in the nineteenth and early twentieth centuries primarily as source material for a number of larger projects—for reconstructing Indo-European mythic patterns, leading to an undue emphasis on seasonal and fertility motifs; for uncovering Germanic prehistory, giving life to forgotten heroes of the Migration Period (AD 400–600), and demonstrating Germanic ethics, customs, and heroic culture. More recently the poems have been acknowledged as worthy objects of study in their own right. Scholars ceased to rearrange or excise the stanzas of the longer mythological poems in order to recreate their vision of the 'original' poem, and began to concentrate on the unity and aesthetic value of the poems as they stand in the manuscripts. Since 1945 the poems have been interpreted according to structuralist, comparative, and, most recently, gender and queer theory. One important approach has been the investigation of how the texts mediate between oral and unrecoverable stages of transmission, as individual unrepeatable performances, and their preservation within a literate and fully Christian culture. Relating poems to 'real life', to particular historical moments, has been hampered by lack of knowledge about pagan religious ritual and the precise dates and origins of the poetry, but attempts at reading enduring Scandinavian social structures—ideas about kingship, the role of women, the function of feud—based on developments in anthropological theory yoked with a more flexible structuralist approach, have been relatively successful. The question of successive moments of reception too has been raised: what might a late thirteenth-century readership for whom the Codex Regius was put together have understood from the poem? How did contemporary poets make use of eddic traditions in composing new Christian poetry, such as the hybrid wisdom-eschatological poem *Solarljod* (*The Song of the Sun*) or the Icelandic translation of Geoffrey of Monmouth's *Prophetiae Merlini* (*The Prophecies of Merlin*) which uses the *Seeress's Prophecy* as one of its models?

The heroic poems are easier to characterize than the mythological ones since they form one long episodic cycle, yoking together Helgi, Sigurd, Gunnar, Gudrun, and her sons in the story of the hero and the valkyrie, in its different versions, and the subsequent history of the Niflung line. The plots centre on honour, revenge, love, and greed in an essentially aristocratic society. The hero is doomed to die young and faces his end with bravura and courage, glad not to die ignominiously in bed at the hands of a woman as Atli does. The heroine is left to grieve passionately for the greatness which has been lost and for her own plight. The women—Sigrun, Gudrun, Oddrun, Brynhild—voice the emotion and passion which the heroic mentality suppresses; effective actors themselves in the unfolding drama, they should not be regarded as mere victims of male power politics.

The mythological poems seem to be organized by main protagonist, with poems featuring Odin followed by *Skirnir's Journey*, a poem about Freyr, poems about Thor, and then poems about marginally divine figures, Volund and Alviss. Twentieth- and twenty-first-century critics have tended to stress the apocalyptic theme in the mythological poems, reading the Odinic poems, in which Odin seems desperate to learn the fate he cannot escape, as driving inexorably towards Ragnarok—a theme particularly congenial to a readership mindful of the perils of nuclear war and ecological catastrophe, a particular focus of A. S. Byatt's *Ragnarok*. Even the less solemn poems, *Harbard's Song* and *Loki's Quarrel*, have been adduced as evidence for the lack of unity and moral corruption among the gods, who thus deserve to be destroyed. Such an interpretation is both unhelpfully Christian and judgemental and also overlooks the space given to comic adventure in the triumphs of Thor over giants in *Thrym's Poem*, *Hymir's Poem*, and *All-wise's Sayings* and the apparently happy ending of *Skirnir's Journey*. Though the theme of Ragnarok is prominent in the *Seeress's Prophecy* and *Vafthrudnir's Sayings*, the mythological poems, despite Snorri's best efforts, cannot be synthesized into a single grand narrative. The poems, composed by different authors, at different times, in different genres, as monologues, dialogues, perhaps brief dramas, and as narrative, a millennium later speak individually to us in comic, tragic, grandiose, crude, witty, profound, and common-sense tones.

NOTE ON THE TRANSLATION

I HAVE used the usual conventions for spelling of Icelandic proper names, omitting accents and the consonantal nominative ending -r, except where it follows a vowel. The special Icelandic characters 'thorn' (þ) and 'eth' (ð) have been rendered as 'th' and 'd', spellings which occur in the *Poetic Edda* itself. Hooked 'o' and 'ø' have been printed as 'o'; 'œ' and 'æ' both as 'æ', in accordance with modern Icelandic pronunciation; 'i' has been used for the semi-consonantal sound often written 'j'. Stress always falls on the first syllable in Norse names.

The Norse text used as the general basis for translation is *Edda: Die Lieder des Codex Regius nebst verwandten Denkmälern*, i: *Text*, ed. G. Neckel, rev. H. Kuhn, 4th edn (Heidelberg, 1962). The translations of the Codex Regius and the Hauksbók versions of the *Seeress's Prophecy* have been made from the electronic texts produced by Karl G. Johansson in the MENOTA corpus; these do not conflate the manuscript witnesses as Neckel–Kuhn does. Proper names are cited according to the normalized orthography of Jón Helgason as used in *Eddadigte*, ed. J. Helgason, 3 vols. (Copenhagen, 1955). *Groa's Chant* and the *Sayings of Fiolsvinn* are translated from Peter Robinson's 1991 Oxford dissertation, 'An Edition of *Svipdagsmál*'. The *Waking of Angantyr* translates the text from Hannah Burrows' edition-in-progress of verses from *Hervarar saga ok Heidreks* and draws upon her notes. The final version of these verses will appear in *Skaldic Poetry of the Middle Ages*, vol. VIII, and may not be identical to the text I have used.

The *Kommentar zu den Liedern der Edda*, an ongoing commentary project from J. W. Goethe-University, Frankfurt, has been constantly at hand during the revision process, and I have also consulted Ursula Dronke's three-volume edition of eddic poems.

A certain amount of cross-referencing to Snorri Sturluson's mythographical treatise, the *Prose Edda*, as it often clarifies or amplifies the material of the *Poetic Edda*, to *Ynglinga saga* (the first legendary saga in Snorri's history of the kings of Norway, *Heimskringla*), to *Volsunga saga*, which covers much of the ground of the heroic poetry, and to Saxo's *History of the Danish People* is included. The editions used are to be found in the Select Bibliography. Comment on particular points of difficulty can be found in the Explanatory Notes;

the Annotated Index of Names gives basic information as to the identity of named characters.

Metre and style

Eddic poetry is essentially the kind of poetry found in the Codex Regius. It is simple, in comparison with the ornate and complex skaldic verse which was the court poetic style, and the subject of the later sections of Snorri's *Edda*. The kind of elaborate phrasing typical of skaldic diction, whereby the term (known as a kenning) 'battle-fish in the hawk's perch' means 'sword in the hand', is normally eschewed in eddic verse. In the heroic poetry a warrior may be denoted as 'powerful apple-tree of strife', but such periphrases are relatively easy to decode. Eddic poetry depends for its effect rather upon stress and alliteration. The poems are composed in a restricted number of metres. *Fornyrdislag* (*old-story metre*) is the most frequent narrative metre, especially in the heroic poetry; it is very similar to what might be described as a common Germanic metre, having affinities with Old English and Old High German poetry. Stanzas consist of a series of lines which fall into two half-lines. These are separated by a pause or caesura. The whole line has four stresses and an alliterating pattern; the first stress of the second half-line will alliterate with one or more of the stressed syllables in the first half-line; the fourth stressed syllable does not alliterate. Rhyme and assonance also contribute to the sound effect. See the example below:

x x	x x
*H*ér má *H*öðbroddr	*H*elga kenna,
x x	x x
*fl*ótta trauðan,	í *fl*ota miðiom;
x x	x x
hann hefir *e*ðli	*æ*ttar þinnar
x x	x x
arf Fiörsunga,	*u*nd sic þrungit.

(*Second Poem of Helgi Hundingsbani*, v. 20)

[Here Hodbrodd may recognize Helgi, | the fighter who does not flee, in the midst of the fleet; | the homeland of your kin, | the inheritance of the Fiorsungs, he has conquered.]

(x indicates the stress while the alliterating letters are italicized; vowels alliterate with one another).

Malahattr (*speech-metre*) is an augmented *fornyrdislag*, found in the *Greenlandic Lay of Atli*. It has five stresses to a line, with double alliteration in the first half-line. Each half-line can contain as many as eight syllables, giving an expansive effect.

Ljodahattr (*song-metre*), used for wisdom and dialogue poetry, has stanzas consisting in two halves (*helmingar*), each composed of a long line with four stresses and up to three alliterating syllables, and a shorter line, with two stresses and two alliterating syllables, as in this example:

>   x   x   x   x
> *Hiarðir þat vito,*   *nær þær heim scolo,*
>
>   x   x
> *oc ganga þá af grasi;*
>
>   x   x   x x
> *enn ósviðr maðr*   *kann ævagi*
>
>   x   x
> *síns um mál maga.*

(Sayings of the High One, v. 21)

[Cattle know when they ought to go home, | and then they leave the pasture; | but the foolish man never knows | the measure of his own stomach.]

Galdralag (literally 'spell-measure') is different again, a repetitive metre found for example in *Sayings of the High One*, v. 144.

Many poems change metre as they move from dialogue to narrative, or wisdom material to conversation. In the *Lay of Fafnir*, the dragon, Fafnir, and the hero, Sigurd, converse mostly in *ljodahattr* as they bandy gnomic sayings, but once the dragon is dead, the nuthatches who advise Sigurd to kill his foster-father, Regin the dwarf, and to set out to look for Sigrdrifa, tend to use *fornyrdislag*. Some poems have prose introductions giving a minimum of information necessary to understand the initial situation. In the cycle of poems about the hero Sigurd, someone, perhaps the compiler of the manuscript, has inserted some explanatory prose passages, covering parts of the story where perhaps no poem exists; elsewhere he draws attention to the conflicting traditions about where Sigurd's death took place. I have not imitated the half-line structure in the translation though, where possible, I have used alliteration and rhythmic patterning.

The state and presentation of the text

Part of the Codex Regius is missing. Some leaves are lost in the Sigurd cycle, so that the end of the *Lay of Sigrdrifa* must be added from the prose account of Sigurd's life in *Volsunga saga*. When the manuscript begins again the story of Sigurd's marriage to Gudrun and Gunnar's wooing of Brynhild has been lost; the next poems deal with the aftermath of Brynhild's realization that she has been tricked into marrying the wrong man. Elsewhere in the manuscript lines have been lost and verses appear to have been misplaced. In the manuscript the poetry is written in continuous lines across the page, as if it were prose, in order to save space. We can only determine the boundaries of verses by applying metrical rules.

The poems included from other manuscripts at the end of this book have varying states of preservation. *Baldr's Dreams* is preserved in the A manuscript; the *List of Rig*, which has some missing verses, and the *Song of Grotti* are found in manuscripts of Snorri's *Edda*, and the *Song of Hyndla* in the late Icelandic compilation Flateyjarbók. The two poems which constitute the *Lay of Svipdag* survive in a large number of late manuscripts offering highly varying readings, while the *Waking of Angantyr*, like the second version of the *Seeress's Prophecy*, is found in the early fourteenth-century Hauksbók compendium; *Hervarar saga ok Heidreks* in which it occurs is also found in other manuscripts.

SELECT BIBLIOGRAPHY

The Poetic Edda

Dronke, Ursula (ed. and trans.), *The Poetic Edda*, 3 vols. (Oxford, 1969–2011). Edition of most of the mythological poems and the last four heroic poems of the Codex Regius.

Jón Helgason (ed.), *Eddadigte*, 3 vols. (Copenhagen, 1955). Contains the poems up to the *Lay of Sigrdrifa*.

La Farge, Beatrice, and Tucker, John (eds.), *Glossary to the Poetic Edda Based on Hans Kuhn's Kurzes Wörterbuch* (Heidelberg, 1992). Glossary to the Neckel–Kuhn edition, expanded and updated.

Neckel, Gustav (ed.), *Edda: Die Lieder des Codex Regius nebst verwandten Denkmälern*, i: *Text*, rev. Hans Kuhn, 5th edn (Heidelberg, 1983). The most up-to-date edition of this standard edition of the complete *Poetic Edda*.

Orchard, Andy (trans.), *The Elder Edda: A Book of Viking Lore* (London, 2011).

Vésteinn Ólason, Jónas Kristjánsson, et al. (eds.), *Eddukvæði* (Reykjavik, forthcoming). A new edition of the Codex Regius and some other eddic poems, with Icelandic commentary.

von See, Klaus, La Farge, Beatrice, et al., *Kommentar zu den Liedern der Edda* (Heidelberg, 1997–). German commentary project, 7 volumes plus introduction and index volume (Vol. 1 and index, forthcoming).

Eddukvæði-website (forthcoming).

Other texts

Egil's Saga, trans. Christine Fell (London, 1975).

Gisli Sursson's Saga and the Saga of the People of Eyri, trans. Martin Regal and Judy Quinn (London, 2003).

Grettir's Saga, trans. Denton Fox and Hermann Palsson (Toronto, 1974).

Njals Saga, trans. Robert Cook (London, 2001).

The Sagas of Icelanders: A Selection, intro. Robert Kellogg (London, 2001). Contains translations of a number of important sagas and shorter tales, including *Egils saga*, *Laxdæla saga*, *Hrafnkels saga*, *Gisla saga*, and the Vinland and Greenland sagas.

The Saga of Thidrek of Bern, trans. Edward Haymes (New York and London, 1988).

The Saga of the Volsungs: The Norse Epic of Sigurd the Dragon Slayer, trans. Jesse Byock (Berkeley and London, 2012).

Saxo Grammaticus, *History of the Danish People*, trans. Peter Fisher, ed. Hilda Ellis Davidson, 2 vols. (Cambridge, 1979). A readable and lively translation with a compendious commentary.

Snorri Sturluson, *Edda*, trans. A. Faulkes (London, 1987). A translation of all of Snorri's poetic treatise.

——, *Edda: Prologue and Gylfaginning*, ed. A. Faulkes (London, 1988).

Tacitus, *The Agricola and the Germania*, trans. H. Mattingly, rev. S. A. Handford (Harmondsworth, 1970).

Ynglinga saga, in Snorri Sturluson, *Heimskringla*, Vol. 1, trans. Alison Finlay and Anthony Faulkes (London, 2011).

On the *Edda, Old Norse myth, and heroic verse*

Abram, Christopher, *Myths of the Pagan North: The Gods of the Norsemen* (London, 2011). An up-to-date discussion of the preservation and transmission of Norse myth.

Acker, Paul, and Larrington, Carolyne (eds.), *The Poetic Edda: Essays on Old Norse Mythology* (New York and London, 2002). A book of essays, some reprinted, some freshly translated and some original, on the mythological poetry.

——, *Revisiting the Poetic Edda: Essays on Old Norse Heroic Legend* (New York and London, 2013). Largely new essays on the heroic poems and their reception in later Icelandic literature, in William Morris and J. R. R. Tolkien.

Andersson, Theodore, *The Legend of Brynhild*, Islandica 43 (Ithaca, NY, 1980). A study of the Brynhild figure, incorporating material from the *Nibelungenlied* and other Scandinavian texts and tracing the probable development of the story.

Bek-Pedersen, Karen, *The Norns in Old Norse Mythology* (Edinburgh, 2011). A useful discussion of the norns, *dísir*, and other female figures in Norse myth.

Clark, David, *Gender, Violence and the Past in Edda and Saga* (Oxford, 2012). Contains some essays on the ethics of the heroic poetry.

Clover, Carol, and Lindow, John (eds.), *Old Norse–Icelandic Literature: A Critical Guide*, 2nd edn (Toronto, 2005). Contains two very valuable essays, one by John Lindow on Norse myth and one by Joseph Harris on the *Poetic Edda*. Also full bibliography to 1984.

Clunies Ross, Margaret, *Prolonged Echoes: Old Norse Myths in Medieval Northern Society*, i: *The Myths*, The Viking Collection 7 (Odense, 1994). A highly readable and learned discussion of the mythological materials in Snorri, the *Poetic Edda*, and other medieval sources.

Gunnell, Terry, 'Eddic Poetry', in *A Companion to Old Norse-Icelandic Literature and Culture*, ed. R. McTurk (Oxford and Malden, Mass., 2004). An introductory account of eddic poems.

Larrington, Carolyne, 'Translating the Poetic Edda', in David Clark and Carl Phelpstead (eds.), *Old Norse Made New* (London, 2007), 21–42. Downloadable at: http://www.academia.edu/265041/Translating_the_Poetic_Edda

McKinnell, John, *Both One and Many: Essays on Change and Variety in Late Norse Heathenism* (Rome, 1994). A book which addresses the mythological poetry.

——, *Meeting the Other in Norse Myth and Legend* (Cambridge, 2005). A thorough exploration of various traditional motifs and structures in eddic poetry, the legendary sagas, and Snorri.

Page, R. I., *Norse Myths* (London, 1990). A sceptical, quirkily written account of the myths.

Simek, Rudolf (ed.), *Dictionary of Northern Mythology*, trans. Angela Hall (Cambridge, 1993). Many entries on the protagonists of the myths, but excluding most human heroes.

Turville-Petre, E. O. G., *Myth and Religion of the North* (London, 1964). A standard introduction to Norse myth.

MAIN GENEALOGIES OF GODS, GIANTS, AND HEROES

Note: in the tables below *m.* denotes 'married'; = denotes 'had sexual relationship with'.

GIANTS

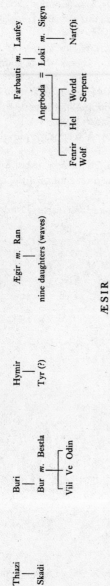
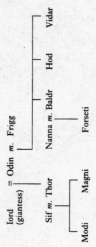

```
Farbauti m. Laufey          Loki m. Sigyn
                                 |
                               Nar(f)i

Angrboda = Loki
     |
  Fenrir   Hel   World
   Wolf          Serpent
```

```
Ægir m. Ran
     |
nine daughters (waves)
```

```
Hymir
  |
Tyr (?)
```

```
Buri
  |
Bur m. Bestla
  |
Vili Ve Odin
```

```
Thiazi
   |
 Skadi
```

Bragi *m.* Idunn

ÆSIR

```
Iord = Odin m. Frigg
(giantess)   |
         Nanna m. Baldr   Hod   Vidar
                   |
               Forseti

Sif m. Thor
     |
 Modi   Magni
```

VANIR

```
Skadi  m.  Niord  =  (sister)
(giantess)   |
        Freyr = Freyia m. Od
          |
Gerd  m. Freyr
(giantess) |
        Fiolnir
```

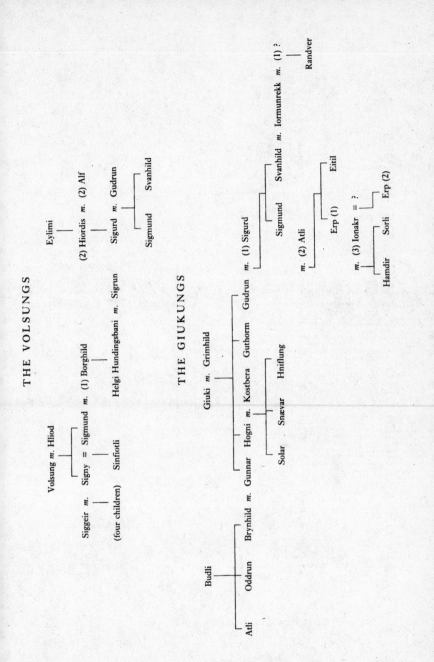

THE VOLSUNGS

Eylimi
|
(2) Hiordis *m.* (2) Alf

Sigurd *m.* Gudrun
|
Sigmund   Svanhild

Volsung *m.* Hliod

Signy = Sigmund *m.* (1) Borghild

Helgi Hundingsbani *m.* Sigrun

Siggeir *m.*

(four children)   Sinfiotli

THE GIUKUNGS

Giuki *m.* Grimhild

Gudrun *m.* (1) Sigurd

Sigmund   Svanhild *m.* Iormunrekk *m.* (1) ?

Randver

m. (2) Atli

Erp (1)   Eitil

m. (3) Ionakr = ?

Hamdir   Sorli   Erp (2)

Guthorm

Hogni *m.* Kostbera   Hniflung

Solar   Snævar

Gunnar

Brynhild *m.*

Oddrun

Budli

Atli

THE POETIC EDDA

THE SEERESS'S PROPHECY

The *Seeress's Prophecy* (*Voluspa*), composed mainly in the *fornyrdislag* metre, is recited by a seeress who can remember before the beginning of the world and who can see as far ahead as after Ragnarok—the Doom of the Gods. Odin ('Father of the Slain' in v. 1) is interrogating the seeress to find out what is to come; her reply moves swiftly and allusively through the history of gods and men. The account begins with the creation of the earth (vv. 3–5), then time is created (v. 6). The gods build temples and enjoy a golden age (vv. 7–8) until they are disrupted by three girls from Giant-land. This somehow leads to the creation of the dwarfs (vv. 9–16). Humanity is created in vv. 18–19 and the fates arrive in v. 20. Now history begins: a mysterious female manifests herself amongst the Æsir, a woman well-versed in magic (vv. 22–3); as a consequence the Æsir find themselves at war with the Vanir (vv. 24–5). Peace is concluded and the gods have to repair damage to Asgard; a giant offers to rebuild the walls in a very short space of time in exchange for the sun, moon, and Freyia. The gods agree, thinking the task impossible, but the builder nearly succeeds and Thor has to destroy him, breaking the gods' promises of safe-conduct (vv. 26–7). At v. 28 we reach the present, with Odin questioning the seeress about what is to come. The Doom of the Gods is signalled by the death of Baldr and its consequences (vv. 32–5); the end of the world by images of punishment and social collapse (vv. 36–44). Ragnarok approaches: the World-Ash Yggdrasill trembles and the giants advance (vv. 45–50). Odin is killed by the wolf Fenrir, Freyr by Surt; Thor and the Midgard-serpent kill each other. Odin is avenged by his son Vidar and the world disappears in fire (vv. 51–5). In the verses which follow, the earth rises anew from the sea and some of the Æsir, including Baldr, return to live peacefully together (vv. 56–62). In the final verse the sinister dragon Nidhogg is seen as the seeress sinks out of her trance. Does evil still exist in the new world, or have we returned to the present where the dragon is a portent of Ragnarok?

The *Seeress's Prophecy* is usually dated to the late tenth century, when the pagan religion was beginning to be superseded by Christianity. One scholar has suggested that the poem is a kind of sacred text of the Scandinavian religion, composed just before the beliefs were to be eradicated by Christianity. The poem exists in two rather different versions; that of the Codex Regius manuscript, given here, and one in the early fourteenth-century Hauksbók, given in the Appendix. Many of the verses are also to be found in Snorri's *Edda*.

1   Hearing I ask from all the tribes,
   greater and lesser, the offspring of Heimdall;*
   Father of the Slain, you wished me well to declare
   living beings' ancient stories, those I remember from furthest
      back.

2   I remember giants born early in time
   those nurtured me long ago;
   I remember nine worlds, I remember nine giant women,*
   the mighty Measuring-Tree below the earth.

3   Early in time Ymir made his settlement,*
   there was no sand nor sea nor cool waves;
   earth was nowhere nor the sky above,
   a void of yawning chaos, grass was there nowhere

4   before the sons of Bur brought up the land-surface,*
   those who shaped glorious Midgard;
   the sun shone from the south on the stone-hall,
   then the ground was grown over with the green leek.

5   From the south, Sun, companion of the moon,
   threw her right hand round the sky's edge;
   Sun did not know where she had her hall,
   the stars did not know where they had their stations,
   the moon did not know what might he had.

6   Then all the Powers went to the thrones of fate,
   the sacrosanct gods, and considered this:
   to night and her children they gave names,
   morning they named and midday,
   afternoon and evening, to reckon up in years.

7   The Æsir met on Idavoll Plain,
   high they built altars and temples;
   they set up their forges, smithed precious things,
   shaped tongs and made tools.

8   They played chequers in the meadow, they were merry,
     they did not lack for gold at all,
     until three ogre-girls came,*
     all-powerful women, out of Giant-land.

9   Then all the Powers went to the thrones of fate,
     the sacrosanct gods, and considered this:
     who should create the lord of the dwarfs
     out of Brimir's blood and from Blain's limbs?*

10   There Motsognir became most famous of
     all dwarfs, and Durin next;
     Many manlike figures the dwarfs made,*
     out of the earth, as Durin recounted.

11   New-moon and Dark-of-moon, North and South,*
     East and West, Master-thief, Dvalin,
     Bivor, Bavor, Bombur, and Nori,
     An and Anar, Great-grandfather and Mead-wolf.

12   Liquor and Staff-elf, Wind-elf and Thrain,
     Known and Thorin, Thror, Colour and Wise,
     Corpse and New-advice: now I have rightly
     —Regin and Counsel-clever—reckoned up the dwarfs.

13   Fili and Kili, Foundling and Nali,
     Haft and Vili, Hanar and Sviur,
     Frar and Hornborer, Fræg and Sea-pool,
     Loam-field, Iari, Oakenshield.

14   Time it is to tally up the dwarfs in Dvalin's troop,
     for the children of men, to trace them back to Lofar;
     those who sought out Frar's Hall-stone,
     the dwelling of Loam-field on Iorovellir.

15   There were Draupnir and Dolgthrasir,
     Greyhair, Mound-river, Lee-plain, Glow,
     Skirvir, Virvir, Skafid, and Great-grandfather.

16   Elf and Yngvi, Oakenshield,
      Fialar and Frosty, Finn and Ginnar;
      they'll be remembered while the world endures,
      the long list of ancestors, going back to Lofar.

17   Until three gods, strong and loving,*
      came from out of that company;
      they found on land capable of little,
      Ash and Embla, lacking in fate.*

18   Breath they had not, spirit they had not,
      blood nor bearing nor fresh complexions;
      breath gave Odin, spirit gave Hænir,
      blood gave Lodur, and fresh complexions.

19   An ash I know that stands, Yggdrasill it's called,
      a tall tree, drenched with shining loam;
      from there come the dews which fall in the valley,
      green, it stands always over Urd's well.*

20   From there come girls, knowing a great deal,
      three from the lake standing under the tree;
      Urd one is called, Verdandi another—
      they carved on a wooden slip—Skuld the third;

21   they laid down laws, they chose lives
      for the sons of men, the fates of men.

22   She remembers the first war in the world,*
      when they stuck Gullveig with spears
      and in the High-One's hall they burned her;*
      three times they burned her, three times she was reborn,
      over and over, yet she lives still.

23   Bright One they called her, wherever she came to houses,*
      the seer with pleasing prophecies, she practised spirit-magic;
      she knew *seid*, *seid* she performed as she liked,
      she was always a wicked woman's favourite.

24 Then all the Powers went to the thrones of fate,
    the sacrosanct gods, and considered this:
    whether the Æsir should yield the tribute
    or whether all the gods should share sacrificial feasts.

25 Odin hurled a spear, sped it into the host;
    that was war still, the first in the world;
    the wooden rampart of the Æsir's stronghold was wrecked;
    the Vanir, with a war-spell, kept on trampling the plain.

26 Then all the Powers went to the thrones of fate,
    the sacrosanct gods, and considered this:
    which people had troubled the air with treachery,
    or given Od's girl to the giant race.*

27 Thor alone struck a blow there, swollen with rage,
    he seldom sits still when he hears such a thing;
    the oaths broke apart, words and promises,
    all the solemn pledges which had passed between them.

28 She knows that Heimdall's hearing is hidden
    under the bright-grown, sacred tree;
    she sees, flowing down, the loam-filled flood
    from Father of the Slain's pledge—do you want to know more:
        and what?*

29 Alone she sat outside, when the old man came,
    the Terrible One of the Æsir and he looked in her eyes:
    'Why do you question me? Why do you test me?
    I know all about it, Odin, where you hid your eye
    in Mimir's famous well.'
    Mimir drinks mead every morning
    from Father of the Slain's pledge—do you want to know more:
        and what?

30 Father of Hosts chose for her rings and necklaces,
    treasure, wise speech, and spirits of divination;
    she saw widely, widely about every world.

31   She saw valkyries coming from far and wide,*
      ready to ride to the gods' realm;
      Skuld shouldered one shield, Skogul was another,
      Gunn, Hild, Gondul, and Geir-skogul—
      now the General's ladies are counted up,
      valkyries ready to ride over the earth.

32   I saw for Baldr, for the bloody god,
      Odin's child, his fate in store;
      there stood grown—higher than the plain,
      slender and very fair—the mistletoe.

33   From that stem which seemed so slender
      there came a dangerous grief-dart: Hod started to shoot;
      Baldr's brother was born quickly;*
      Odin's son started killing at one night old.

34   He never washed his hands nor combed his hair,
      until he brought Baldr's adversary to the funeral pyre;
      and in Fen-halls Frigg wept
      for Valhall's woe—do you want to know more: and what?

35   A captive she saw lying under Cauldron-grove,
      an evil-loving figure, unmistakable as Loki;
      there sits Sigyn, getting very little
      joy from her husband—do you want to know more: and what?

36   From the east there flows, through poison valleys,
      a river with knives and swords, Fearful it is called.
      To the north there stood on Dark-of-moon Plains,
      a hall of gold, of Sindri's lineage;*
      and another stood on Never-Cold,
      the beer-hall of a giant called Brimir.

37   A hall she saw standing far from the sun,
      on Corpse-strand; its doors look north;
      poison-drops fall in through the roof-vents,
      the hall is woven of serpents' spines.

38   There she saw wading in turbid streams
      false-oath swearers and murderers,
      and the seducer of another man's close confidante;
      there Nidhogg sucks the corpses of the dead—
      a wolf tears at men—do you want to know more: and what?

39   In the east sat the old woman in Iron-wood
      and gave birth there to Fenrir's offspring;
      one of them in trollish shape
      shall be snatcher of the moon.

40   It gluts itself on doomed men's lives,
      reddens the gods' dwellings with crimson blood;
      sunshine becomes black all the next summers,*
      weather all vicious—do you want to know more: and what?

41   He sat on the mound and struck his harp,
      the giantess's herdsman, cheerful Eggther;
      near him crowed in Gallows-wood,
      that bright-red rooster who is called Fialar.

42   Golden-comb crowed near the Æsir,
      he wakens the warriors at Father of Hosts' hall;*
      and another crows below the earth,
      a sooty-red cock in the halls of Hel.

43   Garm bays loudly before Gnipa-cave,*
      the fetter will break and the ravener run free,
      much wisdom she knows, I see further ahead*
      to the mighty Doom of the Gods, of the victory-gods.

44   Brother will fight brother and be his slayer,
      sister's sons will violate the kinship-bond;
      hard it is in the world, whoredom abounds,
      axe-age, sword-age, shields are cleft asunder,
      wind-age, wolf-age, before the world plunges headlong;
      no man will spare another.

45   The sons of Mim are at play and the Measuring-Tree is
          kindled*
      at the resounding Giallar-horn;
      Heimdall blows loudly, his horn is in the air.
      Odin speaks with Mim's head.
      The ancient tree groans and the giant gets loose,
      Yggdrasill shudders, the tree standing upright.

46   Now Garm bays loudly before Gnipa-cave,
      the fetter will break and the ravener run free,
      much wisdom she knows, I see further ahead
      to the mighty Doom of the Gods, of the victory-gods.

47   Hrym drives from the east, heaves his shield before him,*
      the great serpent writhes in giant rage;
      the serpent churns the waves, the eagle shrieks in anticipation,
      pale-beaked he rips the corpse, Naglfar breaks free.*

48   A ship journeys from the east, Muspell's troops are coming*
      over the ocean, and Loki steers.
      All the giant-sons advance along with the ravener,
      Byleist's brother goes in company with them.*

49   What disturbs the Æsir? What disturbs the elves?
      All Giant-land is roaring. The Æsir are in council.
      The dwarfs groan before their rocky doors,
      wise ones of the mountain wall—do you want to know more:
          and what?

50   Surt comes from the south with branches-ruin,*
      the slaughter-gods' sun glances from his sword;
      rocky cliffs clash together and the troll-women are abroad,
      heroes tread the hell-road and the sky splits apart.*

51   Then Frigg's second sorrow comes about*
      when Odin advances to fight against the wolf,
      and Beli's bright slayer against Surt;*
      then Frigg's dear-beloved must fall.

52 Then comes Victory-father's strong son,
   Vidar, to battle the Beast of Slaughter;
   With his hand he sends to Loki's son's heart*
   his sword to stab: then his father is avenged.

53 Then comes Hlodyn's glorious boy:
   Odin's son advances to fight the serpent,*
   he strikes in wrath Midgard's-protector,*
   all men must abandon their homesteads;
   nine steps Fiorgyn's child takes,
   exhausted, from the serpent which fears no shame.

54 The sun turns black, land sinks into the sea,
   the bright stars vanish from the sky;
   steam rises up in the conflagration,
   hot flame plays high against heaven itself.

55 Now Garm bays loudly before Gnipa-cave,
   the fetter will break and the ravener run free,
   much wisdom she knows, I see further ahead
   to the mighty Doom of Gods, of the victory-gods.

56 She sees, coming up a second time,
   earth from the ocean, eternally green;
   the waterfalls plunge, an eagle soars above them,
   over the mountain hunting fish.

57 The Æsir find one another on Idavoll
   and they converse about the mighty Earth-girdler,*
   and Fimbultyr's ancient runes.

58 There will be found again in the grass
   the wonderful golden chequers,
   those which they possessed in the bygone days.

59 Without sowing the fields will grow,
   all evil will be healed, Baldr will come;
   Hod and Baldr will settle down in Hropt's victory-homesteads,
   the slaughter-gods are well—do you want to know more: and
      what?*

60   Then Hænir will choose a wooden slip for prophecy,
      and two brothers' sons build a settlement
      in the wide wind-realm—do you want to know more: and what?

61   A hall she sees standing, fairer than the sun,
      thatched with gold, at Gimle;
      there the noble fighting-bands will dwell
      and enjoy the days of their lives in pleasure.

62   There comes the shadow-dark dragon flying,
      the gleaming serpent, up from Dark-of-moon Hills;
      Nidhogg flies over the plain, in his pinions
      he carries corpses; now she will sink down.

SAYINGS OF THE HIGH ONE

Human social wisdom, teasing allusion to runic mysteries, spells, and charms combine in this poem to give a conspectus of different types of wisdom. Most of the poem is taken up with instruction on the subject of social behaviour, common sense and folly, moderation and friendship, composed in *ljodahattr*, the usual metre of wisdom verse. At times the poet steps forward to speak in his own voice, at times the first person merges with Odin, the god of wisdom, speaking from his own experience of questing after knowledge. The wisdom stanzas are organized by themes, connections made by juxtaposition or contrast. Towards the end of the poem Odin speaks more, of his sacrifice to learn the secrets of the runes (vv. 138–45) and of his knowledge of spells (vv. 146–64); the magical subject-matter is related in a different metre. Earlier Odin narrates two adventures with women—Billing's girl who outwits him (vv. 96–102) and Gunnlod, whose love he exploits to win the mead of poetry (vv. 104–10). *Sayings of the High One* (*Havamal*) is, no doubt, a redaction of several different poems unified by the theme of wisdom and by the central figure of Odin.

1   All the doorways, before one enters,
    should be looked around,
    should be spied out;
    it can't be known for certain where enemies are sitting
    in the hall ahead.

2   'Blessed be the givers!' A guest has come in,
    where is he going to sit?
    He's in great haste, the one who by the log-stack
    is going to try his luck.

3   Fire is needful for someone who's come in
    and who's chilled to the knee;
    food and clothing are necessary for the man
    who's journeyed over the mountains.

4   Water is needful for someone who comes to a meal,
    a towel and a warm welcome,
    a friendly disposition, if he could get it,
    speech and silence in return.

5   Wits are needful for someone who wanders widely,
    anything will pass at home;
    he becomes a laughing-stock, the man who knows nothing
    and sits among the wise.

6   About his intelligence no man should be boastful,
    rather cautious of mind;
    when a wise and silent man comes to a homestead
    blame seldom befalls the wary;
    for no more dependable friend can a man ever get
    than a store of common sense.

7   The careful guest, who comes to a meal,
    keeps silent, with hearing finely attuned;
    he listens with his ears, and looks about with his eyes;
    so every wise man spies out what's ahead.

8   He's lucky, the man who can get himself
    praise and good will;
    very difficult it is when a man lays claim to
    what's in another's breast.

9   He's lucky, the man who keeps in himself
    praise and wit while he lives;
    for bad advice men have often received
    from another's breast.

10 No better burden a man bears on the road
    than a store of common sense;
    better than riches it will seem in an unfamiliar place,
    such is the resort of the wretched.

11 No better burden a man bears on the road
    than a store of common sense;
    no worse journey-provision could he carry over the plain
    than over-much drinking of ale.

12 It isn't as good as it's said to be,
    ale, for the sons of men;
    for the more a man drinks, the less he knows
    about his own mind.

13 The forgetfulness-heron it's called
who hovers over ale-drinking;
he steals a man's mind;
with this bird's feathers I was fettered
in the court of Gunnlod.*

14 Drunk I was, I was more than drunk
at wise Fialar's;
that's the best about ale-drinking that afterwards
every man gets his mind back again.

15 Silent and thoughtful a prince's son should be
and bold in fighting;
cheerful and merry every man should be
until he comes to death.

16 The cowardly man thinks he'll live for ever,
if he keeps away from fighting;
but old age won't grant him a truce
even if spears spare him.

17 The fool stares when he comes on a visit,
he mutters to himself or hovers about;
but it's all up with him if he gets a swig of drink;
the man's mind is exposed.

18 Only that man who wanders widely
and has journeyed a great deal knows
what sort of mind each man controls;
he who's sharp in his wits.

19 Let no man hold onto the cup, but drink
mead in moderation,
let him say what's necessary or be silent;
no man will scold you
because you go off early to bed.

20 The greedy man, unless he guards against this tendency,
will eat himself into lifelong trouble;
often when he comes among the wise,
the foolish man's stomach is laughed at.

21 Cattle know when they ought to go home,
and then they leave the pasture;
but the foolish man never figures
the measure of his own stomach.

22 He's a wretched man, of evil disposition,
the one who makes fun of everything;
he doesn't know the one thing he ought to know:
that he is not devoid of faults.

23 The stupid man stays awake all night
and worries about everything;
he's tired out when the morning comes
and all's just as bad as it was.

24 The foolish man thinks that everyone
is his friend who laughs with him;
he doesn't notice though they say nasty things about him
when he sits among the wise.

25 The foolish man thinks that everyone
is his friend who laughs with him;
but then he finds when he comes to the Assembly*
that he has few to speak on his behalf.

26 The foolish man thinks he knows everything
if he cowers in a corner;
he doesn't know what he can say in return
if people ask him questions.

27 The foolish man in company
does best if he stays silent;
no one will know that he knows nothing,
unless he talks too much;
but the man who knows nothing does not know
even if he is talking too much.

28 Wise he esteems himself who knows how to question
and how to answer as well;
the sons of men cannot keep secret
what's going around about folk.

29 Quite enough baseless blather comes
   from the man never silent;
   a quick tongue, unless it's held in check,
   often talks itself into trouble.

30 Into a laughing-stock no man should make another,
   if he comes to visit the household;
   many a man seems wise if he isn't asked questions
   and he manages to lurk unscathed.

31 Wise that man seems who retreats
   when one guest is insulting another;
   the man who mocks at a feast doesn't know for sure
   whether he shoots off his mouth amid enemies.

32 Many men are devoted to one another
   and yet they fight at feasts;
   amongst men there will always be strife,
   guest squabbling with guest.

33 An early meal a man should usually eat,
   unless he is visiting friends;
   he sits and gazes round hungrily, acts as if he's starving,
   and doesn't make conversation.

34 It's a great detour to a bad friend's house,
   even though he lives on the route;
   but to a good friend's house the ways lie straight,
   even though he lives far off.

35 A man must go, he must not remain a guest
   always in one place;
   the loved man is loathed if he sits too long
   in someone else's hall.

36 A farm of your own is better, even if small,
   everyone's someone at home;
   though he has two goats and a twig-roofed room,
   that is still better than begging.

37   A farm of your own is better, even if small,
     everyone's someone at home;
     a man's heart bleeds when he has to beg
     for food for himself at meal-times.

38   From his weapons on open land
     no man should step one pace away;
     for it can't be known for certain, out on the road,
     when a man might have need of his spear.

39   I never found a generous man, nor one so unstingy with food,
     that he wouldn't accept what was given;
     or one so open-handed with possessions
     that he disliked a gift when offered.

40   His piled-up property
     a man shouldn't go without;
     what you meant for those you love is often saved for those you
         hate;
     much goes worse than is expected.

41   With weapons and gifts friends should gladden one another,
     those which can be seen on them;*
     mutual givers and receivers are friends for longest,
     if the friendship keeps going well.

42   To his friend a man should be a friend
     and repay gifts with gifts;
     laughter men should accept with laughter
     but return deception for a lie.

43   To his friend a man should be a friend
     and to his friend's friend too;
     but no man should be a friend
     to the friend of his enemy.

44   You know, if you've a friend whom you really trust
     and from whom you want nothing but good,
     you should mix your soul with his and exchange gifts,
     go and see him often.

45 If you've another, whom you don't trust,
    but from whom you want nothing but good,
    speak fairly to him, but think falsely
    and repay treachery with a lie.

46 Again, concerning the one you don't trust,
    and whose mind you suspect:
    you should laugh with him and disguise your thoughts:
    a gift should be repaid with a like one.

47 I was young once, I travelled alone,
    then I found myself going astray;
    rich I thought myself when I met someone else,
    for man is the joy of man.

48 Generous and brave men live the best,
    seldom do they harbour sorrow;
    but the cowardly man is afraid of everything,
    the miser always worries when he gets gifts.

49 My clothes I gave out in the field
    to two wooden men;*
    champions they thought themselves when they had clothing,
    the naked man is despised.

50 The fir-tree withers that stands on the farmstead,*
    neither bark nor needles protect it;
    so it is with the man whom no one loves,
    how should he live for long?

51 Hotter than fire between bad friends
    burns fondness for five days;
    but it dies down when the sixth day comes,
    and all that friendship goes to the bad.

52 A man need not give only a big gift,
    often you buy praise with a little;
    with half a loaf and a tilted cup
    I've got myself a companion.

53   Of small sands, of small seas,
     small are the minds of men;
     thus all men aren't equally wise:
     half wise, half not, everywhere.

54   Averagely wise a man ought to be,
     never too wise;
     for those men have the best sort of life
     who know a fair amount.

55   Averagely wise a man ought to be,
     never too wise;
     for a wise man's heart is seldom cheerful,
     if he who owns it's too wise.

56   Averagely wise a man ought to be,
     never too wise;
     let no one know his fate beforehand,
     for he'll have the most carefree spirit.

57   One brand takes fire from another, until it is consumed,
     a flame's kindled by flame;
     one man becomes clever by talking with another,
     but foolish through being reserved.

58   He should get up early, the man who means to take
     another's life or property;
     seldom does the loafing wolf snatch the ham,
     nor a sleeping man victory.

59   He should get up early, the man who has few workers,
     and set about his work with thought;
     much gets held up for the man sleeping in in the morning;
     wealth is half-won by activity.

60   Of dry wood and thatching-bark
     a man can know the measure;
     and of the wood which can get one through
     a quarter- or a half-year.

61 Washed and fed, a man should ride to the Assembly,
though he may not be very well dressed;
of his shoes and breeches no man should be ashamed,
nor of his horse, though he doesn't have a good one.

62 He snaps and cranes his neck when he comes to the sea,
the eagle to the ancient ocean;*
so does a man who comes among the multitude
and has few people to speak for him.

63 Asking and answering every wise man should do,
he who wants to be reputed intelligent;
one shall know, a second shall not,
the whole world knows, if three know.

64 Every man wise in counsel
should use his power in moderation;
for when he mingles with the brave he finds
that no one is boldest of all.

65 For those words which one man says to another,
often he gets paid back.*

66 Much too early I've come to many places,
but sometimes too late;
the ale was all drunk, or sometimes it wasn't yet brewed,
the unpopular man seldom hits on the right moment.

67 Here and there I might be invited home
when I had no need of food that mealtime;
or two hams would be hanging in a trusty friend's house
when I'd already eaten one.

68 Fire is best for the sons of men,
and the sight of the sun
his health, if a man can manage it,
living without disgrace.

69   No man is completely wretched, even if he has bad luck;
     one man is blessed with sons,
     another with kinsmen, another has enough money,
     another feels good from his deeds.

70   It is better to live than not to be alive,
     it's the living man who gets the cow;
     I saw fire blaze up for the wealthy man,
     and he was dead outside the door.

71   The lame man rides a horse, the handless man drives a herd,
     the deaf man fights and succeeds;
     to be blind is better than to be burnt:
     a corpse is of no use to anyone.

72   A son is better, even if he is born late,
     when the father is dead;
     seldom do memorial stones stand by the wayside,
     unless one kinsman raises them for another.

73   Two are destroyers of one, the tongue is the head's slayer,
     hidden under every fur coat I expect to find a hand.*

74   Night is eagerly awaited by him who can rely on his provisions;
     short are a ship's yards,
     changeable are autumn nights,
     many kinds of weather in five days,
     and more in one month.

75   The man who knows nothing does not know this:
     that many are fooled by money;
     one man is rich, another is not rich,
     he should not be blamed for that.

76   Cattle die, kinsmen die,*
     the self must also die;
     but the glory of reputation never dies,
     for the man who can get himself a good one.

77 Cattle die, kinsmen die,
  the self must also die;
  I know one thing which never dies:
  the reputation of each dead man.

78 Fully stocked folds I saw for Fitiung's sons,*
  now they carry a beggar's staff;
  wealth is like the twinkling of an eye,
  it is the most unreliable of friends.

79 The foolish man, if he manages to get
  money or the love of a woman,
  his arrogance increases, but not his common sense;
  on he goes deeply sunk in delusion.

80 That is now proved, what you asked of the runes,
  of divine origin
  which the great gods made
  and the mighty sage coloured;*
  then it is best for him if he stays silent.

81 At evening should the day be praised, the woman when she is
     cremated,
  the blade when it is tested, the girl when she is married,
  the ice when it is crossed, the ale when it is drunk.

82 In a wind one should cut wood, in fine weather row on the sea,
  in darkness chat with a girl: many are day's eyes;
  use a ship to glide along, a shield for defence,
  a sword for blows, and a girl for kisses.

83 By the fire one should drink ale, one should slide over the ice,
  buy a lean horse and a rusty blade,
  fatten the horse at home and the dog at someone else's.

84 The words of a girl no one should trust,
  nor what a woman says;
  for on a whirling wheel their hearts were made,*
  deceit lodged in their breasts.

85 A breaking bow, a burning flame,
    a gaping wolf, a cawing crow,
    a grunting pig, a rootless tree,
    a rising wave, a boiling kettle,

86 a flying dart, a falling wave,
    ice of one night, a coiled serpent,
    the bed-talk of a woman, or a broken sword,
    the playing of a bear, or a king's child,

87 a sick calf, an independent-minded slave,
    a seer who prophesies good, a newly killed dead man

88 an early-sown field let no man trust,
    nor too soon in a son;
    the weather rules the field and brains the son,
    both of them are risky.

89 A brother's killer, if met on the road,
    a house half-burned, a too swift horse—
    the mount is useless if a leg breaks—
    let no man be so trusting as to trust all these.

90 Such is the love of women, of those with false minds;
    it's like driving a horse without spiked shoes over slippery ice,
    a frisky two-year-old, badly broken in,
    or like steering, in a stiff wind, a rudderless boat
    or trying to catch when you're lame a reindeer on a thawing
        hillside.

91 I can speak frankly since I have known both:
    men's hearts are fickle towards women;
    when we speak most fairly, then we think most falsely,
    that entraps the wise mind.

92 He has to speak fairly and offer precious things,
    the man who wants a lady's love;
    praise the body of the radiant woman:
    he who flatters, gets.

93 No man should ever reproach
   another for being in love;
   often the wise man is seized, when the foolish man is not,
   by a desire-arousing appearance.

94 Not at all should one man reproach another
   for what is common among men;
   among men's sons the wise are made into fools
   by that mighty force: desire.

95 The mind alone knows what lies near the heart,
   he is alone with his spirit;
   no sickness is worse for the sensible man
   than to find no contentment in anything.

96 That I found when I sat among the reeds
   and waited for my beloved;
   body and soul the shrewd girl was to me,
   nonetheless I didn't win her.

97 Billing's girl I found on the bed,*
   sleeping, sun-radiant;
   no nobleman's pleasure could I imagine
   except to live beside that body.

98 'Towards evening, Odin, you should come again,
   if you want to talk a girl round;
   all will be lost unless only we know
   of such shamelessness together.'

99 Back I turned, and thought that I loved,
   turned back from my certain pleasure;
   this I thought: that I would have
   all her heart and her love-play.

100 When next I came, all the keen
    warrior-band were awake,
    with burning torches and barricading wood:
    such a wretched path was determined for me.

101   And near morning, when I came again,
       then the hall-company were asleep;
       a bitch I found then tied on the bed
       of that good woman.

102   Many a good girl when you know her well
       is fickle of heart towards men;
       I found that out, when I tried to seduce
       that sagacious woman into shame;
       every degradation the clever woman devised for me,
       and I got nothing from the girl at all.

103   At home a man should be cheerful and merry with his guest,
       he should be shrewd about himself,
       with a good memory and eloquent, if he wants to be very wise,
       often should he speak of good things;
       a nincompoop that man is called, who can't say much for
           himself,
       that is the hallmark of a moron.

104   I visited the old giant, now I've come back,*
       I didn't get much there from being silent;
       with many words I spoke to my advantage
       in Suttung's halls.

105   Gunnlod gave me on her golden throne
       a drink of the precious mead;
       a poor reward I let her have in return,
       for her open-heartedness,
       for her sorrowful spirit.

106   With Rati the auger's mouth I made space for myself*
       and made it gnaw through the rock;
       over me and under me went the giants' paths,
       thus I risked my head.

107   That bargain-bought beauty I made good use of,
       the wise lack for little;
       for Odrerir has now come up*
       to the rim of men's sanctuaries.

108 I am in doubt as to whether I would have come
back from the giants' courts,
if I had not used Gunnlod, that good woman,
and put my arms about her.

109 The next day the frost-giants went
to ask for the High One's advice, in the High One's hall;
they asked about Bolverk: whether he was amongst the gods,*
or whether Suttung had slaughtered him.

110 I think Odin will have sworn a sacred ring-oath,*
how can his pledge be trusted?
He left Suttung defrauded of the drink
and made Gunnlod weep.

111 It is time to declaim from the sage's high-seat,
at Urd's spring;
I saw and was silent, I saw and I considered,
I heard the speech of men;
I heard talk of runes nor were they silent about interpretation,
at the High One's hall, in the High One's hall;
thus I heard them speak:

112 I advise you, Loddfafnir, to take this advice,*
it will be useful if you learn it,
do you good, if you have it:
don't get up at night, except if you're on watch
or if you need to visit somewhere outside.*

113 I advise you, Loddfafnir, to take this advice,
it will be useful if you learn it,
do you good, if you have it:
in a witch's arms you should never sleep,
so she encloses you with her limbs;

114 she'll bring it about that you won't care
about the Assembly or the king's business;
you won't want food nor the society of people,
sorrowful you'll go to sleep.

115 I advise you, Loddfafnir, to take this advice,
     it will be useful if you learn it,
     do you good, if you have it:
     never entice another's wife to you
     as a close confidante.

116 I advise you, Loddfafnir, to take this advice,
     it will be useful if you learn it,
     do you good, if you have it:
     on mountain or fjord should you feel like travelling,
     make sure you've enough food along.

117 I advise you, Loddfafnir, to take this advice,
     it will be useful if you learn it,
     do you good, if you have it:
     never let a wicked man know
     of any misfortune you suffer;
     for from a wicked man you will never get
     a good thought in return.

118 I saw a man terribly wounded
     by a wicked woman's words;
     a malicious tongue brought about his death,
     and by no means through proven guilt.

119 I advise you, Loddfafnir, to take this advice,
     it will be useful if you learn it,
     do you good, if you have it:
     you know, if you've a friend, one whom you trust well,
     go to see him often;
     for brushwood grows, and tall grass,
     on the road which no man treads.

120 I advise you, Loddfafnir, to take this advice,
     it will be useful if you learn it,
     do you good, if you have it:
     draw to you a good man in friendly intimacy
     and learn helpful charms all your life.

121   I advise you, Loddfafnir, to take this advice,
it will be useful if you learn it,
do you good, if you have it:
with your friend never be
the first to tear fine friendship asunder;
sorrow eats the heart if you don't have someone
to whom to tell all your thoughts.

122   I advise you, Loddfafnir, to take this advice,
it will be useful if you learn it,
do you good, if you have it:
you should never bandy words
with a stupid fool;

123   for from a wicked man you will never get
a good return;
but a good man will make you
assured of favour through his praise.

124   That is the true mingling of kinship when a man can tell
someone all his thoughts;
anything is better than to be fickle;
he is no true friend who only says pleasant things.

125   I advise you, Loddfafnir, to take this advice,
it will be useful if you learn it,
do you good, if you have it:
not three quarrelsome words should you bandy with an
    inferior;
often the better retreats
when the worse man fights.

126   I advise you, Loddfafnir, to take this advice,
it will be useful if you learn it,
do you good, if you have it:
be neither a shoemaker nor a shaftmaker
for anyone but yourself;
if the shoe is badly fitting or if the shaft be crooked,
then curses are called down on you.

127   I advise you, Loddfafnir, to take this advice,
      it will be useful if you learn it,
      do you good, if you have it:
      where you recognize evil, call it evil,
      and give no truce to your enemies.

128   I advise you, Loddfafnir, to take this advice,
      it will be useful if you learn it,
      do you good, if you have it:
      never be made glad by wickedness
      but please yourself with good things.

129   I advise you, Loddfafnir, to take this advice,
      it will be useful if you learn it,
      do you good, if you have it:
      you should never look upwards in battle:*
      —men's sons become madmen—
      and people may try to bewitch you.

130   I advise you, Loddfafnir, to take this advice,
      it will be useful if you learn it,
      do you good, if you have it:
      if you want to talk a good woman into secret love with you,
      and to get pleasure from her,
      make fair promises and keep them well:
      no man tires of good, if he can get it.

131   I advise you, Loddfafnir, to take this advice,
      it will be useful if you learn it,
      do you good, if you have it:
      I tell you to be cautious but not over-cautious;
      be most wary of ale, and of another's wife,
      and, thirdly, lest thieves beguile you.

132   I advise you, Loddfafnir, to take this advice,
      it will be useful if you learn it,
      do you good, if you have it:
      never hold up to scorn or mockery
      a guest or a wanderer.

133   Often they don't know for certain, they who sit inside,
whose kin those newcomers are;
no man is so good that he has no blemish,
nor so bad that he is good for nothing.

134   I advise you, Loddfafnir, to take this advice,
it will be useful if you learn it,
do you good, if you have it:
at a grey-haired sage you should never laugh!
Often what the old say is good;
often from a wrinkled bag come judicious words,
from the one who hangs around with the hides
and skulks among the skins
and lurks about the low-born.

135   I advise you, Loddfafnir, to take this advice,
it will be useful if you learn it,
do you good, if you have it:
don't bark at your guests or drive them from your gate,
treat the indigent well!

136   Mighty is that door-bar which has to move aside
to open up for everyone;
give a ring, or there'll be called down on you
a curse in every limb.

137   I advise you, Loddfafnir, to take this advice,
it will be useful if you learn it,
do you good, if you have it:
where you drink ale, choose yourself earth's power!*
For earth soaks up drunkenness, and fire works against
    sickness,
oak against constipation, an ear of corn against witchcraft,
the hall against household strife, for hatred the moon should
    be invoked—
earthworms for inflamed parts, and runes against evil;
land must take up the flood.

138   I know that I hung on a windswept tree*
     nine long nights,
     wounded with a spear, dedicated to Odin,
     myself to myself,
     on that tree of which no man knows
     from where its roots run.

139   With no bread did they refresh me nor a drink from a horn,
     downwards I peered;
     I took up the runes, screaming I took them,
     then I fell back from there.

140   Nine mighty spells I learnt from the famous son
     of Bolthor, Bestla's father,*
     and I got a drink of the precious mead,
     I, soaked from Odrerir.

141   Then I began to quicken and be wise,
     and to grow and to prosper;
     one word from another word found a word for me,
     one deed from another deed found a deed for me.

142   The runes you must find and meaningful letters,
     very great letters,
     very stiff letters,
     which the mighty sage coloured
     and the huge Powers made
     and the runemaster of the gods carved out.

143   Odin among the Æsir, and Dain among the elves,
     Dvalin among the dwarfs,
     Asvid among the giants,
     I myself carved some.

144   Do you know how to carve, do you know how to interpret,
     do you know how to colour, do you know how to question,
     do you know how to ask, do you know how to sacrifice,
     do you know how to dispatch, do you know how to slaughter?

145 Better not to pray than to sacrifice too much:
one gift always calls for another;
better not dispatched than too many slaughtered.
So Thund carved before the close of nations' history,*
where he rose up, when he came back.

146 I know those spells which a ruler's wife doesn't know,*
nor any man's son;
'help' one is called,
and that will help you against
law-suits and sorrows
and every sort of anxiety.

147 I know a second one which the sons of men need,
those who want to live as physicians.

148 I know a third one if there's great need for me
that my furious enemies are fettered;
the edges of my foes I can blunt,
neither weapons nor cudgels will bite for them.

149 I know a fourth one if men put
bonds upon my limbs;
I can chant so that I can walk away,
fetters spring from my feet,
and chains from my hands.

150 I know a fifth if I see, shot in malice,
an arrow fly amid the army:
it cannot fly so hard that I cannot hinder it
if I see it with my eyes.

151 I know a sixth one if a man wounds me
using roots of the sap–filled wood:
and that man who conjured to harm me,
the evil consumes him, not me.

152 I know a seventh one if I see towering flames
in the hall about my companions:
it can't burn so widely that I can't counteract it;
I know the spells to chant.

153 I know an eighth one, which is most useful
for everyone to acquire;
where hatred flares up between the sons of warriors,
then I can quickly bring settlement.

154 I know a ninth one if I am in need,
if I must save my ship when afloat;
the wind I can quieten upon the wave
and lull all the sea to sleep.

155 I know a tenth one if I see witches
playing up in the air;
I can bring it about that they wander astray
from their shapes left at home,
from their minds left at home.

156 I know an eleventh if I have to lead
long-loyal friends into battle;
under the shields I chant, and they journey confidently,
safely to the battle,
safely from the battle,
safely they come back from everywhere.

157 I know a twelfth one if I see, up in a tree,
a dangling corpse in a noose:
I can so carve and colour the runes
that the man walks
and talks with me.

158 I know a thirteenth if I must pour water
over a young warrior:
he will not fall though he goes into battle,
before swords that man will not sink.

159 I know a fourteenth if I have to reckon up
the gods before a group of men:
of Æsir and elves, I know every detail,
few who are not wise know that.

160   I know a fifteenth, which the dwarf Thiodrerir
       chanted before Delling's doors:
       power he sang for the Æsir and advancement for the elves,
       thoughtfulness to Hroptatyr.

161   I know a sixteenth if I want to have all
       a clever woman's heart and love-play:
       I can turn the thought of the white-armed woman
       and change her mind entirely.

162   I know a seventeenth, so that any young woman
       will scarcely want to shun me.
       Of these spells, Loddfafnir,
       you will long be in want;
       though they'd be good for you, if you get them,
       useful if you learn them,
       handy, if you have them.

163   I know an eighteenth, which I shall never teach
       to any girl or any man's wife—
       it's always better when just one person knows,
       that follows at the end of the spells—
       except that one woman who embraces me in her arms,
       or who may be my sister.

164   Now the High One's song is recited, in the High One's hall
       very useful to the sons of men,
       quite useless to the sons of men,*
       luck to him who recited, luck to him who knows!
       May he benefit, he who learnt it,
       luck to those who listened!

VAFTHRUDNIR'S SAYINGS

As the *Seeress's Prophecy*, *Sayings of the High One*, and *Grimnir's Sayings* show, Odin is characterized by his obsessive quest for wisdom, particularly for information about Ragnarok. In this poem he sets off, against his wife's advice, disguised as a poor wanderer, to test his wisdom against the giant Vafthrudnir, known only from this poem. Once Odin has proved his mettle, by answering questions which the giant puts to him, he is invited to risk his head in questioning the giant. *Vafthrudnir's Sayings* (*Vafthrudnismal*) belongs to the genre of the wisdom contest, known in many other cultures. Two protagonists ask each other questions or riddles, until one fails to answer. Thus the questioner must know the answer to his question; the answerer corroborates the interlocutor's information, rather than providing new facts. The trick question with which Odin wins the contest seems to be a favourite of his, since he also uses it to secure victory in a riddle contest against King Heidrek in *Heidreks saga*. Vafthrudnir's questions elicit simple mythological facts: the names of the horses who draw the day and the night, the name of the river which divides giants and gods and of the field on which the battle of Ragnarok will be fought. Odin's questions are more pointed: he draws out the history of the universe, its past (vv. 20–35), and present (36–43), culminating in questions about the future and Ragnarok (44–54). Some scholars have speculated that Odin's real aim is to discover his own fate (52–3); once he hears about the wolf, he brings the contest to a speedy end with his unanswerable question. Odin alone knows what he whispered into Baldr's ear, but it has been guessed that Baldr is assured of his return after Ragnarok, as the *Seeress's Prophecy*, v. 59, tells us, to rule over the gods who survive. As a contest between god and giant, *Vafthrudnir's Sayings* is mimetic of Ragnarok. Vafthrudnir's answers emphasize the ancientness and authority of the giants as the first of beings, but Odin's questions lead away from the giants and their claims, to the final triumph of gods and men. It is they, Odin's descendants and creations, if not Odin himself, who will survive the final conflagration. The giants may have had a past, but they have no future; Vafthrudnir's defeat in the contest symbolizes the final defeat in time of the giant race.

Odin said:

1   'Advise me now, Frigg, for I long to journey
      to visit Vafthrudnir;
      I've a great curiosity to contend in ancient matters
      with that all-wise giant.'

Frigg said:

2   'I'd rather keep the Father of Hosts
      at home in the courts of the gods,
      for I know no giant to be as powerful
      as Vafthrudnir is.'

Odin said:

3   'Much I have travelled, much have I tried out,
      much have I tested the Powers;
      this I want to know: what kind of company
      is found in Vafthrudnir's hall.'

Frigg said:

4   'Journey safely! Come back safely!
      Be safe on the way!
      May your mind be sufficient when, Father of Men,
      you speak with the giant.'

5   Then Odin went to try the wisdom
      of the all-wise giant;
      to the hall he came which Im's father owned;*
      Odin went inside.

Odin said:

6   'Greetings, Vafthrudnir! Now I have come into the hall
      to see you in person;
      this I want to know first, whether you are wise
      or very wise, giant.'

Vafthrudnir said:

7   'What man is this who addresses me in hostile fashion
    in my hall?
    May you not come out of our halls alive
    unless you should be the wiser one.'

Odin said:

8   'Gagnrad I am called; now I have come walking,
    thirsty to your hall;
    in need of hospitality and of your welcome,
    I have journeyed long, giant.'

Vafthrudnir said:

9   'Why, Gagnrad, do you speak thus from the floor?
    Come take a seat in the hall!
    Then we shall test which one knows more,
    the guest or the old sage.'

Odin said:

10 'The poor man who comes to the wealthy one
    should speak when needful or be silent;
    to be too talkative I think will bring bad results
    when one comes to the cold-ribbed man.'

Vafthrudnir said:

11 'Tell me, Gagnrad, since on the hall-floor
    you want to try your skill,
    what that horse is called who draws every
    day over mankind.'

Odin said:

12 'Shining-mane, the shining one is called
    who draws day over mankind;
    the best of horses he is held to be among the Hreid-Goths,*
    always that horse's mane gleams.'

Vafthrudnir said:

13 'Tell me, Gagnrad, since on the hall-floor
   you want to try your skill,
   what that horse is called who from the east draws night
   to the beneficent Powers.'

Odin said:

14 'Frost-mane he is called, who draws every night
   to the beneficent Powers;
   foam from his bit he lets fall every morning;
   from there dew comes to the valleys.'

Vafthrudnir said:

15 'Tell me, Gagnrad, since on the hall-floor
   you want to try your skill,
   what that river is called which divides the land
   between the sons of giants and the gods.'

Odin said:

16 'Ifing the river is called, which divides the land
   between the sons of giants and the gods;
   freely it will flow through all time,
   ice never forms on the river.'

Vafthrudnir said:

17 'Tell me, Gagnrad, since on the hall-floor
   you want to try your skill,
   what that plain is called where in battle
   Surt and the good-tempered gods will meet.'

Odin said:

18 'Vigrid the plain is called, where in battle
   Surt and the good-tempered gods will meet;
   a hundred leagues it is in each direction;
   that is the field ordained for them.'

Vafthrudnir said:

19　'Wise you are, guest, come to the giant's bench,
　　　and we will speak together in the seat;
　　　we shall wager our heads in the hall,
　　　guest, on our wisdom.'

Odin said:

20　'Tell me this one thing if your mind is sufficient
　　　and you, Vafthrudnir, know,
　　　from where the earth came or the sky above,
　　　first, O wise giant.'

Vafthrudnir said:

21　'From Ymir's flesh the earth was shaped,*
　　　and the mountains from his bones;
　　　the sky from the skull of the frost-cold giant,
　　　and the sea from his blood.'

Odin said:

22　'Tell me this second thing if your mind is sufficient
　　　and you, Vafthrudnir, know,
　　　from where the moon came, so that it journeys over men,
　　　and likewise the sun.'

Vafthrudnir said:

23　'Mundilfaeri he is called, the father of Moon
　　　and likewise of Sun;
　　　they must circle through the sky, every day
　　　to count the years for men.'

Odin said:

24　'Tell me this third thing, since you are said to be wise,
　　　and you, Vafthrudnir, know,
　　　where day comes from, he who passes over mankind,
　　　or night with its new moons.'

Vafthrudnir said:

25 'Delling he is called, he is Day's father,
and Night was born of Norr;
new moon and dark of the moon the beneficent Powers made
to count the years for men.'

Odin said:

26 'Tell me this fourth thing, since you are said to be wise,
and you, Vafthrudnir, know,
from where winter came or warm summer,
first among the wise Powers.'

Vafthrudnir said:

27 'Wind-cool he is called, Winter's father,
and Mild One, the father of Summer.'

Odin said:

28 'Tell me this fifth thing, since you are said to be wise,
and you, Vafthrudnir, know,
who was the eldest of the Æsir or of Ymir's descendants
in bygone days.'

Vafthrudnir said:

29 'Uncountable winters before the earth was made,
then Bergelmir was born,
Thrudgelmir was his father,
and Aurgelmir his grandfather.'

Odin said:

30 'Tell me this sixth thing, since you are said to be wise,
and you, Vafthrudnir, know,
from where Aurgelmir came among the sons of giants,*
first, the wise giant.'

Vafthrudnir said:

31   'Out of Elivagar sprayed poison-drops,*
      so they grew until a giant came of them;
      [from there arose all our clan,
      thus they are all always terrifying.']*

Odin said:

32   'Tell me this seventh thing, since you are said to be wise,
      and you, Vafthrudnir, know,
      how he got children, that fierce giant,
      when he had no sport with giantesses.'

Vafthrudnir said:

33   'They said that under the frost-giant's arms
      a girl and boy grew together;
      one foot with the other, of the wise giant,
      begot a six-headed son.'

Odin said:

34   'Tell me this eighth thing, since you are said to be wise,
      and you, Vafthrudnir, know,
      what you first remember or what you know to be earliest,
      you are all-wise, giant.'

Vafthrudnir said:

35   'Uncountable winters before the world was made,
      then Bergelmir was born;
      that I remember first when the wise giant
      was first laid in his coffin.'*

Odin said:

36   'Tell me this ninth thing, since you are said to be wise,
      and you, Vafthrudnir, know,
      where the wind comes from which blows over the waves,
      which men never see itself.'

Vafthrudnir said:

37 'Carrion-swallower he is called, who sits at heaven's end,
    a giant in eagle's shape;
    from his wings, they say, the wind blows
    over all men.'

Odin said:

38 'Tell me this tenth thing, since all the fate of the gods
    you, Vafthrudnir, know,
    from where Niord came to the sons of the Æsir;
    he rules over very many temples and sanctuaries
    and he was not raised among the Æsir.'

Vafthrudnir said:

39 'In Vanaheim the wise Powers made him
    and gave him as hostage to the gods;
    at the doom of men he will come back
    home among the wise Vanir.'*

Odin said:

40 'Tell me that eleventh thing, where men fight
    in the courts every day.'

Vafthrudnir said:

41 'All the Einheriar fight in Odin's courts*
    every day;
    they choose the slain and ride from the battle;
    then they sit the more at peace together.'

Odin said:

42 'Tell me this twelfth thing, why all the fate of the gods
    you, Vafthrudnir, know;
    of the secrets of the giants and of all the gods
    tell most truly,
    all-wise giant.'

Vafthrudnir said:

43 'Of the secrets of the giants and of all the gods,
I can tell truly,
for I have been into every world;
nine worlds I have travelled through to Mist-hell,
there men die down out of hell.'

Odin said:

44 'Much I have travelled, much have I tried out,
much have I tested the Powers;
which humans will survive when the famous
Mighty Winter is over among men?'

Vafthrudnir said:

45 'Life and Lifthrasir, and they will hide
in Hoddmimir's wood;*
they will have the morning dew for food;
from them generations will spring.'

Odin said:

46 'Much I have travelled, much have I tried out,
much have I tested the Powers;
from where will a sun come into the smooth heaven
when Fenrir has destroyed this one?'

Vafthrudnir said:

47 'Elf-radiance will bear a daughter,
before Fenrir destroys her;
she shall ride, when the Powers die,
the girl on her mother's paths.'

Odin said:

48 'Much I have travelled, much have I tried out,
much have I tested the Powers;
who are those girls who glide over the sea,*
wise in spirit, they journey?'

Vafthrudnir said:

49 'Three mighty rivers flow over the settlement*
    of Mogthrasir's girls;*
    theirs are the only protective spirits in this world,*
    although they were raised among giants.'

Odin said:

50 'Much I have travelled, much have I tried out,
    much have I tested the Powers;
    which Æsir will rule over the gods' possessions,
    when Surt's fire is slaked?'

Vafthrudnir said:

51 'Vidar and Vali will live in the gods' sanctuaries,
    when Surt's fire is slaked;
    Modi and Magni shall have Miollnir*
    and demonstrate battle-strength.'

Odin said:

52 'Much I have travelled, much have I tried out,
    much have I tested the Powers;
    what will Odin's life's end be,
    when the Powers are torn apart?'

Vafthrudnir said:

53 'The wolf will swallow the Father of Men,
    Vidar will avenge this;
    the cold jaws of the wolf
    he will sunder in battle.'

Odin said:

54 'Much I have travelled, much have I tried out,
    much have I tested the Powers;
    what did Odin say into his son's ear*
    before he mounted the pyre?'

Vafthrudnir said:

55   'No man knows what you said in bygone days
        into your son's ear;
        with doomed mouth I've spoken my ancient lore
        about the fate of the gods;
        I've been contending with Odin in words of wisdom;
        you'll always be the wisest of beings.'

GRIMNIR'S SAYINGS

The prose introduction to *Grimnir's Sayings* (*Grimnismal*) gives an unexpected account of Odin and Frigg as rival patrons to two kingly candidates, the lost sons of King Hraudung. Odin uses cunning to give his foster-son an unfair advantage, and then precipitates a matrimonial quarrel by pointing out the different fates which have overtaken their protégés. Frigg is swift to get her own back, accusing Odin's favourite of stinginess, a serious charge, given the near-sacred character which Germanic societies ascribed to hospitality. Frigg duplicitously ensures that Geirrod does mistreat his guest, relying on Odin's practice of disguising himself when visiting strange halls. Odin arrives at Geirrod's hall calling himself Grimnir (the Masked One). Geirrod's methods of torture, starvation, and heat have been thought to recall shamanistic rituals allowing access to arcane knowledge kept hidden from the uninitiated; such practices could have been known to the Scandinavians from their northern neighbours, the Lapps. On the ninth night (nine is a magical number), Odin reveals himself. Geirrod realizes his mistake too late; as eventually happens to most Odinic protégés, the hero has lost his patron's favour and is doomed to die. Geirrod's son, Agnar, who, significantly, bears his uncle's name and is now the same age as his uncle was when the brothers encountered their divine protectors, has recognized the responsibilities of the host in giving Odin a drink, and the god's favour now falls on him.

Like *Vafthrudnir's Sayings*, *Grimnir's Sayings* is obsessed with mythological facts: the topography of the world of the gods, rather than its history, is revealed in Odin's monologue. Stimulated by heat and hunger, Odin gradually reveals his divinity, first through demonstrating his mastery of arcane knowledge, wide-ranging and compendious, thematically arranged to allude to his physical torment and the judgement and revenge which will result from it. Finally, after the crucial v. 45, in which Odin asserts that right relations of sacrifice and patronage have been restored between gods and men by Agnar's action, he identifies himself in all his guises. Like *Sayings of the High One*, *Grimnir's Sayings* intends both to reveal mythological knowledge and to teach wisdom, a wisdom which comes too late for Geirrod, but which qualifies Agnar to become king in his father's place. The acquisition of all sorts of wisdom: runic, magical, gnomic, and mythological, as evidenced by the poems recounting Sigurd's youth, is necessary for the hero to achieve the transition from fighter to ruler. In its context in the *Poetic Edda*, *Grimnir's Sayings* both completes the exposition of Odinic wisdom and looks forward to the exploration of kingship which develops in the heroic poems.

About the Sons of King Hraudung   *King Hraudung had two sons;
one was called Agnar, and the other Geirrod. Agnar was 10 years old,
and Geirrod 8. They both rowed out in a boat with rods and trailing
lines to catch small fish. The wind drove them out into the ocean. In the
dark that night, they made land-fall, and went ashore; they found a
crofter. They stayed there for the winter. The old woman fostered Agnar,
and the old man Geirrod. In the spring, the old man got them a ship.
And when he and the old woman took them down to the shore, then the
old man spoke privately to Geirrod. They got a breeze and came to their
father's harbour. Geirrod was forward in the ship, he jumped ashore and
pushed the ship out and said: 'Go where the evil one may take you!' The
ship was driven out, and Geirrod went up to the house. He was greeted
joyfully; his father had died. Then Geirrod was taken as king and
became a splendid man.*

Odin and Frigg sat in Hlidskialf and looked into all the worlds.
Odin said, 'Do you see Agnar, your foster-son, there raising children with
a giantess in a cave? But Geirrod, my foster-son, is king and rules over
the land.' Frigg says: 'He is so stingy with food that he tortures his guests
if it seems to him that too many have come.' Odin says that is the greatest
lie. They wagered on the matter.*

*Frigg sent her handmaid, Fulla, to Geirrod. She told the king to
beware lest a wizard, who had come into the country, should bewitch
him, and said he could be known by this sign: that no dog was so fierce
that it would leap on him. And that was the greatest slander that
Geirrod was not generous with food; however, he had that man arrested
whom no dog would attack. He was wearing a blue cloak and called
himself Grimnir, and would say nothing more about himself, though he
was asked. The king had him tortured to make him speak and set him
between two fires, and he sat there eight nights.*

*Geirrod the king had a son who was 10 years old, and he was called
Agnar after Geirrod's brother. Agnar went to Grimnir and gave him a
full horn to drink from, saying that the king was acting wrongly to have
him, an innocent man, tortured. Grimnir drank it up. Then the fire had
come so close that Grimnir's cloak burned. He said:*

1   'Hot you are, hurrying fire, and rather too fierce;
    go away from me, flame!
    My fur cloak singes, though I lift it up,
    my mantle burns before me.

2   'Eight nights I have sat here between the fires,
    yet no one offered me food,
    except Agnar alone, and he alone shall rule,
    the son of Geirrod, the land of the Goths.

3   'Blessed shall you be, Agnar,
    since Odin bids you be blest;
    for one drink you shall never
    get a better reward.

4   'The land is sacred which I see lying
    near the Æsir and elves;
    but in Thrudheim Thor shall remain,
    until the Powers are torn asunder.

5   'Yewdale it is called, the place where Ull*
    has made a hall for himself;
    Alfheim the gods gave to Freyr
    in bygone days as tooth-payment.*

6   'There is a third home where the cheerful Powers
    roofed the rooms with silver;
    Valaskialf it is called, which the God designed for himself*
    in bygone days.

7   'Sokkvabekk a fourth is called and cool waves
    resound over it;
    there Odin and Saga drink every day,*
    joyful, from golden cups.

8   'Gladsheim a fifth is called, there gold-bright Valhall
    extends out widely;
    there Odin chooses every day
    those dead in combat.

9   'It's very easy to recognize for those who come to Odin
     to see how his hall's arranged;
     spear-shafts the building has for rafters, it's roofed with shields,
     mail-coats are strewn on the benches.

10   'It's very easy to recognize for those who come to Odin
     to see how his hall's arranged;
     a wolf hangs west of the door
     and an eagle hovers above.*

11   'Thrymheim the sixth is called, where Thiazi lived,*
     the all-powerful giant;
     but now Skadi, the shining bride of the gods,*
     lives in her father's ancient courts.

12   'Breidablik is the seventh, where Baldr has
     made a hall for himself,
     in that land where I know there
     are the fewest runes of ill-omen.

13   'Himinbiorg is the eighth, and there, they say,
     Heimdall rules over his sanctuaries;
     there the gods' glad watchman drinks good mead
     in the peaceful hall.

14   'Folkvang is the ninth, and there Freyia fixes
     allocation of seats in the hall;
     half the slain she chooses every day,
     and half Odin owns.

15   'Glitnir is the tenth, it has golden buttresses,
     and likewise is roofed with silver;
     and there Forseti lives most days*
     and puts to sleep all quarrels.

16   'Noatun is the eleventh, where Niord has
     made a hall for himself,
     the prince of men, lacking in malice,
     rules a high-timbered temple.

17 'Brushwood grows and high grass
and woods in Vidar's land;
and there the son proclaims from his horse's back
his keenness to avenge his father.

18 'Andhrimnir has Sæhrimnir boiled
in Eldhrimnir,*
the best of pork; but few know
on what the Einheriar are nourished.

19 'Geri and Freki he satiates,*
the glorious Father of Hosts, trained in battle;
but on wine alone the weapon-magnificent
Odin always lives.

20 'Hugin and Munin fly every day*
over the vast-stretching world;
I fear for Hugin that he will not come back,
yet I tremble more for Munin.

21 'Thund roars, the Great Wolf's fish*
swims happily in the stream;
the river's current seems too strong for
the slaughter-horse to wade.

22 'Valgrind it's called, standing on the plain,
sacred before the sacred door:
ancient is that gate, but few men know
how it is closed up with a lock.

23 'Five hundred doors and forty
I think there are in Valhall;
eight hundred Einheriar will pass through a single door*
when they march out to fight the wolf.

24 'Five hundred daises and forty,
so I think Bilskirnir has in all;*
of all those halls which I know to be roofed,
my son's I know is the greatest.

25   'Heidrun is the goat's name, who stands on Father of Hosts' hall
     and browses on Lærad's branches;*
     she will fill a vat of shining mead;
     that liquor cannot ever diminish.

26   'Eikthyrnir is the hart's name, who stands on Father of Hosts'
         hall
     and browses on Lærad's branches;
     and from his antlers there's dripping into Hvergelmir,
     from thence all waters make their way:

27   'Sid and Vid, Sækin and Eikin,*
     Svol and Gunnthro,
     Fiorm and Fimbulthul,
     Rin and Rennandi,
     Gipul and Gopul,
     Gomul and Geirvimul,
     they flow round the gods' treasure-hoard,
     Thyn and Vin, Tholl and Holl,
     Grad and Gunnthorin.

28   'Vina is one's name, another Vegsvinn,
     a third Thiodnuma,
     Nyt and Not, Nonn and Hronn,
     Slid and Hrid, Sylg and Ylg,
     Vid and Van, Vond and Strond,
     Gioll and Leipt, they fall close to men,
     and flow down from here to hell.

29   'Kormt and Ormt and the two Kerlaugar,
     these Thor must wade
     every day, when he goes to give judgements
     at Yggdrasill's ash,
     for the Æsir's bridge burns all with flames,
     the sacred waters boil.

30 'Glad and Golden, Glassy and Skeidbrimir,
    Silvertuft and Sinir,
    Gils and Hidden-hoof, Goldtuft and Lightfoot,
    these horses the Æsir ride
    every day, when they go to give judgements,
    at Yggdrasill's ash.

31 'Three roots there grow in three directions
    under Yggdrasill's ash;
    Hel lives under one, under the second, the frost-giants,
    under the third, humankind.

32 'Ratatosk is the squirrel's name, who must scurry
    about on Yggdrasill's ash;
    the eagle's utterance he must bring from above
    and tell to Nidhogg below.*

33 'There are four harts too, who browse on its shoots,
    with their necks tilted back;
    Dain and Dvalin,
    Duneyr and Durathror.

34 'More serpents lie under Yggdrasill's ash
    than any numbskull fool can imagine:
    Goin and Moin, they are Grafvitnir's sons,
    Grabak and Grafvollud,
    Ofnir and Svafnir I think for ever will
    erode the tree's branches.

35 'Yggdrasill's ash suffers agony
    more than men know:
    a stag nibbles it above, but at its side it's decaying,
    and Nidhogg rends it beneath.

36 'Hrist and Mist, I wish would bear a horn to me,*
    Skeggiold and Skogul,
    Hild and Thrud, Hlokk and Herfiotur,
    Goll and Geirolul,
    Randgrid and Radgrid, and Reginleif;
    they bear ale to the Einheriar.

37 'Arvak and Alsvid, the slender ones, must pull
    the sun up from here;
    and under their shoulders the cheerful gods,
    the Æsir, have installed cooling-iron.*

38 'Svalin he's called, he stands before the sun,
    a shield for the shining goddess;
    mountain and sea I know would burn up
    if he fell away from there.

39 'Skoll a wolf is called who pursues the shining goddess
    to the protecting woods;
    and another is Hati, he is Hrodvitnir's son,*
    who must run before heaven's bright bride.

40 'From Ymir's flesh the earth was made,*
    and from his blood, the sea,
    mountains from his bones, trees from his hair,
    and from his skull, the sky.

41 'And from his eyelashes the cheerful gods
    made Midgard for men's sons;
    and from his brain the hard-tempered clouds
    were all created.

42 'Ull's protection, and that of all the gods,
    he has, the first one to seize the flames;*
    for the worlds lie open over the sons of the gods
    when the kettles are lifted off.*

43 'Ivaldi's sons in bygone days*
    went to create Skidbladnir,
    the best of ships, for shining Freyr,
    Niord's beneficent son.

44 'Yggdrasill's ash is the most pre-eminent of trees,
    as is Skidbladnir of ships,
    Odin of the Æsir, Sleipnir of horses,
    Bilrost of bridges, Bragi of poets,
    Habrok of hawks, and Garm of dogs.*

45 'Fleeting visions I have now revealed before the victory-gods'
    sons,*
now the wished-for protection will awaken;
to all the Æsir it will become known
on Ægir's benches,
at Ægir's feast.*

46 'I was called Mask, I was called Wanderer,*
General and Helm-wearer,
Known and Third, Thund and Ud,
Hellblind and High;

47 'Steady and Svipal and Sanngetal,
War-merry and Hnikar,
Weak-eyed, Flame-eyed, Bolverk, Fiolnir,
Mask and Masked One, Glapsvid and Much-wise;

48 'Broadhat, Broadbeard, Victory-father, Hnikud,
All-Father, Father of the Slain, Atrid and Burden-god;
by one name I have never been known
since I went among the people.

49 'Grimnir they called me at Geirrod's
and Ialk at Asmund's,
and then Kialar, when I pulled the sledge;
Thror at the Assembly,
Vidur in battle,
Oski and Omi, Equal-high and Biflindi,
Gondlir and Harbard among the gods.

50 'Svidur and Svidrir I was called at Sokkmimir's,*
and I tricked the old giant then,
when I became of Midvidnir's famous son
the sole slayer.

51 'Drunk are you, Geirrod! You've drunk too much;
you are bereft of much, of my support,
that of all the Einheriar, and Odin's favour.

52   'Much I told you but little you remember;
       friends have played you false;
       I see my friend's sword lying
       all spattered with his blood.

53   'The Terrible One will now take the weapon-weary slaughtered
            man;
       I know your life is over;
       the *disir* are against you, now you may see Odin,*
       draw near to me if you can!

54   'Odin I am called now, Terrible One I was called before,
       they called me Thund before that,
       Vak and Skilfing, Vafud and Hroptatyr,
       Gaut and Ialk among the gods,
       Ofnir and Svafnir, all these I think stem
       from me alone.'

*Geirrod the king sat with a sword on his lap, half drawn from the sheath.
But when he heard that it was Odin who had come there, he stood up
and intended to pull Odin away from the fire. The sword slipped from his
hand, hilt downwards. The king lost his footing and plunged forwards,
and the sword pierced him through, and he was killed. Odin disappeared.
And Agnar was then king for a long time afterwards.*

SKIRNIR'S JOURNEY

Freyr falls in love with a giant's daughter whom he sees from Odin's high-seat, Hlidskialf. According to Snorri (*Edda*, pp. 31–2) his love-sickness is a punishment for usurping Odin's place, though the poem does not suggest this. Freyr's concerned parents, Niord and Skadi,* ask their son's old friend and servant Skirnir ('Shining One') to help. Skirnir volunteers to go on a wooing mission and, after a remarkably smooth journey, effectively bullies the reluctant girl into agreeing to a rendezvous with Freyr. Snorri tells us in *Ynglinga saga*, ch. 10, that the pair married and had a son called Fiolnir who was the ancestor of the Yngling dynasty of Norwegian kings, and that in handing his sword over to Skirnir, Freyr leaves himself weaponless at Ragnarok. Although the poem has no especial connection with wisdom, it is composed mostly in *ljodahattr* dialogue. Several scholars have thought that, with its succession of lively scenes, *Skirnir's Journey* may well have been intended for dramatic presentation.

Freyr, the son of Niord, had seated himself in Hlidskialf and looked over all the worlds. He looked into Giant-land and saw there a beautiful girl, as she was walking from her father's hall to an outbuilding. From that he caught great sickness of heart. Skirnir was the name of Freyr's page. Niord asked him to go and have a conversation with Freyr. Then Skadi said:

1 'Get up now, Skirnir, and go and ask to speak
　　with our son
　　and ask this: with whom the wise man
　　is so terribly angry.'

Skirnir said:

2 'Harsh words I expect from your son
　　if I go to talk to the young man
　　and ask this: with whom the wise man
　　is so terribly angry.

3 'Tell me, Freyr, war-leader of the gods,
　　for I would like to know,
　　why do you sit alone in the long hall,
　　my lord, day after day?'

Freyr said:

4 'Why should I tell you, young man,
about my great sorrow of heart,
for the elf-radiance shines day after every day,*
but not according to my desires.'

Skirnir said:

5 'I don't think your desires can be very great,
that you, sir, can not tell me,
for we were young together in bygone days;
you and I may well trust each other.'

Freyr said:

6 'In Gymir's courts I saw walking
a girl pleasing to me.
Her arms shine and from them
all the sea and air catch light.

7 'More pleasing to me is the girl than any girl to any young man,
in bygone days;
of all the gods and the elves, no one wishes
that we should be together.'

Skirnir said:

8 'Give me that horse which will carry me through the knowing,
dark, flickering flame,
and that sword which fights by itself
against the giant race.'

Freyr said:

9 'I'll give you that horse which will carry you through the
knowing,
dark, flickering flame,
and that sword which will fight by itself
if he who wields it is wise.'

Skirnir said to the horse:

10 'It is dark outside, I declare it's time for us to go
over the dewy mountain,
through giant realms;
we'll both get there or the all-powerful giant
will seize us both.'

*Skirnir rode to Giant-land to Gymir's courts. There were savage dogs
tied in front of the gate in the wooden fence surrounding Gerd's hall. He
rode to where a herdsman was sitting on a mound and greeted him:*

11 'Tell me this, herdsman, as you sit on the mound*
and watch all the ways,
how I may come to converse with the young girl,
despite the dogs of Gymir.'

The herdsman said:

12 'Are you doomed or are you dead already?
Conversation you shall never have
with Gymir's excellent daughter.'

Skirnir said:

13 'The choices are better than simply sobbing,
for a man who is eager to advance;
for on one day all my life-span was shaped,
all my days laid down.'

Gerd said:

14 'What is that noise of noises which I hear now
making a noise in our dwellings?
The earth trembles and all Gymir's courts
shudder before it.'

The serving-maid said:

15 'There is a man out here, dismounted from a horse,
he is letting his horse graze.'

Gerd said:

16   'Tell him to come in into our hall
      and drink the famous mead;
      though I am afraid that out here may be
      my brother's slayer.*

17   'Who are you, of the elves or of the Æsir's sons,
      or of the wise Vanir?
      Why do you come alone over the wild fire
      to see our company?'

Skirnir said:

18   'I am not of the elves or of the Æsir's sons,
      or of the wise Vanir,
      though I come alone over the wild fire
      to see your company.

19   'Eleven apples here I have all of gold,*
      those I will give you, Gerd,
      to buy your favour, that you may say that to you
      Freyr's the least loathsome man alive.'

Gerd said:

20   'Eleven apples I will never accept
      at any man's desire,
      nor will Freyr and I settle down together
      as long as our lives last.'

Skirnir said:

21   'I shall give you a ring, the one which was burnt
      with Odin's young son;
      eight are the equally heavy ones, that drop from it
      every ninth night.'*

Gerd said:

22   'I won't accept a ring, even if it was burnt
      with Odin's young son;
      I lack no gold in Gymir's courts,
      my father's wealth at my disposal.'

Skirnir said:

23   'Do you see this sword, girl, slender, inlaid,
      which I have here in my hand?
      Your head I shall strike from your neck
      unless you declare we are reconciled.'

Gerd said:

24   'Coercion I shall never endure
      at any man's desire;
      though I reckon this, if you and Gymir meet,
      keen fighters, a battle is bound to occur.'

Skirnir said:

25   'Do you see this sword, girl, slender, inlaid,
      which I have here in my hand?
      Before these edges the old giant will fall,
      your father will be doomed.

26   'I strike you with a taming wand, and I will tame you,
      girl, to my desires;
      there you shall go where the sons of men
      will never see you again.

27   'On an eagle's mound you shall sit from early morning,
      looking out of the world, hankering towards hell;
      food shall be fouler to you than is
      the shining serpent to all living men.

28 'May you become a spectacle when you come out;
    may Hrimnir glare at you, may everything stare at you,
    better known may you be than the watchman among the
        gods,*
    may you gape through the bars!

29 'Madness and howling, tearing affliction and unbearable
        desire,
    may tears well up for you with grief!
    Sit down, for I shall tell you
    heavy tormenting craving
    and twofold grief:

30 'Fiends will oppress you all the long weary day,
    in the giants' courts;
    to the halls of the frost-giants every day you shall
    creep without choice,
    without hope of choice;
    weeping you shall have for pleasure,
    and misery shall go with your tears.

31 'With a three-headed ogre you shall linger out your life,
    or else be without a man!
    May your spirit be seized!
    May pining waste you away!
    Be like the thistle which is crushed
    at the end of the harvest!

32 'I went to the forest, to the sap-rich tree,
    to get a magic twig;
    a magic twig I got.

33 'Odin is angry with you, Thor is angry with you,
    Freyr will hate you;
    most wicked girl, you have brought down upon you
    the magic-mighty wrath of the gods.

34   'Hear O giants, hear O frost-ogres,
      Suttung's sons, the Æsir-band itself,
      how I forbid, how I deny
      pleasure in men to the girl,
      benefit from men to the girl.

35   'Hrimgrimnir he's called, the giant who'll possess you
      down below the corpse-gates,
      where bondsmen will give you
      goat's piss at the tree-roots;*
      finer drink you will never get,
      girl, at your desire,
      girl, at my desire!

36   ' "Ogre" I carve for you and three runes:*
      lewdness and frenzy
      and unbearable desire;
      I can carve that off, as I carved that on,
      if there is need of this.'

Gerd said:

37   'Be welcome now, lad, and receive the crystal cup,
      full of ancient mead;
      though I had never thought that I should ever love
      one of the Vanir well.'

Skirnir said:

38   'All my errand will I know
      before I ride home from here,
      when you'll grant a tryst
      to Niord's vigorous son.'

Gerd said:

39   'Barri is the name, as we both know,
      of a wind-calm grove;
      and after nine nights, there to Niord's son
      Gerd will give love's pleasure.'

Then Skirnir rode home. Freyr stood outside and greeted him and asked for news:

40   'Tell me, Skirnir, before you fling the saddle from the horse
         and you step a foot further,
         what you achieved in Giant-land,
         your desire or mine.'

Skirnir said:

41   'Barri is the name, as we both know,
         of a wind-calm grove;
         and after nine nights, there to Niord's son
         Gerd will give love's pleasure.'

Freyr said:

42   'Long is one night, long are two,
         how shall I long through three?
         Often a month to me has seemed less
         than half one of these wedding-eves.'

HARBARD'S SONG

Odin, in disguise, and Thor meet at a fjord crossing. Odin refuses to ferry Thor over the water and the two engage in a ritual exchange of insults. *Harbard's Song* (*Harbardzljod*) is both typical and atypical of this kind of exchange or 'flyting': a verbal battle common in Germanic literature. The best known examples are the exchange between Beowulf and Unferth in *Beowulf* or between Hagen and the ferryman in the *Nibelungenlied*. Typically the winner is the contestant best able to prove his courage and manhood, while demonstrating the cowardice, laziness, and effeminacy of his opponent. In *Harbard's Song*, however, such is Odin's use of strategy and rhetoric, and so slow-witted is Thor, that Odin emerges a clear winner, despite the obvious advantages Thor has in strength and courage in battling against giants. The nub of *Harbard's Song* may be the statement in v. 24 that 'Odin owns the nobles who fall in battle | and Thor owns the race of thralls', establishing the difference between the cults of the two deities, or, as Carol Clover has suggested, the poem may be intended as a parody of the usual 'flyting' poem. The poem is composed in a motley collection of metres, *ljodahattr*, *malahattr*, some unrecognizable metres, and some odd bits of prose. Many of the episodes alluded to by the two gods are unknown from any other sources; where additional information exists, it is outlined in the notes.

Thor was travelling from the east and he came to an inlet. On the other side of the inlet was the ferryman with his ship. Thor called:

1   'Who is that lad of lads who stands on that side of the inlet?'*

He answered:

2   'Who is that churl of churls who calls over the gulf?'

Thor said:

3   'Ferry me over the water and I'll feed you in the morning;
     I've a basket on my back, no food could be better;
     I ate at leisure before I left home,
     herrings and oatmeal—I've eaten my fill of these.'

The ferryman said:

4   'As your morning's work you praise your breakfast!
    You don't know clearly what's before you;
    sad is your household, I think your mother's dead.'*

Thor said:

5   'What you say now would seem great news
    to most people, that my mother is dead.'

The ferryman said:

6   'It doesn't look as if you own three decent farms;
    barelegged you stand, wearing your beggar's gear,
    you don't even have any breeches.'

Thor said:

7   'Steer the oaken ship here—
    I'll direct you to the landing stage—
    anyway, who owns the ship which you keep next to the bank?'

The ferryman said:

8   'Hildolf he's called, the man who ordered me to keep it,
    that warrior wise in counsel, who lives in Counsel-island
        Sound;
    he told me not to ferry highwaymen or horse-thieves
    but good men alone, and those whom I recognized clearly;
    tell me your name if you want to cross the inlet.'

Thor said:

9   'I'd tell my name, even if I were outlawed,
    and my origin to all: I am Odin's son,
    brother of Meili, father of Magni,
    powerful gods-leader; with Thor you converse here!
    This I'll ask now, what you are called.'

The ferryman said:

10 'I am called Harbard, I seldom conceal my name.'

Thor said:

11 'Why should you conceal your name, unless you are in
        a dispute?'

Harbard said:

12 'Whether or not I have a dispute, I'd defend my life
        from such as you are, unless I were doomed.'

Thor said:

13 'It seems to me that it'd be an unpleasant labour
        to wade over the water to you, and wet my prick.*
        I'll pay you back, you babe in arms,
        for your jeering words, if I get over the water.'

Harbard said:

14 'Here I'll stand and wait for you;
        you've encountered no tougher man since Hrungnir's death.'*

Thor said:

15 'This is what you're talking about: that Hrungnir and
            I fought—
        the great-spirited giant whose head was made of stone:
        and yet I brought him down and made him fall before me.
        What were you doing meanwhile, Harbard?'

Harbard said:

16 'I was with Fiolvar five winters long
        on that island called All-green;
        we fought there and wreaked slaughter,
        we tried out many things,
        had our choice of girls.'

Thor said:

17 'How did it turn out with your women?'

Harbard said:

18 'We had frisky women, if only they were well-disposed to us;
      we had clever women, if only they were faithful to us;
      they wound a rope out of sand,
      and from a deep valley
      they dug out the ground;
      only I was superior to them all with my shrewdness;
      I slept with the seven sisters,*
      and I got all their hearts, and pleasure from them.
      What were you doing meanwhile, Thor?'

Thor said:

19 'I killed Thiazi, the powerful-minded giant,*
      I threw up the eyes of Allvaldi's son*
      into the bright heaven;
      they are the greatest sign of my deeds,
      those which since all men can see.
      What were you doing meanwhile, Harbard?'

Harbard said:

20 'Mighty love-spells I used on the witches,
      those whom I seduced from their men;
      a tough giant I think Hlebard was,
      he gave me a magic twig,
      and I bewitched him out of his wits.'

Thor said:

21 'Malevolently you repaid him for his good gifts.'

Harbard said:

22 'One oak-tree thrives when another is stripped,
      each is for himself in such matters.
      What were you doing meanwhile, Thor?'

Thor said:

23 'I was in the east, and I fought against giants,
malicious women, who roamed in the mountains;
great would be the giant race if they all survived:
there'd be no humans within Midgard.
What were you doing meanwhile, Harbard?'

Harbard said:

24 'I was in Valland, and I followed the war,
I incited the princes, never reconciled them;
Odin owns the nobles who fall in battle
and Thor owns the race of thralls.'

Thor said:

25 'Unequally you'd share out warriors among the Æsir,
if you had as much power as you'd like.'

Harbard said:

26 'Thor has quite enough strength, and no guts;
in fear and cowardice you were stuffed in a glove,*
and you didn't then seem like Thor;
you dared in your terror neither
to sneeze nor fart in case Fialar might hear.'

Thor said:

27 'Harbard, you pervert! I would knock you into hell
if I could stretch over the water.'

Harbard said:

28 'Why should you stretch over the water, since we have no
dispute?
What were you doing meanwhile, Thor?'

Thor said:

29   'I was in the east and I defended the river
      where Svarang's sons attacked me;*
      they pelted me with stones, yet they didn't rejoice in advantage,
      before me they had to sue first for peace.
      What were you doing meanwhile, Harbard?'

Harbard said:

30   'I was in the east and I was consorting with someone,
      I sported with a linen-white lady and set up a secret meeting,
      I made the gold-bright one happy, the girl enjoyed her
           pleasure.'

Thor said:

31   'You had good dealings with the girl there.'

Harbard said:

32   'I could have done with your help, Thor,
      to hold the linen-white girl.'

Thor said:

33   'I'd have helped you with that, if I could have managed it.'

Harbard said:

34   'I'd have trusted you then, if you didn't betray my trust.'

Thor said:

35   'I'm not a heel-biter like an old leather shoe in spring.'

Harbard said:

36   'What were you doing meanwhile, Thor?'

Thor said:

37 'Berserk women I battled in Hlesey;
    they'd done the worst things, betrayed the whole people.'

Harbard said:

38 'That was a shameful deed, Thor, to fight against women.'

Thor said:

39 'They were she-wolves, and scarcely women,
    they rattled my ship which I'd beached on trestles,
    they threatened me with an iron club, and chased Thialfi.
    What were you doing meanwhile, Harbard?'

Harbard said:

40 'I was in the army, which set out here
    to raise battle-banners
    and to redden the spear.'

Thor said:

41 'This is tantamount to saying that you set out to bring us harm.'

Harbard said:

42 'I'll compensate you for that with an arm-ring*
    which arbitrators use, those who want to settle things between us.'

Thor said:

43 'Where did you find such despicable words?
    I've never heard words more despicable!'

Harbard said:

44 'I learned them from those ancient men who have their home in
    the woods.'*

Thor said:

45 'That's giving a good name to burial cairns, when you call them
the "home in the woods".'

Harbard said:

46 'That's how I talk of such things.'

Thor said:

47 'Your glibness with words will bring evil upon you,
if I decide to wade over the sound;
louder than the wolf I think you'll howl,
if you get a blow from my hammer.'

Harbard said:

48 'Sif has a lover at home, he's the one you want to meet,*
that's the test of strength you ought to attempt, that's more
pressing for you.'

Thor said:

49 'You say just what comes into your mouth, so that it seems the
worst to me,
coward, I think you're lying.'

Harbard said:

50 'Truth I think I'm saying, you're slow in your journey,
you'd now be well on your way, Thor, if you'd travelled by day
and night.'

Thor said:

51 'Harbard, you pervert, you've held me up too long!'

Harbard said:

52 'I never thought Asa-Thor would let
a herdsman hold up his journeys.'

Thor said:

53 'I'll give you some advice now: row the boat here,
let's stop this quarrelling, come and meet Magni's father!'

Harbard said:

54 'Go further away from the inlet,
you shall be refused passage!'

Thor said:

55 'Show me the way since you won't ferry me over the water!'

Harbard said:

56 'It's a little thing to refuse: it's a long time to travel;
a while to the stock, another to the stone,
keep to the left-hand road until you come to Verland;
there Fiorgyn will meet Thor, her son,*
and she will show him the kinsmen's road, to get to Odin's land.'

Thor said:

57 'Can I get there today?'

Harbard said:

58 'With toil and difficulty you'll get there, while the sun's in the
sky,
since I think it's thawing.'

Thor said:

59 'Short will our conversation be now, since you answer me only
with jeers.
I'll reward you for refusing to ferry me, if we meet another time.'

Harbard said:

60 'Go where the monsters'll get you!'

HYMIR'S POEM

Hymir's Poem (*Hymiskvida*) is badly preserved in the manuscript, but we can fill in the gaps from Snorri. The gods decide to have a feast and compel the giant Ægir to prepare it; this may reflect Scandinavian royal practices in which the king enforces his authority on his subordinates by visiting their homes and demanding to be feasted. Cunningly, Ægir demands an enormous cauldron in which to brew beer for the feast. This can only be obtained with great danger from the giant Hymir. Tyr, who was probably not the original protagonist of the poem, and Thor set off to try to obtain the cauldron. Like most encounters between Thor and the giants the adventure turns into a trial of strength. The gods are aided by a giant woman who gives them advice at crucial moments. Embedded in the adventure of 'Fetching the Cauldron' is the tale of Thor and Hymir's fishing expedition, in which Thor almost catches the Midgard-serpent and demonstrates his strength. This is an ancient tale, depicted on several Viking-age picture-stones.

1   In bygone days the slaughter-gods had a good bag from
        hunting,
    they were keen to drink before they got enough;
    they shook the twigs and looked at the augury,*
    they found that at Ægir's was an ample choice of cauldrons.

2   The mountain-dweller sat there, cheerful as a child,
    very like the mash-blender's son;*
    Odin's son looked into his eyes in defiance:
    'You shall often prepare a feast for the Æsir.'

3   The contentious man annoyed the giant;
    he thought how to avenge himself soon on the god;
    he asked Sif's husband to fetch him a cauldron,
    'in which I can brew the ale for all of you'.

4   Nor could the glorious gods,
    the mighty Powers, get one anywhere,
    until privately Tyr in trustworthy friendship
    gave vital good advice to Hlorridi.*

5 'To the east of Elivagar
   lives Hymir the very wise, at the sky's end;
   my father, the brave man, owns a cauldron,*
   a capacious kettle, a league deep.'

6 'Do you know if we can get that liquid-boiler?'
   'If, friend, we use trickery to do it.'

7 They journeyed hard that day, and far
   from Asgard, until they came to Egil.
   He secured their goats with splendid horns,*
   they headed for the hall which Hymir owned.

8 The lad found his grandmother, very ugly she seemed to him,*
   nine hundred heads she had;
   and another woman, all gold-decked, walked forward
   with shining brows, bearing beer to her boy.

9 'Kinsman of giants, I'd like to seat you
   two valiant men under the cauldrons.
   My beloved, on many occasions,
   is stingy to guests, prone to enmity.'

10 Misshapen, stern-minded Hymir
   came late back from hunting.
   He entered the hall, the icicles tinkled
   when he came in: the old man's cheek-forest was frozen.*

11 'Greetings, Hymir, be of good humour!
   Now our son has come to your hall,
   he whom we've expected on his long journeyings.
   Hrod's adversary accompanies him,*
   the friend of warriors, Veor is his name.

12 'See where they sit under the hall-gable,
   they protect themselves so with a pillar in front of them.'
   Asunder the pillar splintered at the giant's gaze,
   just before the cross-beam broke in two.

13   Eight kettles smashed to pieces, but one of them,
     a strong-forged cauldron, fell whole from the peg.
     Forward they went, and the ancient giant
     turned his gaze on his enemy.

14   His mind didn't speak encouragingly to him, when he saw
     the one who makes the giantess weep walking across the floor.*
     Then three bulls were taken.
     The giant ordered them quickly to be boiled up.

15   Each one they made shorter by a head
     and bore them off to the cooking-pit.
     Sif's husband ate before he went to bed,
     on his own he ate right up two of Hymir's oxen.

16   It seemed to Hrungnir's grey-haired friend*
     that Hlorridi had consumed a considerable amount.
     'Tomorrow evening we three must live on
     food that we have hunted ourselves.'

17   Thor said he wanted to row out in the bay,
     if the bold giant would give him bait.
     'Go to the herds, if you've the guts for it,
     mountain-giant-breaker, to look for bait!

18   'I expect that it'll be easy for you
     to get bait from the oxen.'
     The young man hastened smartly to the woods,
     there stood an ox, jet-black before him.

19   That ogre-slayer broke off from the bull
     the horns' high meadow, tore off its head.*

     .   .   .   .

     (Hymir said)
     'Your deed seems much worse,
     captain of ships, than if you had sat still quietly.'

20   The lord of goats told the ape's offspring
     to row the launchway-horse out further;*
     but the giant said, for his part,
     he wasn't eager to row further out.

21   The brave and famous Hymir alone caught
     two whales at once on his hook,
     and back in the stern Odin's kinsman,
     Thor, cunningly laid out his line.

22   The protector of humans, the serpent's sole slayer,*
     baited his hook with the ox's head.
     The one whom the gods hate, the All-Lands-Girdler
     from below gaped wide over the hook.

23   Then very bravely Thor, doer of great deeds,
     pulled the poison-gleaming serpent up on board.
     With his hammer he violently struck, from above
     the hideous one, the wolf's intimate-brother's head.*

24   The sea-wolf shrieked and the rock-bottom re-echoed,
     all the ancient earth was collapsing*

     .   .   .   .

     then that fish sank itself into the sea.

25   The giant wasn't jolly as they rowed back,
     at first Hymir didn't say a word;
     he swung round the rowing, completely changed tack:

26   'You'll be doing half the work with me
     if you carry the whales home to the farm
     or pen up our floating-goat.'*

27   Hlorridi went forward and gripped the prow,
     alone he lifted the sea-stallion with its bilge-water,
     with oars and bailer;
     he brought the giant's sea-pigs home to the farm,*
     through the hollow in the wooded ridge.

28 And still the giant, habitually contentious,
    strove with Thor about his strength;
    he said no man was strong, even if he could row
    mightily, if he could not smash the goblet.

29 And quickly Thor, when he laid hands on it,
    smashed through the towering stone with the glass;
    sitting, he slung it through the columns;
    they carried it whole back to Hymir.

30 Until the beautiful beloved lady gave him
    vital friendly advice which she knew:
    'Smash it on Hymir's skull, the food-sated giant's,
    that's harder than any goblet!'

31 The strong man, lord of goats, rose, bracing his knees
    brought all his divine power to bear;
    whole was the old man's helmet-stump above,*
    and the round wine-vessel broke apart.

32 'Great treasures I know I've lost,
    when I see the goblet leaving my lap',
    the old man announced: 'Never again
    can I say, "ale, you are brewed!"

33 'Now it's up to you, if you can manage
    to take the beer-boat out of our court.'
    Tyr tried twice to move the cauldron,
    both times the cauldron stayed immovable.

34 Modi's father took it by the rim,
    and he stamped down through the floor in the hall;*
    Sif's husband lifted the kettle up on his head,
    the handle-rings jingled at his heels.

35 They had gone a long way
    when Odin's son looked once behind him;
    he saw from the boulder-heaps, from the east with Hymir
    a many-headed army marching along.

36   He lifted from his shoulders the outstanding cauldron,
     he swung Miollnir before him, keen to kill,
     and he struck down all the lava-whales.*

37   They hadn't gone a long way, before Hlorridi's goat
     collapsed, half-dead, in front of them;
     the draught-beast was lamed through a curse,
     this malevolent Loki had caused.*

38   But you have heard this—anyone wiser about the gods
     may tell it more clearly—
     what recompense he got from the lava-dweller,
     how he paid for it with both his children.*

39   The mighty one came to the gods' assembly,
     bringing the kettle which Hymir had owned;
     and the gods will drink in delight
     ale at Ægir's every winter.

LOKI'S QUARREL

Excluded from the feast at Ægir's hall, where all the other gods except Thor are celebrating, Loki forces his way in, compels Odin to assign him a seat, and insults each of the gods and goddesses in turn—hence the title *Loki's Quarrel* (*Lokasenna*). No one escapes his scorn and it is only when Thor returns from his journeying in Giant-land and threatens Loki with his hammer Miollnir that Loki falls silent and consents to leave. The poem is cleverly structured so that Loki has two stanzas of insult, countered by one uttered by the victim in his or her defence; the next verse uttered to support the victim or to attack Loki by another of the company serves to draw Loki's attention to the new speaker. In so far as we can verify the charges Loki lays against the gods and goddesses, they appear to have some foundation, though Loki speaks as if the gods were wayward human beings rather than divinities whose actions are attributes of their separateness and power. The poem may be early—and thus the composition of a poet who believes in the divinities he burlesques: a little comedy cannot hurt divinities whose cult is secure—or it may be late, and the mockery be directed by a Christian poet at heathen divinities whose immorality contrasts with the stern morality of the new religion. The prose introduction seems to misunderstand the poem; the latter suggests that Loki was never invited to the feast and gatecrashes it, insulting Ægir's servant as he does so.

About Ægir and the Gods *Ægir, who is also called Gymir, had brewed ale for the Æsir, when he got the great cauldron which has just been told about. To this feast came Odin and Frigg, his wife. Thor did not come, because he was away in the east. Sif was there, Thor's wife, Bragi, and Idunn, his wife. Tyr was there; he was one-handed, for Fenrir the wolf tore his hand off when he was bound. There was Niord and his wife, Skadi, Freyr and Freyia, Vidar, son of Odin; Loki was there and the servants of Freyr, Byggvir and Beyla. Many of the Æsir and elves were there. Ægir had two servants, Fimafeng and Eldir. Shining gold was used instead of firelight; ale went round by itself; that was a great place of peace. People praised the excellence of Ægir's servers. Loki could not bear to hear that, and he killed Fimafeng. Then the Æsir shook their shields and shrieked at Loki and chased him out to the woods, and they set to drinking.*

Loki came back and met Eldir outside; Loki greeted him:

1 'Tell me, Eldir, before you step
a single foot forward,
what the sons of the victory-gods here inside
talk about over their ale.'

Eldir said:

2 'They discuss their weapons and their readiness for war,
the sons of the victory-gods;
among the Æsir and elves who are within,
no one has a friendly word for you.'

Loki said:

3 'In I shall go, into Ægir's halls
to have a look at that feast;
quarrelling and strife I'll bring to the Æsir's sons
and thus mix their mead with malice.'

Eldir said:

4 'You know, if in you go, into Ægir's halls
to have a look at that feast,
if accusation and scandal you pour over the loyal gods,
they'll wipe it off on you.'

Loki said:

5 'You know, Eldir, that if you and I should
contend with wounding words,
I'll be rich in my replies
when you say too much.'

*Afterwards Loki went into the hall. And when those inside saw who had
come in, they all fell silent.*

Loki said:

6   'Thirsty I come to this hall,
    Loki, come a long way,
    to ask the Æsir that they should give me
    one drink of magnificent mead.

7   'Why are you so silent, you pride-swollen gods,
    that you are unable to speak?
    Assign me a place to sit at the feast,
    or tell me to go away!'

Bragi said:

8   'A place to sit at the feast
    the Æsir will never assign you,
    for the Æsir know for whom they should
    provide their potent feast.'

Loki said:

9   'Do you remember, Odin, when in bygone days
    we blended our blood together?*
    You said you'd never imbibe beer
    unless it were brought to both of us.'

Odin said:

10 'Get up then, Vidar, and let the wolf's father*
    sit down at the feast,
    lest Loki speak words of blame to
    us in Ægir's hall.'

*Then Vidar stood up and poured a drink for Loki, and before he drank,
he toasted the Æsir:*

11 'Hail to the Æsir, hail to the Asynior
    and all the most sacred gods!
    —except for that one god who sits further in,*
    Bragi, on the benches.'

Bragi said:

12   'A horse and a sword I'll give you from my possessions,
       and Bragi will recompense you with a ring too,
       so you don't repay the Æsir with hatred;
       don't make the gods exasperated with you!'

Loki said:

13   'Both horses and arm-rings you'll always
       be short of, Bragi;
       of the Æsir and the elves who are in here,
       you're the wariest of war
       and shyest of shooting.'

Bragi said:

14   'I know if I were outside, just as now I am inside
       Ægir's hall,
       your head I'd be holding in my hand;
       I'd see that as reward for your lies.'

Loki said:

15   'You're brave in your seat, but you won't be doing that,
       Bragi the bench-ornament!
       You go and fight, if you are so furious,
       the truly bold man doesn't think twice!'

Idunn said:

16   'I beg you, Bragi, that kin ties will hold
       between the children and those who are adopted,*
       so you shouldn't speak words of blame to Loki
       in Ægir's hall.'

Loki said:

17   'Be silent, Idunn, I declare that of all women
       you're the most man-mad,
       since you wound your arms, washed bright,
       around your brother's killer.'*

Idunn said:

18   'I'm not speaking words of blame to Loki
       in Ægir's hall;
       I am quietening Bragi, made talkative with beer;
       I don't want you two angry men to fight.'

Gefion said:

19   'Why should you two Æsir in here
       fight with wounding words?
       isn't it known of Loki that he likes a joke
       and all the gods love him?'

Loki said:

20   'Be silent, Gefion, I'm going to mention this,
       how your spirit was seduced;
       the white boy gave you a jewel
       and you laid your thigh over him.'*

Odin said:

21   'Mad you are, Loki, and out of your wits,
       when you make Gefion angry with you,
       for I think she knows all the fate of the world,
       as clearly as I myself.'

Loki said:

22   'Be silent, Odin, you could never
       apportion war-fortune among men;
       often you've given what you shouldn't have given,
       victory, to the faint-hearted.'*

Odin said:

23   'You know, if I gave what I shouldn't have given,
       victory, to the faint-hearted,
       yet eight winters you were, beneath the earth,
       a milchcow and a woman,
       and there you bore children,
       and that I thought the hallmark of a pervert.'*

Loki said:

24 'But you, they say, practised *seid* on Samsey,*
and you beat on the drum as seeresses do,
in the likeness of a wizard you journeyed over mankind,
and that I thought the hallmark of a pervert.'

Frigg said:

25 'The fates you met should never be
told in front of people,
what you two Æsir underwent in past times;
the living should keep their distance from ancient matters.'

Loki said:

26 'Be silent, Frigg, you're Fiorgyn's daughter
and you've always been man-mad:
Ve and Vili, Vidrir's wife,*
you took them both in your embrace.'

Frigg said:

27 'You know that if I had in here in Ægir's hall
a boy like my son Baldr,
you wouldn't get away from the Æsir's sons;
there'd be furious fighting against you.'

Loki said:

28 'Frigg, you want me to say more about
my wicked deeds;
for I brought it about that you will never again
see Baldr ride to the halls.'*

Freyia said:

29 'Mad are you, Loki, when you reckon up your
ugly, hateful deeds;
Frigg knows, I think, all fate,
though she herself does not speak out.'

Loki said:

30   'Be silent, Freyia, I know all about you;
      you aren't free of faults:
      of the Æsir and the elves, who are in here,
      each one has been your lover.'

Freyia said:

31   'False is your tongue, I think that soon
      it will chant out disaster for you;
      the Æsir are furious with you, and the Asynior,
      you'll go home discomfited.'

Loki said:

32   'Be silent, Freyia, you're a witch
      and much imbued with malice,
      you were with your brother, all the cheerful gods surprised you,
      and then, Freyia, you farted.'*

Niord said:

33   'That's harmless, if a woman has a husband,
      or a lover, or one of each;
      what's surprising is that a pervert god comes here
      and he has borne children!'

Loki said:

34   'Be silent, Niord, you were sent from here
      eastwards as hostage to the gods;
      the daughters of Hymir used you as a pisspot
      and pissed in your mouth.'*

Niord said:

35   'That was my comfort, when I, from far away,
      was sent as hostage to the gods,
      that I fathered that son, whom no one hates
      and is thought the protector of the Æsir.'

Loki said:

36 'Stop now, Niord, keep some moderation!
I won't keep it secret any longer:
with your sister you got that son,
though that's no worse than might be expected.'

Tyr said:

37 'Freyr is the best of all the bold riders
in the courts of the Æsir;
he makes no girl cry nor any man's wife,
and looses each man from captivity.'

Loki said:

38 'Be silent, Tyr, you could never
deal straight between two people;
your right hand, I must point out,
is the one which Fenrir tore from you.'*

Tyr said:

39 'I've lost a hand, but you've lost the famous wolf;
evil brings pain to us both;
it's not pleasant for the wolf, who must in shackles
wait for the twilight of the gods.'

Loki said:

40 'Be silent, Tyr, it happened that your wife*
had a son by me;
not an ell of cloth nor a penny have you ever had
for this injury, you wretch.'

Freyr said:

41 'A wolf I see lying before a river mouth,
until the Powers are torn asunder;
next you shall be bound—unless you fall silent—
smith of evil!'

Loki said:

42   'With gold you had Gymir's daughter bought*
      and so you gave away your sword;
      but when Muspell's sons ride over Myrkwood,*
      you don't know then, wretch, how you'll fight.'

*Byggvir said:**

43   'You know, if I had the lineage of Freyr,
      and such a blessed dwelling,
      smaller than marrow I'd have ground that hateful crow
      and mangled all his limbs into pieces.'

Loki said:

44   'What's that little creature I see wagging its tail
      and snapping things up snappily?
      At Freyr's ears you're always found
      and twittering under the grindstones.'

Byggvir said:

45   'Byggvir I'm called, and I'm said to be busy
      by all the gods and men;
      thus I'm proud here that Odin's sons are
      all drinking ale together.'

Loki said:

46   'Be silent, Byggvir, you could never
      share out food among men;
      and in the bench-straw they can never find you
      when men are going to fight.'

Heimdall said:

47   'Drunk you are, Loki, so that you're out of your wits,
      why don't you stop speaking?
      For too much drinking affects every man
      so he doesn't notice his talkativeness.'

Loki said:

48 'Be silent, Heimdall, for you in bygone days
a hateful life was decreed:
a mucky back you must always have*
and watch as guard of the gods.'

Skadi said:

49 'You're light-hearted, Loki; you won't for long
play with your tail wagging free,
for on a rock-edge, with your ice-cold son's guts,
the gods shall bind you.'*

Loki said:

50 'You know, if on a rock-edge, with my ice-cold son's guts,
the gods shall bind me,
first and foremost I was at the killing
when we seized Thiazi.'*

Skadi said:

51 'You know, if first and foremost you were at the killing
when you seized Thiazi,
from my sanctuaries and meadows cold counsel
shall always come to you.'

Loki said:

52 'Gentler in speech you were to Laufey's son
when you had me invited to your bed;*
we must mention such things when we reckon up
our shameful deeds.'

Then Sif went forward and poured out mead for Loki into a crystal goblet and said:

53 'Welcome, now, Loki, and take the crystal goblet
full of ancient mead,
you should rather admit, of the Æsir's children,
that Sif alone is blameless.'

He took the horn and drank it down:

54   'You would be the only one, if you were so,
      were cautious and reluctant with a man;
      I know one—and I think I do know—
      a lover besides Thor,
      and that was the malevolent Loki.'*

Beyla said:

55   'All the mountain-range shakes; I think Thor must be
      on his way from home;
      he'll bring peace to the one who badmouths here
      all the gods and men.'

Loki said:

56   'Be silent, Beyla, you're Byggvir's wife
      and much imbued with malice;
      no worse disgrace came among the Æsir's children,
      you dung-splattered dairy-maid.'

Then Thor arrived and said:

57   'Be silent, perverse creature, my mighty hammer
      Miollnir shall deprive you of speech;
      your shoulder-rock I shall strike off your neck,*
      and then your life will be gone.'

Loki said:

58   'The son of Earth has now come in;
      why are you raging so, Thor?
      But you won't be daring when you must fight against the wolf,
      when he swallows Odin all up.'

Thor said:

59   'Be silent, perverse creature, my mighty hammer
      Miollnir shall deprive you of speech;
      I shall throw you up on the roads to the east,*
      afterwards no one will ever see you.'

Loki said:

60 'Your eastern journeys you should never
relate to people
since in the thumb of a glove you crouched cowering, you hero!*
And then you didn't seem like Thor.'

Thor said:

61 'Be silent, perverse creature, my mighty hammer
Miollnir shall deprive you of speech;
with my right hand I'll strike you, with Hrungnir's killer,*
so that every one of your bones will break.'

Loki said:

62 'I intend to live for a good time yet,
though you threaten me with a hammer;
strong leather straps you thought Skrymir had,
and you couldn't get at the food,
and you starved, unharmed but hungry.'*

Thor said:

63 'Be silent, perverse creature, my mighty hammer
Miollnir shall deprive you of speech;
Hrungnir's killer will send you to hell,
down below the corpse-gate.'

Loki said:

64 'I spoke before the Æsir, I spoke before the Æsir's sons
what my spirit urged me,
but for you alone I shall go out,
for I know that you do strike.

65 'Ale you brewed, Ægir, but you'll never again
prepare a feast;
all your possessions that are here inside—
may flame play over them,
and your back be burnt!'

About Loki   *And after that Loki hid himself in the waterfall of Franangr, in the shape of a salmon. There the Æsir caught him. He was bound with the guts of his son Nari. But his son Narfi* turned into a wolf. Skadi took a poisonous snake and fastened it over Loki's face; poison dripped down from it. Sigyn, Loki's wife, sat there and held a basin under the poison. But when the basin was full, she carried the poison out; and meanwhile the poison fell on Loki. Then he writhed so violently at this that all the earth shook from it; those are now called earthquakes.*

THRYM'S POEM

The comedy of *Thrym's Poem* (*Thrymskvida*) depends upon the characterization of Freyia and Thor, who are compelled to act against their reputations. Freyia is indignant when Loki and Thor suggest that she might marry a giant, though her reputation for promiscuity is such that taking a giant as a sexual partner might not be regarded as out of the question. Thor is the most masculine of the gods, and dressing up as a woman causes him acute embarrassment. Thrym, who has stolen Thor's hammer, is a giant with considerable social pretensions. The simple structure and repetitiveness of the poem proved suitable for adaptation into the ballad form and a number of versions of it are found among Danish and Swedish ballads.

1   Furious was Thor when he awoke
    and missed his hammer;
    he shook his beard, he tossed his hair to and fro,
    Earth's son began to grope about.

2   And these were the very first words he spoke:
    'Listen, Loki, to what I'm saying,
    what no one knows, nowhere on earth
    nor in heaven: the God has been robbed of his hammer.'

3   They went to the beautiful courts of Freyia
    and these were the very first words he spoke:
    'Will you lend me, Freyia, your feather-shirt,*
    to see if I can find my hammer?'

Freyia said:

4   'I'd give it you even if it were made of gold,
    I'd lend it to you even if it were made of silver.'

5   Then Loki flew off, the feather-shirt whistled,
    until he came outside the courts of the Æsir
    and he came inside Giant-land.

6   Thrym sat on a grave-mound, lord of the ogres,
       plaiting golden collars for his bitches;
       he was trimming his horses' manes.

Thrym said:

7   'What's up with the Æsir, what's up with the elves?
       Why have you come alone into Giant-land?'
       'Bad news among the Æsir, bad news among the elves;
       have you hidden Thor's hammer?'

8   'I have hidden Hlorridi's hammer*
       eight leagues under the earth;
       no man will ever take it back again,
       unless he brings me Freyia as my wife.'

9   Then Loki flew off, the feather-shirt whistled,
       until he came outside Giant-land
       and he came inside the courts of the Æsir.
       He met Thor in the middle of the court,
       and these were the very first words he spoke:

10   'Have you had any success for your efforts?
       Tell me all the news while you're still in the air!
       For tales often escape the sitting man,
       and the man lying down barks out lies.'

11   'It was an effort and I've had some success:
       Thrym has your hammer, lord of the ogres;
       no man will ever take it back from him again,
       unless he brings him Freyia as his wife.'

12   Then they went to see the beautiful Freyia,
       and these were the very first words he spoke:
       'Tie on yourself, Freyia, a bridal head-dress!
       We two shall drive to the land of the giants.'

13   Furious then was Freyia and snorted in rage,
     the whole hall of the Æsir trembled at that,
     the great necklace of the Brisings fell from her:*
     'You'll know me to be the most man-mad of women,
     if I drive with you to the land of the giants.'

14   All together the Æsir came in council,
     and all the Asynior in consultation,
     and what they debated, those mighty gods,
     was how they should get back Hlorridi's hammer.

15   Then Heimdall said, the whitest of the gods—
     he knows the future as do the Vanir too:
     'Let's tie on Thor a bridal head-dress,
     let him wear the great necklace of the Brisings.

16   'Let keys jingle by his side*
     and women's clothing fall down over his knees,
     and on his breast display jewels,
     and we'll put a pointed head-dress properly on his head!'

17   Then said Thor, the vigorous god:
     'The Æsir will call me perverse,
     if I let you tie a bridal head-dress on me.'

18   Then said Loki, Laufey's son:
     'Be quiet, Thor, don't speak these words!
     The giants will be settling in Asgard
     unless you get your hammer back.'

19   Then they tied on Thor a bridal head-dress
     and the great necklace of the Brisings,
     they let keys jingle by his side
     and women's clothing fall down over his knees,
     and on his breast they displayed jewels,
     and put a pointed head-dress properly on his head.

20   Then said Loki, Laufey's son:
      'I'll go with you to be your maid,
      we two shall drive to Giant-land.'

21   Quickly the goats were driven home,*
      hurried into the harness, they were going to gallop fast;
      the mountains split asunder, the earth flamed with fire,
      Odin's son was driving to Giant-land.

22   Then said Thrym, lord of ogres:
      'Be upstanding, giants, and strew the benches!
      Now they are bringing me Freyia as my wife,
      Niord's daughter from Noatun!

23   'Gold-horned cows walk here in the yard,
      jet-black oxen to the giant's delight;
      heaps I have of treasures, heaps I have of luxuries,
      only Freyia seemed to be missing.'

24   They came together there early in the evening,
      and ale was brought for the giants;
      he ate one whole ox, eight salmon,
      all the dainties meant for the women;
      Sif's husband drank three casks of mead.

25   Then said Thrym, lord of ogres:
      'Where have you seen brides eating more ravenously?
      I've never seen any brides with a broader bite,
      nor any girl drink so much mead.'

26   The very shrewd maid sat before him,
      she found an answer to the giant's speech:
      'Freyia ate nothing for eight nights,
      so madly eager was she to come to Giant-land.'

27   He bent under the head-dress, he was keen to kiss her,
      instead he sprang back right along the hall:
      'Why are Freyia's eyes so terrifying?
      It seems to me fire is burning from them.'

28 The very shrewd maid sat before him,
   she found an answer to the giant's speech:
   'Freyia did not sleep for eight nights,
   so madly eager was she to come to Giant-land.'

29 In came the wretched sister of the giants,
   she dared to ask for a gift from the bride:
   'Let the red-gold rings flow from your arms,
   if you want to merit my love,
   my love and all my favour.'

30 Then said Thrym, lord of ogres:
   'Bring in the hammer to sanctify the bride,
   lay Miollnir on the girl's lap,
   consecrate us together by the hand of Var!'*

31 Hlorridi's heart laughed in his breast,
   when he, stern in courage, recognized the hammer;
   first he killed Thrym, lord of ogres,
   and battered all the race of giants.

32 He killed the old sister of the giants,
   she who'd asked for the gift from the bride;
   striking she got instead of shillings,
   and hammer-blows instead of heaps of rings.

So Odin's son got the hammer back.

THE POEM OF VOLUND

The Poem of Volund (*Volundarkvida*) appears to be a combination of two poems: the first, the tale of the swan-maidens, the second, the tale of Volund's imprisonment and his revenge. Volund is a strange character, neither human nor divine At one point he is referred to as 'prince of elves'; since we know so little about elves in the Norse mythic scheme we cannot prove or disprove this attribution. Volund's story was known in England as well as Scandinavia. The Old English poem *Deor* refers allusively to the sufferings of 'Weland', and the misery of 'Beadohild' (Bodvild), while high-quality swords are sometimes called in Old English poetry 'Weland's work'. The smith is often regarded as an outsider and as possessing supernatural powers in a wide range of cultures. The antisocial noisiness of his work and the mysterious ability to transform unpromising lumps of metal into precious tools, weapons, and jewellery may account for this. Another version of the story is given in *Thidreks saga*.

Nidud was the name of a king among the Swedish people. He had two sons and one daughter. She was called Bodvild. There were three brothers, sons of the Lappish king. One was called Slagfid, the second Egil, the third Volund. They went on skis and hunted wild animals. They came to Wolfdale and there built themselves a house. There is a lake there called Wolf-lake. Early in the morning, they found three women on the lake-shore, and they were spinning linen. Near them were their swan's garments; they were valkyries.* There were two daughters of King Hlodver—Hladgud the swan-white, and Hervor, the strange creature—the third was Olrun, the daughter of Kiar of Valland. They took them home to the hall with them. Egil took Olrun, and Slagfid Swanwhite [i.e. Hladgud], and Volund Strange-Creature [i.e. Hervor]. They lived together seven winters. Then the women flew off to go to battles and did not come back. Then Egil skied off to look for Olrun, and Slagfid went looking for Swanwhite, and Volund sat in Wolfdales. He was the most skilful of men, that men know of, in the ancient stories. King Nidud had him seized, as is told of here:

1   Girls flew from the south across Myrkwood,
      strange, young creatures, to fulfil fate;
      there on a lake shore they sat to rest,
      the southern ladies spun precious linen.

2 One of them began to enclose Egil in her arms,
the fair living girl in bright embrace;
Another was Swanwhite, she wore swan feathers;
and the third, their sister,
wound her arms around Volund's white neck.

3 They stayed thus for seven winters,
but all the eighth they suffered anguish,
and in the ninth necessity parted them;
the girls yearned for the dark wood,
the strange, young creatures, to fulfil fate.

4 Then came from hunting the weather-eyed shooter;*
Slagfid and Egil found the halls empty;
they went in and out and looked about.
Egil skied off east after Olrun,*
and Slagfid went south after Swanwhite.

5 But Volund sat alone in Wolfdales.
He struck red gold about a firm-set gem,
he closed up all the serpent-rings well;*
so he waited for his shining woman
if she were to make her way back to him.

6 Nidud heard, lord of the Niarar,
that Volund sat alone in Wolfdales.
By night men journeyed, their corslets studded,
their shields glinted in the waning moon.

7 They dismounted from their saddles at the hall's gable-wall,
they went in there all along the hall,
they saw on the bast-rope rings threaded,
seven hundred in all, which this warrior owned.

8 And they took them off and they put them back,
all but one, which they left off.
Then there came from hunting the weather-eyed shooter,
Volund, travelling over the long road.

9   He went to roast the flesh of the brown she-bear;
    high burned with kindling the very dry fir,
    the wind-dried wood in front of Volund.

10 He sat on a bearskin, counted rings,
    the prince of elves; he missed one.
    He thought that Hlodver's daughter,
    the strange, young creature, had come back again.

11 He sat so long that he fell asleep,
    and he awoke deprived of joy,
    he felt on his hands pressing, heavy bonds,
    and on his feet a fetter clasped.

12 'Who are the princes, those who have placed upon me
    this bast-rope and bound me?'

13 Now Nidud called, lord of the Niarar:
    'Where did you get, Volund, lord of elves,
    this gold of ours in Wolfdales?'

14 'The gold was not there in Grani's road,*
    far I think is our land from the hills of the Rhine.
    I remember that we owned greater riches
    when the couples were all together at home:

15 'Hladgud and Hervor, children of Hlodver,
    Olrun, Kiar's daughter, was famous.'

16 She went in right along the hall,*
    stood on the floor, said with low voice:
    'He is not very friendly, this one who came out of the forest.'

King Nidud gave Bodvild, his daughter, the gold ring which he took from the bast-rope at Volund's, and he himself wore the sword which Volund owned. But the queen said:

17 'He bares his teeth when the sword is shown before him
    and he recognizes Bodvild's ring;
    his eyes are like those of a shining serpent.
    Cut from him the might of his sinews*
    and afterwards put him in Sævarstad!'

*Thus it was done: the sinews were cut through at the back of his knees
and he was put on an island, near the land, called Sævarstad. There he
made all kinds of treasures for the king. No man dared go to him except
the king alone.*

Volund said:

18 'There shines at Nidud's belt a sword,
    which I sharpened most skilfully as I knew how,
    and I tempered as seemed to me best;
    that gleaming blade is forever borne far from me,
    I shall not see that brought to Volund in the smithy;

19 'now Bodvild wears my bride's—
    I don't expect redress for this—red-gold rings.'

20 He sat, nor did he sleep, ceaselessly he struck with his hammer,
    subtle things he shaped quite quickly for Nidud.
    The two young men came to see precious things,
    the sons of Nidud, to Sævarstad.

21 They came to the chest, demanded the keys;
    the evil was patent when they looked inside;
    a multitude of treasures, which seemed to the boys
    to be red gold, and jewellery.

22 'Come alone, you two, come another day!
    I shall have that gold given to you;
    don't tell the girls, nor the household,
    nor any man, that you'll visit me!'

23   Early called one lad to the other,
      brother to brother: 'Let's go to see the rings!'
      They came to the chest, demanded the keys;
      the evil was patent when they looked inside.

24   He cut off the heads of those young cubs,
      and under the mud of the forge he laid their limbs;
      and their skulls which were under the hair,
      he chased with silver, gave to Nidud.

25   And the precious stones from their eyes,
      he sent to Nidud's cunning wife;
      and from the teeth of the two
      he struck round brooches; sent them to Bodvild.

26   Then Bodvild began
      to praise the ring she'd broken.
      'I dare not tell anyone except you alone.'

Volund said:

27   'I will so repair the break in the gold,
      that your father will think it fairer,
      and your mother much better,
      and you yourself as good as before.'

28   He overcame her with beer, because he was cleverer,*
      so that on the couch she fell asleep.
      'Now I have avenged my sorrow,
      all except one of the wicked injuries!

29   'Good for me', said Volund, 'if I were on my webbed feet,*
      of which Nidud's warriors deprived me!'
      Laughing, Volund rose into the air;
      weeping, Bodvild went from the island,
      she grieved for her lover's departure and her father's fury.

30 Outside stood Nidud's cunning wife,
and she went inside, all along the hall;
and he on the hall-wall perched to rest himself:*
'Are you awake, Nidud, lord of the Niarar?'

31 'I am always awake, deprived of joy,
I sleep very little since my sons' deaths;
it's icy in my head, cold are your counsels to me,
I wish now that I could talk with Volund.

32 'Tell me, Volund, prince of elves,
what became of my healthy young cubs?'

33 'First you shall give me all these oaths:
by the side of a ship and the rim of a shield,
the back of a horse and the edge of a blade,
that you will not torment Volund's lady,
nor be the slayer of my bride,
though I have a wife who is known to you,
and we have a child inside your hall.

34 'Go to the smithy, the one you built,
there you'll find bellows spattered with blood:
I cut off the heads of your young cubs,
and in the mud of the forge I laid their limbs.

35 'And their skulls which were under their hair,
I chased with silver, sent them to Nidud:
and the precious stones from the eyes,
I sent to Nidud's cunning wife;

36 and from the teeth of the two
I struck round brooches; sent them to Bodvild.
Now Bodvild is with child,*
the only daughter of you both!'

37 'You could say no words that would grieve me more,
    nor, Volund, would I deny you any worse a fate;
    there is no man so tall that he could reach you from horse-back,
    nor so powerful that he could shoot you down from below,
    there where you hover against the cloud!'

38 Laughing, Volund rose in the air,
    and Nidud sadly sat there behind.

39 'Get up, Thakkrad, my best thrall;
    ask Bodvild, the white-lashed girl,
    to come in splendid clothes to speak with her father.

40 'Is it true, Bodvild, what they said to me:
    did you and Volund sit together on the island?'

41 'It is true, Nidud, what he said to you:
    Volund and I sat together on the island,
    alone for a tide-turning time; it should never have happened!
    I did not know how to strive against him,
    I was not able to strive against him!'

ALL-WISE'S SAYINGS

Thor intercepts a dwarf who apparently, and unbeknown to Thor, is intending to marry the latter's daughter. Thor proposes a wisdom contest in which he tests the dwarf's knowledge of the terminology used by the different races of being for natural phenomena. The dwarf knows a striking range of kennings and, perhaps, taboo words, but Thor's secret aim is to delay him until the sun comes up and turns him to stone. *All-wise's Sayings* (*Alvíssmál*) is a catalogue poem, rather like *Vafthrudnir's Sayings* and *Grimnir's Sayings*, but it is not mythological information which is at issue; rather the interest is in the range of poetic synonyms which the dwarf has at his disposal.

1 'To deck the benches the bride is coming with me,
   coming home now in this company;
   a precipitate in-lawship it might seem to everyone;
   at home our rest won't be wrecked.'

2 'What sort of creature is that, why so pale about the nostrils,
   did you spend the night with a corpse?
   The image of an ogre you seem to me,
   you were not born for a bride.'

3 'All-wise is my name, I live below the earth,
   my dwelling is under a rock;
   to the lord of wagons I've come on a visit,*
   let no man break people's sworn pledges!'

4 'I shall break them, since I've most authority
   over the bride as her father;
   I wasn't at home when she was promised to you,
   the only one among the gods who can give this gift.'

5 'Which man is this who claims to decide the match
   of the beautifully glowing lady?
   —A vagabond, few people know you,
   who bore you to possess arm-rings?'

6   'Ving-Thor I'm called; I've journeyed far and wide—
    I'm the son of Sidgrani;*
    not with my consent will you gain that young woman
    and get a bridal agreement.'

7   'Your consent I'd quickly like to gain
    and to get a bridal agreement;
    I had rather have her than go without
    the snow-white girl.'

8   'The love of the girl, wise guest,
    you won't be refused,
    if you know how to tell me from all the worlds,
    all that I want to know.

9   'Tell me this, All-wise—I reckon, dwarf,
    that you have wisdom about all beings—
    what the earth is called, which lies in front of men,
    in each world.'

10 'Earth it's called among men, and ground by the Æsir,
    the Vanir call it ways;
    the giants splendid-green, the elves the growing one,
    the Powers above call it loam.'

11 'Tell me this, All-wise—I reckon, dwarf,
    that you have wisdom about all beings—
    what the sky is called, known of old,
    in each world.'

12 'Sky it's called among men, planet-home by the gods,
    wind-weaver the Vanir call it,
    the giants call it the world above, the elves the lovely roof,
    the dwarfs the dripping hall.'

13 'Tell me this, All-wise—I reckon, dwarf,
    that you have wisdom about all beings—
    what the moon is called, which men can see,
    in each world.'

14   'Moon it's called by men, and ball by the gods,
in hell it's the whirling wheel,
the giants call it the hastener, the dwarfs the shiner,
elves call it counter of years.'

15   'Tell me this, All-wise—I reckon, dwarf,
that you know all the fates of men—
what the sun is called, which the sons of men see,
in each world.'

16   'Sun it's called by men, and sunshine by the gods,
for the dwarfs it's Dvalin's plaything,*
the giants call it everglow, the elves the lovely wheel,
the sons of the Æsir all-shining.'

17   'Tell me this, All-wise—I reckon, dwarf,
that you know all the fates of men—
what those clouds are called which mix with showers,
in each world.'

18   'Clouds they're called by men, and hope-of-showers by the
     gods,
the Vanir call them wind-floaters,
hope-of-dew the giants call them, power-of-storms the elves,
in hell the concealing helmet.'

19   'Tell me this, All-wise—I reckon, dwarf,
that you know all the fates of men—
what the wind is called, which blows so widely,
in each world.'

20   'Wind it's called by men, the waverer by the gods,
the mighty Powers say whinnier,
whooper the giants, din-journeyer the elves,
in hell they call it guster.'

21 'Tell me this, All-wise—I reckon, dwarf,
that you know all the fates of men—
what calm is called, which lies quiet,
in all the worlds.'

22 'Calm it's called by men, and lull by the gods,
the Vanir call it wind-end,
the great lee the giants, day-soother the elves,
the dwarfs call it day's retreat.'

23 'Tell me this, All-wise—I reckon, dwarf,
that you know all the fates of men—
what the ocean is called, which men row upon,
in each world.'

24 'Sea it's called by men, and ever-lier by the gods,
the Vanir call it rolling one,
eel-land the giants, liquid-fundament the elves,*
the dwarfs the deep ocean.'

25 'Tell me this, All-wise—I reckon, dwarf,
that you know all the fates of men—
what fire is called, burning before the sons of men,
in each world.'

26 'Fire it's called among men, and flame by the Æsir,
waverer by the Vanir,
ravener by the giants, burner-up by the dwarfs,
in hell they call it hurrier.'

27 'Tell me this, All-wise—I reckon, dwarf,
that you know all the fates of men—
what wood is called, growing before the sons of men,
in each world.'

28 'Wood it's called by men, and mane of the plains by the gods,
slope-seaweed by humankind,
fuel by the giants, lovely boughs by the elves,
wand the Vanir call it.'

29   'Tell me this, All-wise—I reckon, dwarf,
     that you know all the fates of men—
     what night is called, whom Norr acknowledged,
     in each world.'

30   'Night it's called among men, and darkness by the gods,
     the masker by the mighty Powers,
     unlight by the giants, sleep-joy by the elves,
     the dwarfs call it dream-goddess.'

31   'Tell me this, All-wise—I reckon, dwarf,
     that you know all the fates of men—
     what that crop is called, which the sons of men sow,
     in each world.'

32   'Barley it's called by men, and grain by the gods,
     the Vanir call it growth,
     food the giants, liquid-fundament the elves,
     in hell they call it head-hanger.'

33   'Tell me this, All-wise—I reckon, dwarf,
     that you know all the fates of men—
     what ale is called, which the sons of men drink,
     in each world.'

34   'Ale it's called among men, and beer by the gods,
     the Vanir call it liquor,
     clear-brew the giants, and mead in hell,
     the sons of Suttung call it drink.'

35   'In one breast I've never seen
     more ancient knowledge;
     with much guile I declare I've beguiled you;
     day dawns on you now, dwarf,
     now sun shines into the hall.'

THE FIRST POEM OF
HELGI HUNDINGSBANI

The two poems about Helgi Hundingsbani—the slayer of Hunding—and his namesake Helgi Hiorvardsson mark the beginning of the heroic poems in the Codex Regius manuscript. The relationship between the two Helgi Hundingsbani poems is unclear; it is quite likely that they represent much the same poem orally produced in different versions. All three Helgi poems centre on the meeting and battle adventures of the hero and his valkyrie lover. Valkyries were depicted as semi-divine figures, living in Valhall, serving mead to the warriors there, and hovering over battle choosing those who were going to die (hence the meaning of their name 'Choosers of the Slain'). But some valkyries were envisaged rather as human or superhuman. They were royal princesses who chose the valkyrie way of life in preference to that of a normal woman. The valkyrie would choose a hero, bring him good luck in battle while flying overhead with her companions, and eventually would become his bride. This would bring him into usually fateful collision with the valkyrie's kindred or with her thwarted suitors. The name 'Helgi' means 'Sacred One'; the Helgi heroes are archetypal in their relation to the valkyrie bride and may even be reincarnated, as is suggested at the end of the poem of Helgi Hiorvardsson. Central to this poem—and to the other Helgi poems—is the 'flyting', here between Sinfiotli and Gudmund. The opponents accuse each other of unnatural behaviour, sexual deviancy, or taboo acts, as a prelude to battle. It is not always clear who is speaking, and I have punctuated the dialogue to reflect my understanding of who is speaking when. This poem ends with Helgi's successfully winning his bride; the other Helgi poems continue after this point. The events of the poem are summarized in *Volsunga saga*, chs. 8–9.

1 It was at the start of time that the eagles shrieked,
   the sacred waters poured down from Himinfell;
   then Helgi, the strong-minded man,
   was born to Borghild in Bralund.

2 Night fell on the estate, then came norns,*
   those who shaped fate for the prince;
   they said the war-leader should be most famous
   and that he'd appear the best of princes.

3   They plied very strongly the strand of fate,
    as strongholds were breaking in Bralund;*
    they prepared the golden threads
    and fastened it in the middle under the moon's hall.*

4   East and west they concealed its ends,
    the prince possessed all the land between;
    Neri's kinswoman to the north*
    threw one fastening; she said it would hold for ever.

5   Just one thing concerned the kinsman of the Ylfings*
    and that girl who'd given birth to the dear boy:
    one raven said to another—he sat on a high tree,
    lacking for food: 'I know something.

6   'The son of Sigmund stands in his mail-coat,
    one day old; now day has dawned!
    sharp his eyes like fighters;
    he's the friend of wolves, we should be cheerful.'*

7   To the men it seemed that he was a prince,
    they said to one another that good years had come;
    the noble leader himself came from the tumult of battle
    to bring a splendid leek to the young lord.*

8   He gave Helgi a name, gave him Hringstadir,
    Sunfell, Snowfell, and Sigarvoll,
    Hringstod, Highmeadow, and Himinvangi,
    a tested blood-snake to Sinfiotli's brother.*

9   Then he began to grow in the bosom of his friends,
    the splendidly-born elm in radiant delight;*
    he paid out and gave gold to the retinue,
    the prince did not spare blood-stained treasure.

10 For a short time the prince waited for war,
    then the leader was fifteen years old;
    he brought about the killing of Hunding the hard,
    long he'd ruled lands and men.

11   Afterwards they demanded, the sons of Hunding,
       riches and rings from Sigmund's son,
       for they intended to repay the prince
       for his great ravaging and their father's death.

12   The prince did not let compensation be in question,
       nor did the kinsmen get a head-price at all;
       he said they should expect an excessive storm
       of grey spears and Odin's wrath.

13   The chieftains go to the sword-meeting
       which they'd set up at Logafell;
       the peace of Frodi was torn between the enemies;*
       corpse-eager on the island ran Odin's hounds.*

14   The prince sat down, when he'd killed
       Alf and Eyiolf, beneath Arastein,
       Hiorvard and Havard, the sons of Hunding;
       he'd brought down all of spear-Mimir's clan.*

15   Then a light shone from Logafell,
       and from that light came lightning-bolts;
       wearing helmets at Himinvangi [came the valkyries].
       Their byrnies were drenched in blood;
       and beams blazed from their spears.

16   Immediately he asked from the wolf-lair,
       the prince asked if the southern ladies
       wished to go home with the warriors
       when night fell; the elm bows were shrilling.

17   But from her horse, Hogni's daughter,
       —the shield-din was over—said to the prince:
       'I think we ought to have other business
       than drinking beer with the breaker of rings.*

18 'My father has promised his girl
    to Granmar's fierce son;
    but, Helgi, I call Hodbrodd
    a king as impressive as the kitten of a cat.*

19 'The prince will come in a few nights
    unless you challenge him to battle
    or seize the girl from the warrior.'

20 'Don't be afraid of the slayer of Isung!
    first there'll be noise of battle, or else I'll be dead.'

21 The all-powerful one sent messengers from there,
    through air and sea, to assemble his army,
    ample river-fire he offered*
    the warriors and their sons.

22 'Tell them quickly to go to their ships
    and to be ready to sail from Brand-island!'
    There the prince waited until there came
    huge numbers of men from Hedins-island.

23 And there from the beaches at Stafnsness
    they pushed out the ships graven with gold;
    Helgi asked Hiorleif this:
    'Have you inspected the impressive young men?'

24 The young king spoke to the others—
    it would take time to count off Crane-bank
    the long-necked ships beneath the sailors,
    journeying outwards on the Orvasund:

25 'Twelve hundred trusty men;
    though in Highmeadow there's twice as many,
    the king's war-troop; we may expect battle din.'

26   So the leader ordered the prow-tents dismantled,
     roused the crowd of warriors,
     and the fighters see the day-break;
     and the noble men hoisted up
     the well-sewn sail in Varinsfjord.

27   There was the splash of oars and the clash of iron,
     shield smashed against shield, the vikings rowed on;
     hurtling beneath the heroes
     surged the leader's ship far from the land.

28   Then it could be heard: they'd met together,
     the sister of Kolga and the longships,*
     as mountains or surf might break asunder.

29   Helgi ordered the high sail to be set,
     his crew did not cringe at the meeting of the waves,
     when Ægir's terrible daughter
     wanted to capsize the stay-bridled wave-horse.

30   And Sigrun above, brave in battle,
     protected them and their vessel;
     the king's sea-beast twisted powerfully
     out of Ran's hand near Gnipalund.*

31   So in Una-bay in the evening
     the splendid ships were floating;
     and the others in person from Svarinshaug*
     with troubled minds came to look at the army.

32   Gudmund asked, divinely-descended,
     'Who is that lord who leads the troop,
     who's brought the dangerous men to shore?'

33   Sinfiotli said—he'd slung on the yard-arm
     his red shield, the rim was all of gold;
     he was a sea-lookout who knew how to answer
     and how to debate with the princes:

34 'Say this evening, when you're feeding pigs
    and calling your bitches to their slops,*
    that the Ylfings have come from the east,
    eager for fighting to Gnipalund.

35 'Hodbrodd will find Helgi there,
    the prince who never flees, amid his fleet,
    a man who's often sated eagles,
    while you were kissing slave-women at the grindstone.'

36 'Little must you recall, lord, the old stories,
    when you taunt the princes with untruths;
    you have eaten wolves' corpse-leavings
    and were the slayer of your brother,
    often you've sucked wounds with a cold snout;
    hated everywhere, you've slunk into a stone-tip.'*

[*Sinfiotli said:*]

37 'You were a sorceress on Varins-island,
    a deceitful woman, you made up slander;
    you said that you did not want to have
    any warrior in his armour except Sinfiotli.*

38 'You were a harmful creature,
    a witch, a valkyrie, horrible, unnatural, with All-Father;
    all the Einheriar had to fight,
    headstrong woman, on your account.*

39 'Nine wolves on Saga's headland
    we engendered; I alone was their father.'

[*Gudmund said:*]

40 'You were not the father of Fenrir-wolves,
    older than them all, as far as I remember,
    after the giant girls castrated you
    on Thorsness by Gnipalund.

41   'You were Siggeir's stepson, you made your home under
           haystacks,*
       used to wolves' howling, out in the woods;
       you turned your hand to hateful deeds,
       when you tore your brother's breast.
       You made yourself infamous for abominable acts.

42   'You were Grani's bride on Bravoll plain,*
       a gold bit in your mouth, you were ready to leap;
       I've ridden you to exhaustion over many a stretch of road,
       a jaded hack under my saddle, down the mountain.'

[*Sinfiotli said:*]

43   'You seemed to be a lad without morals,
       when you milked Gullnir's goats,
       and another time as Imd's daughter*
       in tattered clothes. Do you want to keep talking?'

[*Gudmund said:*]

44   'Rather I'd like to sate ravens
       on your corpse, at Frekastein,
       than call your bitches to their slops
       or be feeding your pigs; may the trolls take you!'

[*Helgi said:*]*

45   'It would be much more fitting for you two, Sinfiotli,
       to go to battle and make the eagle happy,
       than to be bandying useless words,
       though the generous princes may have a quarrel to resolve.

46   'I don't like the look of Granmar's sons,
       though it befits princes to tell the truth;
       they have proved at Moinsheim,
       that they have the temperament for wielding swords.'

47   They allowed Svipud and Sveggiud*
     to run powerfully to Solheim,
     over the dew-sprinkled dales, the dark slopes,
     the valkyrie's airy sea trembled where the kinsmen passed.

48   They met the excellent prince at the courtyard-door,
     they said with excitement that the lord had come;
     Hodbrodd stepped forward, wearing his helmet,
     he pondered his kinsmen riding towards him:
     'Why do the Niflungs look so troubled?'

49   'They've beached on the sand swift ships,
     harts of mast-rings, long rowlocks,
     many shields, smooth-planed oars,
     the king's splendid troop, the cheerful Ylfings.

50   'Fifteen companies came on shore;
     yet out in Sogn there are seven thousand,
     pulled up by the palisade before Gnipalund,
     dark-coloured surf-beasts all decked with gold.
     By far the most of their mighty host is there.
     Helgi will not delay the meeting of swords.'

51   'Let the bridled horses gallop to the main assembly-places;
     Spurwolf ride to Sparins-heath,
     Melnir and Mylnir to Myrkwood,
     let no man linger behind,
     those who know how to brandish wound-flames.*

52   'Summon Hogni and the sons of Hring,
     Atli and Yngvi, Alf the old;
     they are eager to advance to war,
     let's offer the Volsungs some resistance!'

53   There was only the flickering—as they came together—
     of pale spear-points at Frekastein;
     always was Helgi, slayer of Hunding,
     foremost in the host, where men were fighting,
     eager in the battle, extremely averse to flight;
     that prince had a hard acorn of a heart.

54   Helmeted valkyries came down from the sky
       —the noise of spears grew loud—those who protected the
          prince;
       then said Sigrun—the wound-giving valkyries flew,
       the troll-woman's mount was feasting on raven-fodder:*

55   'Unscathed, prince, you'll unleash men,
       upholder of Yngvi's line, and enjoy your life,
       since you have brought low the king who scorns flight,
       the one who dealt death to the dread-bringing man.

56   'And it's fitting, lord, that you should have
       both red-gold rings and the powerful girl;
       unscathed, lord, you'll enjoy both
       Hogni's daughter and Hringstadir,
       lands and victory; now the battle is over.'

THE POEM OF HELGI HIORVARDSSON

Helgi Hiorvardsson is a kind of doublet of Helgi Hundingsbani whose two poems surround his in the manuscript. The *Poem of Helgi Hiorvardsson* (*Helgakvida Hiorvardssonar*) follows the basic plot of the other Helgi poems, with an added prelude telling of the winning of Helgi's mother. This sets up Helgi's first adventure, killing his mother's disgruntled former wooer; then comes a 'flyting' between the hero's lieutenant, Atli, and a troll-woman, Hrimgerd, the marriage with the valkyrie, and death at the hands of the son of his former enemy. Compared with the other two Helgi poems, the plot in this poem is less coherent. The flyting between Atli and Hrimgerd parallels that in the previous poem, and Hedin's vow has no clear tragic consequences—he simply acquires his brother's bride after his death. The poem ends before we know whether Hedin dies avenging Helgi or whether he and Svava find love together.

About Hiorvard and Sigrlinn   *Hiorvard was the name of a king. He had four wives. One was called Alfhild, their son was Hedin; the second was called Særeid, their son was called Humlung; the third was called Sinriod, their son was Hymling. King Hiorvard had sworn an oath to marry the woman whom he knew to be the most beautiful. He heard that King Svafnir had a daughter who was loveliest of all, who was called Sigrlinn.*

Idmund was the name of his earl. Atli was his son and he went to ask for Sigrlinn on the king's behalf. He spent the whole winter with King Svafnir. There was an earl called Franmar, Sigrlinn's foster-father; his daughter was called Alof. The earl advised that the girl not be betrothed and Atli went home.

Atli, the earl's son, was standing one day in a certain grove; there was a bird sitting in the branches up above him and it had heard that his men were saying that the most beautiful women were those married to Hiorvard. The bird squawked; Atli listened to what it said. It said:

1   'Have you seen Sigrlinn, daughter of Svafnir,
      the loveliest girl in Munarheim?
      even if the wives of Hiorvard seem pleasing
      to men in Glasilund.'

Atli said:

2 'Will you speak further, bird so wise-minded,
   to Atli, Idmund's son?'

The bird said:

   'I will, if the chieftain will sacrifice to me,
   and I may choose what I wish from the king's court.'

Atli said:

3 'Don't choose Hiorvard, nor his sons,*
   nor the lovely brides of the king,
   nor the brides who belong to the ruler;
   let's make a good bargain, that's the hallmark of friends.'

The bird said:

4 'I'll choose a temple with many sanctuaries,
   gold-horned cattle from the prince's farm,
   if Sigrlinn sleeps in his arms
   and willingly goes with the prince.'

*This was before Atli set off, and when he got home and the king asked him
for news, he said:*

5 'We've had difficulties, not achieved our mission,
   exhausted our horses on mighty mountains,
   then we had to ford the Sæmorn;
   Svafnir's daughter was refused us,
   the ring-adorned girl whom we wished to have.'

*The king commanded them to go a second time and he himself went. And
when they came up on top of the mountain, in Svævaland they saw the
country all on fire and dust-clouds from horses' hoofs. The king rode on
down the mountain and encamped for the night by a river. Atli kept watch
and went over the river. He found a house. A great bird was sitting on the
house, keeping watch, but it had fallen asleep. Atli hurled a spear at the*

bird and killed it, and in the house he found Sigrlinn, the king's daugh-
ter, and Alof, the earl's daughter, and took them away with him. Earl
Franmar had changed himself into an eagle and had been keeping them
safe from the army by magic. Hrodmar was the name of a king who was
Sigrlinn's suitor. He had killed the king of Svávaland and was raiding and
burning the land. King Hiorvard married Sigrlinn, and Atli married Alof.

Hiorvard and Sigrlinn had a tall and handsome son. He did not speak
and no name would stick to him.* He sat on a burial-mound* and saw
nine valkyries ride past. One was the most striking of all. She said:

6   'It'll be a long time, Helgi, before you dispose of rings,
       apple-tree of strife, or rule over Rodulsvoll*
       —an eagle shrieked early—if you are always silent,
       even if, helmeted prince, you have a stern temperament.'

7   'What will you give me with the name Helgi,*
       bright-faced lady, since you have bestowed it?
       Consider well before you answer!
       I won't accept it unless I can have you also.'

8   'I know of swords lying on Sigarsholm,
       four less than fifty;
       one is better than all the rest,
       baleful among battle-needles, inlaid with gold.

9   'There's a ring on the hilt, there's courage in the middle,
       and terror in its point, for him who can own it;
       a blood-dyed snake lies along the edge,
       on the boss an adder chases its tail.'

Eylimi was the name of a king. His daughter was Sváva. She was
a valkyrie and rode through the air and over the sea. She gave Helgi
that name and often protected him in battles. Helgi said:

10   'You aren't, Hiorvard, a well-advised king,
       war-band leader, though you are famous;
       you let fire consume the princes' settlements,
       though they have done you no harm.

11   'But Hrodmar will distribute rings,
      those which our kinsmen used to own;
      that king is little anxious about his life,
      he expects to dispose of the dead men's inheritance.'

*Hiorvard answered that he would give Helgi a troop of men if he wanted
to avenge his maternal grandfather. Then Helgi went to look for the
sword to which Svæva had directed him. Then he and Atli set off and
killed Hrodmar and did many brave deeds. He killed the giant Hati,
who was sitting on a certain cliff. Helgi and Atli moored their ships in
Hatafjord. Atli kept watch for the first part of the night. Hrimgerd,
Hati's daughter, said:*

12   'Who are those men in Hatafjord?
      Shields are hanging outside your ships;
      you're acting rather boldly, I don't think you're afraid of much;
      tell me the name of the king!'

Atli said:

13   'Helgi is his name, and you can never*
      bring harm to the prince;
      iron plates protect the prince's ships,
      no troll-women can attack us.'

14   'What is your name (said Hrimgerd), terrifying warrior,
      what do men call you?
      The prince trusts you, since he lets you take your stand
      in the ship's pleasant prow.'

15   'Atli I'm called, atrocious I shall be to you,*
      I am most hostile to ogresses;
      I've often stayed at the dew-washed prow
      and tormented night-riding witches.

16   'What is your name, corpse-greedy hag?
      Troll-woman, name your father!
      You ought to be nine leagues underground
      with fir-trees growing from your breast!'

17   'Hrimgerd I'm called, Hati is my father,
     the most all-powerful giant I know of;
     many brides he's had taken from their dwellings,
     until Helgi hacked him down.'

18   'Ogress, you stood before the prince's ships
     and lurked in the fjord's mouth;
     the king's men you were going to give to Ran,*
     if a spear hadn't quite thwarted you.'

19   'Deluded are you now, Atli, I reckon you're dreaming,
     you're scowling with drooping brow;
     my mother lurked ahead of the prince's ships,
     I drowned Hlodvard's sons in the ocean.

20   'You'd neigh, Atli, if you hadn't been gelded,*
     Hrimgerd's raising up her tail;
     I think your heart, Atli, is in your hindquarters,
     though you have a stallion's voice.'

21   'I'd seem like a stallion to you if you wanted to try it,
     if I came on land from this ship;
     I'd lame every part of you if I were in earnest,
     you'd drop your tail, Hrimgerd!'

22   'Atli, come on land, if you trust in your strength,
     and let's meet at Varins-bay!
     Warrior, you'd get your ribs straightened out,
     if you came into my clutches.'

23   'I can't come before the warriors awake
     and keep watch for the king;
     nor should I be surprised if a witch came close,
     and bobbed up under our ship.'

[*Hrimgerd said:*]

24 'Wake up, Helgi, and give Hrimgerd compensation,
    since you struck down Hati;
    if for one night she can sleep with the prince,
    then she'll have redress for her wrongs.'

25 'Shaggy is the name of the one who'll have you, you're hideous
        to humankind;
    that monster lives on Tholley;
    a very wise giant, but the worst of lava-dwelling ogres,
    he's a fitting mate for you.'

26 'You'd rather have her, Helgi, the one who was spying out the
        harbours
    the other night with the men;
    the sea-golden girl seemed to surpass me in strength;
    here she landed from the sea
    and secured your ships so.
    She alone prevents me from destroying
    the prince's men.'

27 'Listen now, Hrimgerd, if I give redress for your grief,
    answer the prince directly:
    was it just one creature who protected the lord's fleet,
    or many journeying together?'

28 'Three times nine girls, but one girl rode ahead,
    white-skinned under her helmet;
    the horses shook themselves, from their manes
    dew fell into the deep valleys,
    hail in the high woods;
    good harvest comes to men from there;
    all that I saw was hateful to me.'

29 'Look east now, Hrimgerd! See if Helgi has struck you with
        fatal runes!
    on land and sea the prince's ships are safe
    and so are the prince's men.

30 'It's day now, Hrimgerd, Atli has kept you talking
until you laid down your life;
as a harbour-mark you look hilarious,
standing there transformed into stone.'

King Helgi was a great fighter. He came to King Eylimi and asked for his daughter, Svava. Helgi and Svava exchanged vows and loved one another very much. Svava stayed at home with her father, and Helgi went raiding. Svava was a valkyrie just as before.

Hedin was at home with his father, King Hiorvard, in Norway. Hedin was going home alone from the woods one Yule evening and he met a troll-woman; she was riding a wolf and had serpents as reins. She offered Hedin her company. 'No', he said. She said: 'You'll pay for this when it comes to drinking to pledges.' In the evening pledges were made. The sacred boar was led out, men put their hands on it and then they made their vows with the pledging-cup. Hedin vowed to have Svava, daughter of Eylimi, Helgi, his brother's beloved, and he repented so much of this that he went wandering away to the southern lands and encountered his brother Helgi. Helgi said:

31 'Welcome, Hedin! What news
do you bring from Norway?
Why, prince, have you been driven from your country
and come alone to meet us?'

32 'A more terrible crime has come upon me:
I have chosen that royally born
bride of yours with the pledging-cup.'

33 'Don't reproach yourself! For both of us, Hedin,
what's said over ale must come true;
a prince has challenged me to an island duel;*
in three nights' time, I shall go there,
I have my doubts as to whether I'll return;
it may turn out well if I don't.'

34 'You're saying, Helgi, that Hedin deserves from you
good will and great gifts;
it would be more fitting to bloody your sword on me
than to grant peace to your enemies.'

*Then Helgi said that he suspected that he was doomed and those were his
fetches* who had come to Hedin when he met the woman riding on the wolf.*

*Alf, son of Hrodmar, was the king who had staked out the duelling-
ground with hazel-poles for Helgi three nights later. Then Helgi said:*

35   'She rode on a wolf, as it grew dark,
        that lady who offered him company;
        she knew that Sigrlinn's son
        would be killed at Sigarsvellir.'

There was a great fight and Helgi received a death-wound.

36   Helgi sent Sigar to ride
        for Eylimi's only daughter;
        told her to get ready quickly
        if she wanted to find the prince alive.

37   'Helgi has sent me here to you, Svava,
        to speak to you in person;
        the helmet-wearing lord says he wants to see you
        before the splendidly born man draws his last breath.'

38   'What has happened to Helgi, Hiorvard's son?
        A grievous sorrow has been brought upon me;
        if the sea has played cruelly with him, or the sword has bitten
            into him,
        I shall wreak vengeance on that man.'

39   'He fell here in the morning at Frekastein,
        the prince who was best under the sun;
        Alf has achieved total victory,
        though there was no need for it to have happened.'

40   'Greetings, Svava! You must steady your feelings,
        this will be our last meeting in the world;
        wounds begin to bleed for the prince,
        a sword has pierced very close to my heart.

41 'I beg you, Svava—bride, do not weep!—
that you will listen to what I say,
that you will share a bed with Hedin
and live in love with the young prince.'

42 'I declared this in Munarheim,
when Helgi chose me, gave me rings,
that I would not willingly, if my lord were gone,
hold a prince of no reputation in my arms.'

[*Hedin said:*]

43 'Kiss me, Svava! Never will I come
to see Rogheim or Rodulsfiall,
until I've avenged Hiorvard's son;
he was best of princes under the sun.'

Helgi and Svava are said to have been reincarnated.

A SECOND POEM OF
HELGI HUNDINGSBANI

The second poem about Helgi Hundingsbani has several elements in common with the first: the hero's gaining of his nickname, his love for the valkyrie, and a very reduced form of the flyting found in the *First Poem of Helgi Hundingsbani*. It is quite likely that the scribe of the manuscript intended readers and reciters to leaf back to the first poem and read the flyting there, rather than recopying it. This poem is notable for the sense of conflict Sigrun feels between her love for Helgi and her loyalty to her family, and for the extravagantly Gothic ending in which Sigrun and Helgi spend a final night together in the burial-mound.

King Sigmund, son of Volsung, married Borghild of Bralund. They called their son Helgi after Helgi Hiorvardsson. Hagal fostered Helgi.

Hunding was a powerful king. Hundland is named after him. He was a great warrior and had many sons who went raiding. There was hostility and enmity between King Hunding and King Sigmund; each killed the other's kinsmen. Sigmund and his clan were known as Volsungs and Ylfings.

Helgi went in disguise to reconnoitre King Hunding's court. Hæming, son of King Hunding, was at home. And when Helgi went away, he met a shepherd boy and said:

1 'Tell Hæming that Helgi remembers
   whom the warriors struck down in his coat-of-mail.
   You've had a grey wolf within your court,
   he whom King Hunding thought was Hamal.'

Hamal was Hagal's son. King Hunding sent men to Hagal to search for Helgi. And since Helgi couldn't escape any other way he put on a serving-woman's clothes and went to grind at the mill. They searched and couldn't find him. Then Blind the malevolent said:

2 'Piercing are the eyes of Hagal's maidservant,*
   that's not a low-born person standing at the grindstone;
   the stones are breaking, the wooden frame is splitting.

3   'Now the prince has got a harsh sentence,
    the noble has to grind foreign barley.
    It would be more fitting to have in that hand
    a sword hilt than a grinding-handle.'

Hagal answered and said:

4   'It's not so distressing that the frame should be juddering,
    as the king's daughter turns the handle;
    she sped above the clouds
    and dared to fight like vikings do,
    before Helgi captured her;
    she's Sigar and Hogni's sister,
    that's why the Ylfing girl has terrifying eyes.'

*Helgi got away onto a warship. He killed King Hunding and after that
was called Helgi Hundings-killer. With his army he lay in Bruna-bay
and there they butchered cattle on the beach and ate them up raw. Hogni
was the name of a king. His daughter was Sigrun; she was a valkyrie
and rode through air and over the sea; she was Sváva reincarnated.
Sigrun rode to Helgi's ships and said:*

5   'Who has brought these ships to anchor by the steep shore,
    where, warriors, do you come from?
    What are you waiting for in Bruna-bay,
    which way do you set your course?'

6   'Hamal has brought these ships to anchor by the steep shore;
    we come from Hlesey;
    we're waiting for a breeze in Bruna-bay,
    to the east we wish to set our course.'

7   'Where have you, prince, stirred up war
    or fed the goslings of Gunn's sisters?*
    Why is your corslet spattered with blood,
    why must you eat raw meat, men wearing helmets?'

8   'The Ylfings' descendant fought most recently
    west of the sea, if you wish to know,
    where I was hunting bears in Bragalund*
    and sated with sword-points the eagle's race.

9 'Now I've told you, girl, where battle came about;
and so by the sea we're eating meat scarcely roasted.'

10 'A killing you declare; King Hunding
fell on the field before Helgi;
it came to battle, in revenge for a relative,
blood streamed along the sword-edges.'

11 'How could you know, wise lady,
that we avenged our relative on them?
There are many keen prince's sons,
who look like us kinsmen.'

12 'I was not far away, battle-leader,
yesterday morning, when the prince lost his life;
though I reckon that Sigmund's clever son
gives battle-news in secret slaughter-runes.

13 'I glimpsed you once before on the longships,
where you were at the ship's bloody bow;
cold and wet the waves were playing.
Now the prince wants to hide himself from me
but Hogni's girl recognizes Helgi.'

*Granmar was the name of a powerful king who lived at Svarinshaug.
He had many sons: Hodbrodd, the second, Gudmund, the third,
Starkad. Hodbrodd was at a meeting of kings; he betrothed himself to
Sigrun, Hogni's daughter. But when she heard that, she rode with her
valkyries through air and over sea to find Helgi.*

*Helgi was at Logafell and had fought with the sons of Hunding.
There he struck down Alf and Eyiolf, Hiorvard and Hervard; he
was exhausted from battle and he was resting below Arastein. There
Sigrun found him and flung her arms around his neck and kissed him
and told him what her errand was, as it says in the 'Old Poem of the
Volsungs':**

14   Sigrun went to see the cheerful prince,
      she caught Helgi by the hand;
      she kissed and greeted the king in his helmet,
      then the king began to love the woman.

15   She said she'd already loved with all her heart
      Sigmund's son before she'd seen him.

16   'I have been betrothed to Hodbrodd among the fighters,
      but another prince I wished to have;
      though, lord, I fear the anger of kinsmen,
      I've destroyed my father's favoured design.'

17   Hogni's girl did not dissemble,
      she said she wanted Helgi's protection.

18   'Don't worry about Hogni's anger,
      nor the wrath of your kinsmen.
      Young girl, you will live with me;
      I've no fear, good lady, of your family.'

Helgi assembled a great fleet and went to Frekastein, and on the ocean they ran into a terribly dangerous storm. Lightning flashed above them and the ships were struck. They saw nine valkyries riding up in the air, and recognized Sigrun among them. Then the storm abated and they got safely to land. The sons of Granmar were sitting up on a cliff, when the ships sailed to land. Gudmund leapt on his horse and rode down to a cliff near the harbour to reconnoitre. The Volsungs lowered their sails. Then Gudmund Granmarsson said, as is written above in the 'Poem of Helgi':

            'Who is that lord who leads the troop,
             who's brought the dangerous men to shore?'

19   'Who is the prince who steers the ships,
      and has a golden war banner at his prow?
      Peace, it seems to me, is not at the forefront of your journey;
      a red battle-glow hangs over the vikings.'

Sinfiotli said:

20   'Here Hodbrodd may recognize Helgi,
      the fighter who does not flee, in the midst of the fleet;
      the homeland of your kin,
      the Fiorsungs' inheritance, he has conquered.'

[*Gudmund said:*]

21   'Thus we should at Frekastein
      meet together, settle the matter;
      Hodbrodd, it's a case for taking revenge,
      where we have long had to take the lower part.'

[*Sinfiotli said:*]

22   'Rather, Gudmund, you'll be herding goats
      and clambering down the rocky clefts,
      in your hand you'll have a hazel switch;
      for you that's jollier than the judgement of swords.'

[*Helgi said:*]

23   'For you, Sinfiotli, it would be more fitting
      to draw up for battle and make the eagles glad,
      than to be bandying useless words,
      even if chieftains have strife to settle.

24   'I don't like the look of Granmar's sons,
      though it befits princes to tell the truth;
      they have proved at Moinsheim,
      that they have the temperament for wielding swords;
      the princes are far too bold.'

*Sinfiotli, Sigmund's son, answered, as is also written. Gudmund rode
home with the news of invasion. Then Granmar's sons assembled an
army. Many kings came to join them. There was Hogni, Sigrun's
father, and his sons, Bragi and Dag. There was a great battle and all
of Granmar's sons were killed and all of the princes, except for Dag,*

Hogni's son, who obtained a truce and swore oaths to the Volsungs.
Sigrun went among the slaughtered and found Hodbrodd on the point of
death. She said:

25 'Sigrun from Sefafell
will not sink into your arms, King Hodbrodd;
ebbing is the life—often the troll-woman's grey horse-herd*
gets the corpses—of Granmar's sons.'

Then she met Helgi and was extremely joyful. He said:

26 'It was not all good fortune for you, strange creature,*
though I reckon the norns had some part in it;*
this morning at Frekastein
Bragi and Hogni were killed, I was their slayer.

27 'And at Styr-cleft King Starkad,
and at Hlebiorg the sons of Hrollaug;
I saw that fiercest-minded of kings
defending his trunk—his head was gone.

28 'All the rest of your kinsmen
were lying on the ground, corpses they'd become;
you did not stop the battle, it was fated for you
that you'd be cause of strife among powerful men.'

Then Sigrun wept. He said:

29 'Be comforted Sigrun! You've been our battle-goddess;
the princes could not struggle against fate.'
'I'd choose now that those who are gone might live again
and that I could still hold you in my arms.'

Helgi married Sigrun and they had sons. Helgi did not live to old age.
Dag, Hogni's son, sacrificed to Odin for revenge for his father. Odin lent
Dag his spear. Dag encountered Helgi, his brother-in-law, at a place
called Fetter-grove. He pierced Helgi with the spear and Helgi fell there.
And Dag rode to the mountains and told this news to Sigrun:

30   'Sister, I am reluctant to tell you of grief,
      for I am forced to make my kinswoman weep:
      there fell this morning below Fetter-grove
      the lord who was the best in the world
      and who stood on the necks of chieftains.'

31   'May all the oaths which you swore
      to Helgi rebound upon you,
      by the bright water of Leift
      and the cold, wet stone of Unn.

32   'May the ship you sail on not go forward,*
      though the wind you need has sprung up behind;
      may the horse you ride on not go forward,
      though you need to escape your enemies.

33   'May the sword that you wield never bite for you,
      unless it's whistling above your own head.
      Helgi's death would be avenged on you,
      if you were a wolf out in the forest
      deprived of wealth and all well-being
      and of food, except when you glutted yourself on corpses.'

Dag said:

34   'You're mad, sister! you're out of your wits,
      that you wish this evil fate on your brother;
      Odin alone caused all the misfortune,
      for he cast hostile runes between kinsmen.

35   'Your brother offers you red-gold rings,
      all Vandilsve and Vigdal;
      take half of our homeland to pay for your loss,
      ring-adorned woman, you and your sons.'

36   'I shall not sit so happily at Sefafell,
      neither early nor at night-time, that I'll desire to live on;
      unless light should shine on the prince's company,
      unless Vigblær should gallop here under the chieftain,
      tamed to his gold bridle, and I could welcome the warrior.

37 'Helgi so terrified
    all his enemies and their kin,
    just as panicking goats run before the wolf
    down from the mountain filled with fear.

38 'So Helgi surpassed the soldiers
    like the bright-growing ash beside the thorn-bush
    and the young stag, drenched in dew,
    who towers above all other animals
    and whose horns glow right up to the sky.'

A burial-mound was made for Helgi. And when he came to Valhall Odin
asked him to rule over everything with him. Helgi said:

39 'Hunding, you shall fetch the foot-bath*
    for every man and kindle the fire,
    tie up the dogs, watch the horses,
    give the pigs slops before you go to sleep.'

One evening Sigrun's maid went past Helgi's mound and saw Helgi
riding into the mound with a large number of men. The maid said:

40 'Are these just delusions, that I think I can see
    dead men riding, or is it Ragnarok?
    where do you spur your horses onward,
    or are the fighters allowed to come home?'

Helgi said:

41 'These are not delusions that you think you see,
    nor the end of mankind, though you gaze upon us,
    though we spur our horses onwards,
    nor are the fighters allowed to come home.'

The maid went home and told Sigrun:

42 'Go outside, Sigrun from Sefafell,
    if you want to meet the army-leader;
    the mound has opened, Helgi has come!
    his wounds are bleeding, the prince asks you
    to staunch his injuries.'

Sigrun went into the mound to Helgi and said:

43 'Now I am so glad, at our meeting,
as are the greedy hawks of Odin*
when they know of slaughter, steaming flesh,
or, dew-gleaming, they see the dawn.

44 'First I want to kiss the lifeless king,
before you throw off your bloody mail-coat;
your hair, Helgi, is thick with hoar-frost,
the prince is all soaked in slaughter-dew,*
Hogni's son-in-law has clammy hands.
How, ruler, can I find a remedy for this?'

45 'You alone, Sigrun from Sefafell,
cause Helgi to be soaked in sorrow-dew;
you weep, gold-adorned lady, bitter tears,
sun-bright southern girl, before you go to sleep;
each falls bloody on the breast of the prince,
cold and wet, burning into me, thick with grief.

46 'We ought to drink precious liquors,*
though we have lost our love and our lands;
no man should sing a lament for me,
though on my breast wounds can be seen;
now the lady is enclosed in the mound,
a human woman with us, the departed.'

Sigrun made up a bed in the mound.

47 'Here I've made you, Helgi, a bed all ready;
descendant of the Ylfings, now free from care
in your arms, lord, I'll sleep,
as I would with the prince, when he was living.'

48 'I declare nothing else could be less expected,
neither early nor late at Sefafell,
that you should sleep in the dead man's arms,
white lady, in the tomb, Hogni's daughter,
and you alive, and royally born.

49   'It is time for me to ride along the blood-red roads,
      to set the pale horse treading the path through the sky;
      I must cross the wind-vault's bridge in the west,
      before Salgofnir awakens the victorious people.'*

*Helgi and his men rode away, and the women went back to the house.
The next evening Sigrun had the maid keep watch by the mound. And at
dusk, when Sigrun came to the mound, she said:*

50   'He would have come by now, if he meant to come,
      Sigmund's son, from Odin's halls;
      I declare that hopes of the prince coming here are fading,
      now the eagles roost on the ash-branches
      and all the household head for the dream-assembly.'*

51   'Do not be so mad as to go alone,
      high-born lady, into the home of ghosts;
      much more powerful at night, lady, are all
      dangerous dead creatures, than by the light of day.'

*Sigrun did not live long from sorrow and grief. There was a belief in
pagan times, which we now reckon an old wives' tale, that people could
be reincarnated. Helgi and Sigrun were thought to have been reborn.
He was called Helgi Haddingia-damager, and she was Kara, Halfdan's
daughter, as is told in the 'Song of Kara',* and she was a valkyrie.*

THE DEATH OF SINFIOTLI

Sigmund, son of Volsung, was king in the land of the Franks. Sinfiotli was his eldest son, the second was Helgi, the third Hamund. Borghild, Sigmund's wife, had a brother called [?].* And Sinfiotli, her stepson, and [?] were both wooing the same woman, and for that reason Sinfiotli killed him. And when he came home, then Borghild told him to go away, but Sigmund offered her compensation, and she had to accept that. But at the funeral feast Borghild was carrying the ale around. She took poison, a great, full horn of it, and gave it to Sinfiotli. But when he looked in the horn, he realized that there was poison in it and he said to Sigmund, 'This drink is cloudy, Dad!' Sigmund took the horn and drank it up. It is said that Sigmund had such a mighty constitution that no poison could harm him, neither outside nor inside; and all his sons could withstand poison on their skin. Borghild brought another horn to Sinfiotli and told him to drink, and everything happened as before. And the third time she brought him a horn and offered him taunting words if he did not drink it up. He spoke to Sigmund as before. He said, 'Let your moustache strain it, son!' Sinfiotli drank it and died immediately. Sigmund carried him in his arms for a long way, and came to a long, narrow fjord, and there was a little ship and a single man on it. He offered to take Sigmund over the fiord. But when Sigmund put the corpse in the ship, it was fully loaded. The man said that Sigmund would have to walk in along the fiord and he pushed out the boat and disappeared.*

Sigmund lived in Denmark, Borghild's kingdom, for a long time after he married her. Then he went south to the land of the Franks, to the kingdom he had there. Then he married Hiordis, daughter of King Eylimi. Sigurd was their son. Sigmund was killed in battle by the sons of Hunding and then Hiordis married Alf, son of King Hialprek. Sigurd lived with them as a child and grew up there.

Sigmund and all his sons surpassed all men in strength and size and courage and all accomplishments. Sigurd, however, was the most remarkable of all, and in the old traditions everyone says he was the greatest of all men and the most redoubtable of war-leaders.

GRIPIR'S PROPHECY

Gripir's Prophecy (*Gripisspa*) is clearly a late poem, dependent upon the other poems which follow it in the Sigurd cycle, and possibly upon an early version of *Volsunga saga*. Its function is to summarize the story of Sigurd, foretelling everything which will happen to him. It introduces the characters which follow, but adds little, artistically or thematically, to the later poems of the cycle. It does however give some clues as to the material contained in the eight missing leaves of the manuscript. *Volsunga saga*, ch. 16, mentions the meeting between uncle and nephew but, wisely, does not destroy narrative suspense by recounting the contents of the prophecy.

Gripir was a son of Eylimi, Hiordis's brother; he ruled over territories and was the wisest of all men, and could foresee the future. Sigurd was riding by himself and came to the hall of Gripir. Sigurd was easy to recognize. He met a man outside the hall and spoke to him. He said his name was Geitir. Then Sigurd addressed him and asked:

1 'Who lives here in these dwellings?
   What do warriors call that mighty king?'
   'Gripir he is called, that leader of men,
   he who rules over the well-secured land and the warriors.'

2 'Is the clever king at home in the land?
   Will the prince come to speak with me?
   An unknowing man needs to speak to him,
   Quickly I'd like to meet Gripir.'

3 'The gracious king will ask Geitir
   who that man might be who'd speak with Gripir.'
   'Sigurd I am called, son of Sigmund,
   and Hiordis is the prince's mother.'*

4 Then Geitir went to say to Gripir:
   'Here is a man outside, an unknown man has come;
   he is striking to look at;
   he would like, lord, to meet you.'

5 The lord of men went out of the hall
   and greeted warmly the prince who'd come:
   'Welcome here, Sigurd, you should have come before now!
   And you, Geitir, look after Grani!'*

6 They began to speak and they discussed many things,
   there where they met, the sagacious men.
   'Tell me if you know, uncle,
   how life will turn out for Sigurd.'

7 'You will be the most glorious man under the sun
   and raised up highest of all princes,
   generous with gold, and reluctant to retreat,
   striking to look at and wise in your words.'

8 'Say, honest king, more plainly than I can ask,
   wise one, tell Sigurd if you think you can foretell:
   what will happen first in my fortune
   when I have gone out of your courtyard?'

9 'First, prince, you'll avenge your father,
   and requite all Eylimi's sorrow;*
   you'll bring down the brave, hard sons of Hunding;
   you'll have the victory.'

10 'Tell me, shining king, kinsman
    so wise, as we speak thoughtfully:
    do you see Sigurd's mighty deeds ahead
    the highest under heaven's corners?'

11 'You alone will kill the shining serpent,
    the greedy one who lies on Gnita-heath;
    you will be the killer of both Regin and Fafnir;
    Gripir tells what is true.'

12 'There'll be wealth enough if I manage that
    killing among men, as you surely say;
    ponder my course and speak at more length;
    what more will be in my life?'

13 'You will find Fafnir's lair
    and gather up the fabulous treasure,
    load the gold on Grani's back;
    ride to Giuki's, the prince prominent in war.'*

14 'Still you must, high-minded hero,
    in thoughtful conversation say more to the lord;
    I am Giuki's guest, and I go away from there;
    what more will be in my life?'

15 'A prince's daughter, bright in her mail-shirt,
    sleeps on the mountain after the killing of Helgi;*
    you must strike with your sharp sword,
    slit the mail-shirt with Fafnir's slayer.'

16 'The mail-shirt is sliced open, the girl begins to speak,
    when the woman woke from sleep;
    what will the lady wish to say to Sigurd,
    which will bring good fortune to the fighter?'

17 'Runes she'll relate to you, the mighty man,
    all those which men wish to know,
    and how to speak every single human tongue,
    medicine with healing knowledge; and now farewell, king!'*

18 'Now that's over, the wisdom is won,
    and I'm ready to ride from there;
    ponder my course and speak at more length;
    what more will be in my life?'

19 'You will come to the dwellings of Heimir
    and be a cheerful guest of the king;
    that is done, Sigurd, what I knew already;
    you should not question Gripir any further!'

20 'Now sorrow seizes me with the words you say,
    for you see further ahead, prince;
    you know of great misery for Sigurd;
    that's why, Gripir, you won't tell me it.'

21 'Your youth lay before me
   most clearly to look over;
   it is not true that I am reckoned to be wise
   or at all prophetic, I've told you what I know!'

22 'I know no man on earth
   who sees further than you, Gripir;
   you must not hide it, though it be horrible,
   or if harm is afoot in my future.'

23 'No shame is laid down for your life;
   accept that from me, shining prince,
   for as long as men survive, portender of arrow-showers,
   your name will be uppermost.'

24 'The worst it must be for me, if Sigurd parts
   from the prince with things as they are;
   show me the road—all is laid down for me—
   if you will, my illustrious uncle.'

25 'Now shall I speak clearly to Sigurd,
   the prince has forced me to this point;
   you must be certain, no word of a lie,
   that one day death is intended for you.'

26 'I don't want the wrath of the powerful king,
   good advice, Gripir, I'd rather accept;
   now I want to know clearly, though it be uncongenial,
   what is seen ahead for Sigurd.'

27 'A lady is at Heimir's, pleasing to look at,
   Brynhild, the brave men call her,*
   Budli's daughter, and the excellent king,
   Heimir has fostered a fierce-minded girl.'

28 'What's it to me, if a girl should be
pleasing to look at, fostered at Heimir's?
That you must, Gripir, say quite clearly,
since you foresee all this fate ahead.'

29 'She'll rob you of most of your happiness,
pleasing to look at, Heimir's foster-child;
you'll get no sleep, adjudge no lawsuits,
you'll notice no one unless you see the girl.'

30 'What comfort is laid down for Sigurd?
Tell me that, Gripir, if you think you see it;
shall I get the girl, obtain her with a dowry,
that beautiful daughter of the prince?'

31 'You two will swear all your oaths
very strongly; few will you keep;
when you've been one night the guest of Giuki
you won't recall the wise fosterling of Heimir.'

32 'What's this, Gripir, that you're putting to me!
Do you see fickleness in this prince's temperament,
if I shall rend asunder the oaths to that girl
whom I thought I loved with all my heart?'

33 'Prince, victim of another's treacheries you'll be,
Grimhild's counsels will prevail;
she'll offer you the bright-haired girl,
her daughter, she'll ensnare the prince with trickery.'

34 'Shall I then become an in-law to Gunnar
and get to marry Gudrun?
Well wived then this prince would be,
if grief for the harm done didn't seize me.'

35 'Grimhild will thoroughly deceive you,
she'll urge you to woo Brynhild
for Gunnar, king of the Goths;
speedily you'll agree to journey for the ruler's mother.'

36 'Harm lies ahead, I can see that,
Sigurd's plans will clearly go astray,
if I shall woo the splendid woman
for another, the woman I love well.'

37 'All of you will swear oaths,
Gunnar and Hogni, and you, prince, the third;
for you'll exchange appearances on the road,
Gunnar and you; Gripir does not lie!'

38 'What's the point of that? Why should we exchange
appearances and behaviour when we're on the road?
Some further deception goes with this,
something quite terrible; tell me more, Gripir!'

39 'Gunnar's appearance you'll have and his bearing,
your own eloquence and powerful intellect;
you'll betroth yourself to the high-minded woman,
Heimir's fosterling; you'll think nothing of this.'

40 'This is the worst I can imagine, I, Sigurd, will be reviled
by men for this; I should not wish
to entrap with cunning the noble bride
whom I know to be the best.'

41 'You'll sleep, leader of the army,
splendid man, with the girl, as if she were your mother;
and so, prince of the people, as long as men survive,
your name will be uppermost.

43 'Together will both weddings be celebrated,*
Sigurd's and Gunnar's in Giuki's halls;
for you'll change back your shapes when you come home,
each of you will have his own mind in this.'

42 'Gunnar will wed a good woman,
   famous among men, so you tell me, Gripir,
   though the warrior's resolute bride has slept
   three nights with me? That would be unexampled!

44 'How can an in-law bond between men
   prosper after this? Tell me Gripir;
   will contentment next be granted to Gunnar
   and to me myself?'

45 Though you recall your oaths you'll keep silent,
   you want a good marriage for Gudrun;
   and Brynhild the bride will think herself disparaged,
   the lady will use treachery to get her revenge.'

46 'What compensation will that bride accept,
   when we've woven for her such deceit?
   From me the lady had oaths I'd sworn,
   none fulfilled, and little pleasure.'

47 'To Gunnar she'll say very clearly
   that you did not truly keep your oaths,
   those in which the shining king, heir of Giuki,
   trusted you, prince, with all his heart.'

48 'What is this, Gripir? What are you telling me!
   Will these stories be proved true of me?
   or will that praiseworthy woman,
   lie about herself and me? Gripir, tell me that!'

49 'In her anger and her great grief
   the powerful lady will not act so well towards you;
   never will you injure the good woman,
   though you plotted treachery against the king's wife.'

50 'Will Gunnar the wise follow her urging
   —and Guthorm and Hogni—after this?
   Shall the sons of Giuki, on me, their in-law,
   bloody their blades? Gripir, tell me more!'

51   'Gudrun will become grim in her heart
      when her brothers bring about your death,
      and no joy will afterwards come
      to the wise lady; Grimhild's the cause of this.

52   'This shall console you, leader of the army,
      this luck's laid down in the prince's life:
      no mightier man will walk on the earth,
      under the sun's dwelling, than you, Sigurd, seem to be.'

53   'Let's part and say farewell, one can't overcome fate;
      now, Gripir, you've done just as I asked you;
      swiftly you'd have told me of a life
      more pleasant, if you'd been able!'

THE LAY OF REGIN

The *Lay of Regin* (*Reginsmal*) consists of a number of different sequences of verses, most of which have little to do with Regin himself. The poet introduces the theme of the cursed gold, the ransom for Otter which forms Fafnir's hoard, and sketches the future strife it will cause; he sets up the prickly relationship between Regin and Sigurd, and introduces Odin as patron of the Volsung clan. Like other poems pertaining to the youth of Sigurd, part of the poem consists of wisdom, signalled by a change in metre from *fornyrdislag* to *ljodahattr*. Loki asks Andvari for mythological information and Sigurd questions Hnikar (Odin) about battle-omens. The narrative moves forward through prose insets, framing the dialogue of the verses. By the end of the poem the narrative groundwork has been done and Sigurd is ready to face the dragon—his greatest adventure.

Sigurd went to Hialprek's stud and chose himself a horse who was afterwards called Grani.* Then Regin came to Hialprek's; he was the son of Hreidmar; he was more skilful in making things than anyone else and a dwarf in height; he was clever, fierce, and knowledgeable about magic. Regin offered to foster Sigurd and to teach him, and he loved him a great deal. He told Sigurd about his parents and these events: Odin, Hænir, and Loki had come to Andvara-falls; in those falls there were a great many fish. There was a dwarf called Andvari; he had spent a long time in the falls in the form of a pike and got himself food that way. 'Otter was the name of our brother,' said Regin, 'and he used often to go in the falls in the form of an otter. He had caught a salmon and was sitting on the river bank, eating it with his eyes shut. Loki struck him with a stone and killed him. The Æsir thought this was great good fortune and flayed off the otter's skin for a bag. The same evening they stayed the night with Hreidmar and showed what they had caught. Then we seized them and made them ransom their lives by filling the otterskin bag with gold and also by covering the outside with red gold. Then they sent Loki to collect the gold. He went to Ran and borrowed her net and then went to Andvara-falls and cast the net ahead of the pike; and he jumped into it. Then Loki said:

1   ' "What sort of fish is that which courses through the water,
     and doesn't know how to avoid danger?
     Your head you can save from hell;
     find the serpent's flame for me!"*

2   ' "Andvari is my name, Oin was my father's name,
     I've swum through many a fall;
     a wretched norn shaped my fate in the early days,*
     that I must wade in the water."

3   ' "Tell me, Andvari," said Loki, "if you want to retain
     your life in the halls of men:
     what requital do the sons of men get,
     if they wound one another with words?"*

4   ' "A mighty requital the sons of men get,
     those who must wade in Vadgelmir;*
     for untrue words, when one man slanders another,
     a long time he'll suffer the consequences."

'Loki saw all the gold which Andvari possessed, and when he had handed over the gold, he had one ring left, and Loki took that from him. The dwarf went into a rock and said:*

5   ' "That gold, which Gust owned,
     will be the death of two brothers,
     and cause of strife between eight princes;*
     my treasure will be no use to anyone."

'The Æsir gave Hreidmar the treasure and stuffed the otterskin and stood it on its legs. Then the Æsir had to heap up the gold to cover it. And when that was done, Hreidmar went forwards and saw a single whisker, and said it must be covered. Then Odin produced the ring, Andvari's Jewel, and covered the hair.

6   ' "The gold now is given to you" (said Loki), "and you have
     a great payment for my head;
     for your son no good fortune is ordained;
     it will be the death of both of you!"

'*Hreidmar said:*

7   '"Gifts you gave, you did not give love-gifts,
you did not give them wholeheartedly;
I would have taken your lives from you
if I'd known of this mischief before."

'*Loki said:*

8   '"It is worse still—or so I think—
the enduring strife of kinsmen;
the princes are not yet born for whom I believe*
this hatefulness is intended."

9   '"Red gold", said Hreidmar, "I reckon I'll have at my disposal
as long as I may live;
your threat doesn't frighten me in the slightest,
now go home! Go away!"

'*Fafnir and Regin demanded a share of the compensation from Hreidmar
for their brother Otter. He refused. And Fafnir stabbed his father with
a sword while he was asleep. Hreidmar called out to his daughters:*

10   '"Lyngheid and Lofnheid!
know that my life is destroyed,
much does need impel!"
Lyngheid answered:
"Little can a sister, even if she loses a father,
avenge her wrong on a brother!"

11   '"Nurture a daughter then" (said Hreidmar), "you
     wolf-hearted woman,
if you don't get a son with a prince;
give the girl to a man in this great need,
then their son will avenge your wrong!"*

'*Then Hreidmar died, and Fafnir took all the gold. Then Regin asked
for his inheritance from his father, and Fafnir refused. Then Regin asked*

*Lyngheid, his sister, for advice, how he should recover his inheritance.
She said:*

12   ' "You should ask your brother cheerfully
        about your inheritance, with a friendlier demeanour;
        it is not fitting that you should demand the treasure
        from Fafnir with a sword!" '

*Regin told Sigurd these things. One day when he came to Regin's house, he
was warmly greeted. Regin said:*

13   'Sigmund's offspring has come here,
        the decisive man, to our halls;
        more courage he has than a mature man,
        I expect winnings from a ravening wolf.

14   'I must nurture the battle-brave prince;
        now Yngvi's offspring has come to us;
        he will be the most powerful prince under the sun,
        his fate-strands extend through all lands.'

*Sigurd stayed with Regin after that, and he told Sigurd that Fafnir
was lying on Gnita-heath in the shape of a dragon; he had a helmet of
dread* which all living creatures were terrified of.*
    *Regin made Sigurd a sword which was called Gram. It was so sharp
that he put it down in the river Rhine and let a hank of wool drift on
the current, and the hank was sliced apart as if it were water. With this
sword, Sigurd split Regin's anvil in two.*
    After that Regin egged Sigurd on to kill Fafnir. He replied:

15   'Loudly would the sons of Hunding laugh,
        they who denied Eylimi his old age,
        if the prince had a greater lust
        for red-gold rings than vengeance for his father.'

*King Hialprek gave Sigurd a ship's crew to avenge his father. They ran
into a great storm and were weathering a certain rocky headland. There
was a man standing on the cliff who said:*

16 'Who is riding there the sea-king's horses
   on the high waves, on the resounding sea?
   The sail-steeds are spattered with spray,
   the ocean-chargers cannot stand up to the wind.'

Regin answered:

17 'Sigurd is here with us on these sea-trees;
   given a wind which will be our death;
   the steep breaker is falling higher than stern and prow,
   the roller-steeds are plunging; who is asking about it?'

18 'Hnikar they called me, when young Volsung*
   gladdened the raven when there was fighting;
   now you may call the old man on the cliff
   Feng or Fiolnir; I would like passage!'

They turned towards the land, and the old man went aboard the ship, and the tempest abated.

19 'Tell me, Hnikar, you know all about two matters:
   omens of gods and men,
   which omens are best, if one has to fight
   when swords are swinging?'

Hnikar said:

20 'There are many good omens if men knew them,
   when swords are swinging;
   a trusty companion for the warrior, I believe,
   is the dark raven.

21 'That is a second omen, if you have gone outside
   and are ready to set off;
   if you see standing on the pathway
   two men eager for glory.

22 'That is a third omen, if you hear a wolf
   howling under ash-branches,
   good luck will be ordained for you against the warriors
   if you catch sight of them first.

23 'No man should fight facing into the late-
      shining sister of the moon;*
      those who can see get the victory,
      those who urge sword-play
      and know how to draw up a wedge-shaped battle-array.*

24 'That is great misfortune, if you stumble
      when you advance towards battle;
      guileful *disir* stand on both sides of you*
      and want to see you wounded.

25 'Combed and washed every thoughtful man should be
      and fed in the morning;
      for one cannot foresee where one will be by evening;
      it is bad to rush headlong before an omen.'

Sigurd fought a great battle against Lyngvi, son of Hunding, and his brothers. There Lyngvi and his three brothers were killed. After the battle Regin said:

26 'Now a bloody eagle is carved on the back*
      of Sigmund's slayer with a sharp sword!
      No one's more successful than the heir of the king,
      who reddened the earth and gave joy to the raven!'

Sigurd went home to Hialprek. Then Regin egged Sigurd on to kill Fafnir.

THE LAY OF FAFNIR

Perhaps unexpectedly, the *Lay of Fafnir* (*Fafnismal*) does not give the details of an exciting dragon-fight like the one at the end of the Old English poem *Beowulf*. Rather, Sigurd stabs Fafnir from below while hiding in a pit and the rest of the poem is taken up with conversation between Sigurd and the dragon he has fatally wounded, a tetchy interchange between Sigurd and Regin, and the advice of the nuthatches, whose conversation Sigurd comes to understand through the accidental tasting of Fafnir's blood. Sigurd and Fafnir's dialogue alternates between hostility and mutual respect; when Regin returns, the seeds of mistrust which Fafnir has sown in Sigurd's mind, and the arrogant way in which the foster-father orders Sigurd about as if he were an apprentice rather than a fully-fledged hero, combine to create resentment in the young man. The motif of wisdom accidentally acquired from licking the thumb when cooking appears also in Irish, in the tales of the hero Finn mac Cool, who gains knowledge when cooking the Salmon of Wisdom for his master. Birds often give prophetic and insightful advice in the *Edda*. In the *Poem of Helgi Hiorvardsson* Atli makes a compact with a bird, and in the *List of Rig* young Kon is directed towards conquest instead of bird-hunting by a wise bird. The nuthatches point Sigurd both towards a match with Gudrun, daughter of Giuki, and to the awakening of the valkyrie Sigrdrifa.

Sigurd and Regin went up onto Gnita-heath and there they found Fafnir's tracks, where he slithered down to the water. Then Sigurd dug a great pit in the path, and he got down into it. And when Fafnir slithered away from the gold, he snorted out poison and it fell down onto Sigurd's head. And as Fafnir slithered over the pit, Sigurd stabbed him to the heart with his sword. Fafnir shook himself and flailed with his head and tail. Sigurd jumped out of the pit and both looked at one another. Fafnir said:

1　'A boy! just a boy! To what young man were you born?
　　Whose son are you,
　　you who have reddened your shining sword on Fafnir?
　　The blade stands in my heart!'

Sigurd concealed his name, because it was an old superstition to believe that the words of a dying man had great power if he cursed his enemy by name. He said:

2 ' "Pre-eminent beast" I'm called, and I go about*
  as a motherless boy;
  I have no father, as the sons of men do,
  I always go alone.'

Fafnir said:

3 'Do you know, if you had no father, as the sons of men do,
  of what wondrous creature you were born?'

Sigurd said:

4 'My lineage, I declare, will be unknown to you,
  as am I myself;
  Sigurd I am called—Sigmund was my father—
  I who've slain you with my weapons.'

Fafnir said:

5 'Who egged you on, why did you let yourself be urged
  to destroy my life?
  Shining-eyed boy, you had a fierce father,
  [innate qualities show quickly].'*

Sigurd said:

6 'My courage whetted me, my hands assisted me
  and my sharp sword;
  few are brave when they become old,
  if they are cowardly in childhood.'

Fafnir said:

7 'I know, if you could have grown up in the bosom of your
     friends,
  you'd be seen to fight furiously;
  but now you are a captive, a prisoner of war;
  they say bound men are always trembling!'

Sigurd said:

8 'You taunt me now, Fafnir, because I'm far away
    from my father's inheritance;
    but I'm no captive, though I was taken prisoner;
    you've found that I'm a free agent!'

Fafnir said:

9 'Spiteful words you reckon to hear in everything,
    but I'll tell you only the truth:
    the resounding gold and the glowing red treasure,
    those rings will be your death!'

Sigurd said:

10 'Power over his property every man shall have
    always until that one day;
    for on one day only shall every man
    depart from here to hell.'

Fafnir said:

11 'The norns' judgement you'll get in sight of land,*
    and the fate of a fool;
    you'll drown in the water even if you row in a breeze;
    all is dangerous for the doomed man.'

Sigurd said:

12 'Tell me, Fafnir, you are said to be wise*
    and to know a great deal;
    which are those norns who go to help those in need
    and bring children forth from their mothers?'*

Fafnir said:

13 'From very different tribes I think the norns come,
    they are not of the same kin;
    some spring from the Æsir, some from the elves,
    some are daughters of Dvalin.'*

Sigurd said:

14 'Tell me, Fafnir, you are said to be wise
    and to know a great deal:
    what that island is called where Surt and the Æsir
    will mingle sword-liquid together.'*

Fafnir said:

15 'Not-yet-made it's called, and there all the gods
    shall sport with their spears;
    Bilrost will break as they journey away,
    and their horses flounder in the great river.

16 'The helm of terror I wore among the sons of men,*
    while I lay upon the neck-rings;
    more powerful than all I thought myself to be,
    I didn't encounter many equals.'

Sigurd said:

17 'The helm of terror protects no one,
    where furious men have to fight;
    a man finds out when he comes among a multitude;
    that no one is bravest of all.'

Fafnir said:

18 'Poison I snorted, when I lay upon
    the mighty inheritance of my father.'

Sigurd said:

19 'Strong serpent, you snorted great blasts
    and you hardened your heart;
    more ferocity grows in men's sons
    when they have that helmet.'

Fafnir said:

20 'Now I advise you, Sigurd, and you take that advice
and ride home from here!
The resounding gold and the glowing red treasure—
those rings will be your death!'

Sigurd said:

21 'You've given your advice, but I shall ride
to where the gold lies in the heather,
and you, Fafnir, lie in mortal fragments,
there where Hel can take you!'

Fafnir said:

22 'Regin betrayed me, he'll betray you,
he'll be the death of us both;
Fafnir, I think, must give up his life;
you had the greater strength.'

*Regin had disappeared while Sigurd was killing Fafnir and came back as
Sigurd was wiping the blood off his sword. Regin said:*

23 'Hail to you, Sigurd, now you've won the victory
and have brought down Fafnir;
of those men who tread upon the earth
I declare you've been raised the least cowardly.'

Sigurd said:

24 'There's no knowing for certain when all are come together,
all the victory-gods' sons,
who has been raised the least cowardly;
many a man is bold who doesn't redden his sword
in another's breast.'

Regin said:

25   'You're cheerful now, Sigurd, pleased with your winnings,
           as you dry Gram on the grass;
       my brother you've wounded,
           yet in part I myself brought it about.'

Sigurd said:

26   'You advised that I should ride here
           over the sacred mountains;
       his treasure and his life the shining serpent would still possess,
           if you hadn't challenged my courage.'

Then Regin went to Fafnir and cut out his heart with a sword called Ridil, and then he drank the blood from his wound. Regin said:

27   'Sit down now, Sigurd, and I'll go to sleep,
           roast Fafnir's heart in the flame!
       that heart I'll have to eat
           after the drink of blood.'

Sigurd said:

28   'You went far off while in Fafnir I was reddening
           my sharp sword;
       my strength I matched against the dragon's might,
           while you lurked in the heather.'

Regin said:

29   'Long you'd have left the old giant*
           lurking in the heather
       if you'd not used the sword which I myself made
           and that sharp blade of yours.'

Sigurd said:

30   'Courage is better than the power of a sword,
           where angry men have to fight;
       for I've seen a brave man, fighting strongly,
           conquer with a blunt sword.

31   'It's better for the keen than the cowardly
      when they go in for battle-sport;
      it's better for the cheerful than the snivellers,
      whatever may be at hand.'

*Sigurd took Fafnir's heart and roasted it on a spit. And when he thought
that it was done, and the juice was dripping out of the heart, he prodded
it with his finger to see if it was done. He burnt himself and stuck his
finger in his mouth. And when Fafnir's heart-blood came on his tongue,
he understood the speech of birds. He heard that there were nuthatches
twittering in the branches. The nuthatch said:*

32   'There sits Sigurd, splattered with blood,
      roasting Fafnir's heart on the fire;
      the destroyer of rings would seem wise to me*
      if he were to eat the shining life-muscle.'

A second nuthatch said:

33   'There lies Regin plotting to himself,
      he intends to betray the boy who trusts him,
      in fury crooked words he cooks up,
      that smith of evil wants to avenge his brother.'

A third one said:

34   'Shorter by a head he should send the old sage
      off to hell from here!
      Then all the gold he alone would possess,
      that heap which lay under Fafnir.'

A fourth one said:

35   'Wise he'd seem to me if he knew how to get
      the friendly vital advice of you sisters;
      if he thought about himself and made the raven happy;
      I expect a wolf when I see his ears.'*

A fifth one said:

36   'The warrior isn't so wise
      as I thought a war-leader ought to be,
      if he lets one brother get away,
      when he's denied the other old age.'

A sixth one said:

37   'He'll be extremely foolish if he still spares
      the murderous enemy;
      there Regin is lying and plotting against him;
      he doesn't know how to guard against such a thing.'

A seventh said:

38   'Shorter by a head he should leave the frost-cold giant*
      and make him lose the rings;
      then the treasure which Fafnir owned
      would be in one man's control.'

Sigurd said:

39   'Fate is not so powerful that Regin will
      find himself reporting my death,
      since those two brothers are going, very quickly,
      to set off for hell from here.'

*Sigurd cut off Regin's head and then he ate Fafnir's heart and drank
the blood of both Regin and Fafnir. Then Sigurd heard the nuthatches
saying:*

40   'Gather up, Sigurd, the red rings;
      it's not kingly to be afraid of anything!
      I know a girl, the fairest by far,
      endowed with gold, if you could win her.

41   'Green paths lie straight towards Giuki,
      fate points forward for a far-travelling man.
      There the lavish king has raised up a daughter.
      Sigurd, you'll win her with a wedding settlement.

42 'There is a hall on high Hindarfell,
   outside it is all surrounded with flame;
   wise men have made it
   out of radiant river-light.*

43 'I know on the mountain the battle-wise one sleeps,
   and the terror of the linden plays above her;*
   Odin stabbed her with a thorn;*
   the goddess of flax had brought down*
   a different fighter from the one he wanted.

44 'Young man, you shall see the girl under the helmet,
   who rode away from battle on Vingskornir.
   Sigrdrifa's sleep may not be broken,
   by a princely youth, except by the norns' decree.'

Sigurd rode along Fafnir's track to his lair and found it open and with doors and door-frames of iron. All the beams of the house were of iron, and they were driven down into the earth. There Sigurd found a huge amount of gold and filled two chests with it. Then he took the helmet of terror and a gold mail-shirt and the sword Hrotti and many other treasures, and loaded Grani with it, but the horse would not proceed until Sigurd climbed onto his back.

THE LAY OF SIGRDRIFA

As directed by the birds at the end of the previous poem, in the *Lay of Sigrdrifa* (*Sigrdrifumal*) Sigurd sets out towards the sleeping valkyrie. Releasing her from her spell, he asks her for advice and Sigrdrifa obliges with runic and gnomic wisdom. Pages are missing from the Codex Regius manuscript towards the end of the poem, so it remains incomplete. The events which occur in the missing pages are summarized at that point.

Sigurd rode up onto Hindarfell and headed south towards the land of the Franks. On the mountain he saw a great light, as if fire were burning, and gleaming up against the sky. And when he came there, there stood a shield-wall with a banner flying over it. Sigurd went into the shield-wall and saw someone lying there asleep and fully armed. First he took off the helmet, then he saw that it was a woman. Her corslet was tight, as if it had grown into her flesh. So with his sword Gram he cut from the neck of the corslet downwards, and so along both the sleeves. Then he took the corslet off her, and she woke up, sat up, looked at Sigurd, and said:

1 'What bit into my corslet? How have I shaken off sleep?
   Who has lifted from me my pallid coercion?'

He answered:

   'Sigmund's son—the sword of Sigurd,
   which a short time ago was cutting the raven's corpse-flesh.'

2 'Long I slept, long was I sleeping,
   long are the woes of men;
   Odin brought it about that I could not break
   the sleep-runes.'

Sigurd sat down and asked her name. She took a horn full of mead and gave him a memory-drink.

3 'Hail to the day! Hail to the sons of day!
   Hail to night and her kin!
   With gracious eyes may you look upon us two,
   and give victory to those sitting here!

4   'Hail to the Æsir! Hail to the goddesses!
      Hail to the mighty, fecund earth!
      May you give eloquence and native wit to this glorious pair
      and healing hands while we live!'

*She was called Sigrdrifa and was a valkyrie. She said that there were
two kings who were fighting one another; one was called Helmet-
Gunnar, he was old and a great warrior and Odin had promised him
victory; and:*

      'the other was Agnar, the brother of Auda,
      whom no creature wanted to protect.'

*Sigrdrifa brought down Helmet-Gunnar in battle. And Odin pricked her
with a sleep-thorn in revenge for this and said that she would never again
fight victoriously in battle and said that she should be married. 'And
I said to him that I had sworn a great counter-oath, to marry no man
who was acquainted with fear.'* He asked her to teach him wisdom, if she
had news from all the worlds. Sigrdrifa said:*

5   'Beer I give you, apple-tree of battle,*
      mixed with magical power and mighty glory;
      it is full of spells and favourable letters,
      good charms and runes of pleasure.

6   'Victory-runes you must cut if you want to have victory,
      and cut them on your sword-hilt;
      some on the blade-guards, some on the handle,
      and invoke Tyr twice.

7   'Ale-runes must you know if you do not want another's wife
      to beguile your trust, if you trust her;
      on a horn they should be cut and on the back of the hand,
      and mark your nail with "Nauð".*

8   'The full cup should be signed over and guarded against
          mischief,
      and leek thrown in the liquid;
      then I know that for you there will never be
      mead blended with malice.

9 'Helping-runes you must know if you want to assist
   and release children from women;
   they shall be cut on the palms and clasped on the joints,
   and then the *disir* asked for help.*

10 'Sea-runes you must cut if you want to have guaranteed
   the sail-horses on the sea;
   on the prow they must be cut and on the rudder,
   and burnt into the oar with fire;
   however steep the breakers or dark the waves,
   yet you'll come safe from the sea.

11 'Limb-runes you must know if you want to be a healer
   and know how to see to wounds;
   on bark they must be cut and of the tree of the wood,
   on those whose branches bend east.

12 'Speech-runes you must know if you want no one to requite
   your sorrow with enmity;
   you wind them about, weave them about,
   set them all together
   at that meeting where people must go
   to fully constituted courts.

13 'Mind-runes you must know if you want to be
   wiser-minded than every other man;
   Hropt interpreted them,
   cut them, thought them out,
   from that liquid which had leaked
   from Heiddraupnir's skull
   and from Hoddrofnir's horn.*

14 'On a cliff he stood with Brimir's sword,*
   a helmet he had on his head;
   then Mim's head spoke*
   wisely the first word
   and told the true letters.

15 ' "On a shield", he said, "they should be cut,
    the one which stands before the shining god,
    on Arvak's ear and Alsvinn's hoof,*
    on that wheel which turns under [H]rungnir's chariot,
    on Sleipnir's teeth and on the sledges' strap-bands;

16 on the bear's paw and on Bragi's tongue,
    on the wolf's claw, and the eagle's beak,
    on bloody wings and at the end of the bridge,
    on hands which deliver and on the trail of a helpful man,

17 on glass and on gold, and on men's amulets,
    in wine and on wort and on a favourite seat,
    on the point of Gungnir and the breast of Grani,
    on the nail of the norn, and the beak of the owl."

18 'All were shaved off, those which were carved on,
    and stirred into the sacred mead
    and sent on wandering ways;
    they are among the Æsir, they are among the elves,
    some are with the wise Vanir,
    some with humankind.

19 'Those are book-runes, those are helping-runes,*
    and all the ale-runes,
    and precious runes of power,
    for those who can, without confusing them, without destroying
        them,
    possess them for good fortune;
    use them, if you get them,
    until the gods are torn asunder!

20 'Now you must choose, since choice is offered to you,
    maple of sharp weapons,*
    speech or silence—you can make up your own mind,
    all harms are measured out.'

21 'I will not flee, even if you know I am doomed
I was not born a coward;
your loving advice I want in its entirety,
as long as I live.'

22 'That I advise you firstly, that towards your kin
you should be blameless;
be slow to avenge although they do harm:
that is said to benefit the dead.

23 'That I advise you secondly, that you do not swear an oath
unless it is truly kept;
terrible fate-bonds attach to the oath-tearer;
wretched is the pledge-criminal.

24 'That I advise you thirdly, that at the Assembly
you do not contend with fools;
for the stupid man often permits himself to say
worse words than he knows.

25 'Everything is lost if you are silent in response:
then you seem to be born a coward
or else it is spoken truly;
dangerous is it to hear rumour at home
unless it be for good;
on another day take his life away
and thus repay his lies in public.

26 'That I advise you fourthly, if a witch, full of malice,
lives on your route,
better to go on than be her guest,
though night overtake you.

27 'Eyes that can spy out ahead are what the sons of men need,
where angry men shall fight;
often malevolent women sit close to the roads,
those who deaden swords and spirits.

28 'That I advise you fifthly, though you see
   fair ladies on the benches,
   silver-decked women, don't let them disturb your sleep
   nor entice them to you to kiss.

29 'That I advise you sixthly, though among men
   talk over ale becomes offensive,*
   when drunk you should not quarrel with a warrior;
   wine steals many a man's wits.

30 'Songs and ale have been cause of sorrow*
   to many a man;
   slayers of some, misfortune for some;
   manifold is the grief of men.

31 'That I advise you seventhly, if you are feuding
   with courageous men,
   for well-provided men it is better to fight
   than to be burnt inside.*

32 'That I advise you eighthly, that you should guard against evil
   and distance yourself from lightmindedness;
   do not entice girls nor any man's wife,
   nor encourage excessive pleasure.

33 'That I advise you ninthly, that you bury corpses
   where you find them on the ground,
   whether they are dead of sickness or else drowned,
   or men killed by weapons.

34 'A warm bath shall be made for those who are departed;
   hands and head be washed,
   combed, and dried before they go in the coffin,*
   and bid them sleep blessedly.

35 'That I advise you tenthly, that you never trust
   the oaths of a wrongdoer's brat;
   whether you are his brother's slayer
   or you felled the father,
   the wolf is in the young son,
   though he may be gladdened by gold.

36 'Quarrels and enmity—don't think they've gone to sleep—
    any more than grief;
    common sense and weapons are necessary for the prince to
       acquire,
    for him who shall be foremost among men.

37 'That I advise you eleventhly, that you beware
    against evil, from whatever direction it comes;
    a long life I think the prince will [not] have;
    powerful quarrels have sprung up.'

The poem ends here; it is possible to reconstruct what must have hap-
pened in the missing leaves of the manuscript from *Volsunga saga*. The
valkyrie (here, Sigrdrifa, in *Volsunga saga*, Brynhild) and Sigurd betroth
themselves to each other—a fact which has no relevance to the story as it
develops—and Sigurd sets off for the court of Giuki. On the way he stops at
the house of Heimir where he falls in love with Brynhild. It seems likely that
two stories are conflated in the Sigurd cycle: in one the hero is betrothed to
the valkyrie won by crossing a flame-wall, in another he becomes entangled
with the Giukung family and is destroyed by his sister-in-law's passion for
him. But the plots are imperfectly merged: in the *Edda* the two separate
women remain, whereas in *Volsunga saga* the author simplifies the story
by making Brynhild the only woman with whom Sigurd becomes involved
before he meets Gudrun. Thus in the saga Sigurd meets Brynhild three
times—on the mountain, at Heimir's, and when he woos her for Gunnar;
his failure to recognize her at the third meeting is explained by a drink of
forgetfulness. Sigurd is made to appear more heartless than he really is, and
the simplified plot involves the author of *Volsunga saga* in an implausible
second meeting at Heimir's: one which nevertheless was known to Gripir
and included in *Gripir's Prophecy*. At the court of Giuki Sigurd is given
a magic drink which makes him forget Brynhild and he agrees to marry
Gudrun, sister of Gunnar. The Codex Regius takes up the story once again
after Sigurd has agreed to help woo Brynhild for Gunnar. The marriages
of Sigurd to Gudrun and Brynhild to Gunnar have taken place; Sigurd
has remembered his previous promise but he resolves silently to make the
best of things. When Gudrun quarrels with Brynhild and reveals to her the
shape-changing deception involved in her wooing, Brynhild decides that
Sigurd must die. Even though, according to *Volsunga saga*, ch. 31, he offers
to leave Gudrun and marry her, Brynhild remains implacable.

FRAGMENT OF A POEM ABOUT SIGURD

The Codex Regius picks up the story of Sigurd some verses into a poem narrating the aftermath of Brynhild's demand that Sigurd be killed. In this poem Sigurd is murdered outside in the forest by Guthorm, younger brother of Gudrun, aided by Gunnar and Hogni, and the focus is on Brynhild's reaction to the death. The speaker of the first stanza seems to be Hogni, responding to Gunnar's request for help in disposing of his brother-in-law. Gunnar elaborates the problem in v. 2.

1 'What has Sigurd done so wrong
    that you want to deprive the brave man of life?'

2 'To me Sigurd gave oaths,
    oaths he gave, and all are broken;*
    thus he deceived me when he should have been
    completely trustworthy in every oath.'

3 'Brynhild is stirring you up to cause disaster,
    she's urging hatred, that wrong be done;
    she begrudges Gudrun her good marriage match,
    and also that she has to take her pleasure with you.'

4 Some men roasted wolf, some sliced up serpent,
    ravener-meat they gave Guthorm to eat,*
    before they could, desiring his ruin,
    lay their hands on the wise man.

5 Dead was Sigurd on the south side of the Rhine,
    a raven called out loudly from a tree:
    'Atli will redden his blades in your blood,
    your oaths will destroy you, you warlike men.'

6 Outside stood Gudrun, daughter of Giuki,
    and these were the first words that she said:
    'Where is Sigurd, lord of warriors,
    since my kinsmen now are riding ahead?'

7 Hogni alone gave her an answer:
'Sigurd we've hacked into pieces with a sword,
still the grey horse droops his head over the dead prince.'

8 Then said Brynhild, Budli's daughter:
'Well may you enjoy the weapons and lands!
Sigurd alone would have had control of all,
if a little longer he'd kept his life.

9 'It wouldn't have been fitting that he should have ruled
over the inheritance of Giuki and all the hosts of Goths,*
when he had fathered five sons,
eager in battle, to rule the people.'

10 Then Brynhild laughed—all the hall resounded—
just one time with all her heart:
'Well may you enjoy the lands and followers,
now you've brought the brave prince to his death.'

11 Then said Gudrun, Giuki's daughter:
'Many abominable words you've said;
may fiends take Gunnar, Sigurd's gravedigger!
Thoughts bent on wickedness shall be revenged.'

12 It was late in the evening, much was drunk,
there all sorts of pleasant words were spoken;
all went to sleep when they went to their bed,
Gunnar stayed awake for a very long time.

13 His foot began to twitch, he muttered many things,
the destroyer of armies began to ponder
what the two of them had said up there in the tree,
the raven and the eagle, as they'd ridden home.*

14 Brynhild awakened, Budli's daughter,
the royal lady, a little before dawn:
'Urge me on or hinder me—the harm is done now—
sorrow to be told of or else let be!'

15 All were silent at these words,
  not one could understand the behaviour of women,
  now she, weeping, began to speak of
  that which, laughing, she'd asked the men for.

16 'I thought, Gunnar, that I had a grim dream,
  it was chilly in the hall, and my bed was cold;
  and you, lord, were riding, bereft of happiness,
  with chains you were fettered among a troop of foes.
  So from all of you of the Niflung line
  your strength will pass away: you are oath-breakers!

17 'You clearly did not remember, Gunnar,
  that you both let your blood run into a trench;*
  now you have repaid him badly for that,
  when he wanted to make himself the most pre-eminent of men.

18 'Then that was proved when the brave man
  came riding to ask for my hand,
  how the destroyer of armies had previously*
  kept his oaths to the young prince.

19 'A wound-wand, braided round with gold,*
  the splendid king laid between us,
  the edges were forged outside in fire,
  and patterned inside with poison-drops.'

About the Death of Sigurd   *In this poem the death of Sigurd is
related and here it sounds as if they killed him outside. But some say this,
that they killed him inside, sleeping in his bed. And Germans say that
they killed him out in the forest. And the 'Old Poem of Gudrun'* says
that Sigurd and the sons of Giuki were riding to the Assembly when he
was killed. But they all say that they treacherously betrayed him and
attacked him when he was lying down and unarmed.*

THE FIRST POEM OF GUDRUN

There are three poems of Gudrun in the *Poetic Edda*; in this, the first (*Gudrunarkvida I*), Gudrun cannot or will not display her grief at Sigurd's death. Other women attempt to rouse her to tears by telling their own sad tales, but it is Gullrond, Gudrun's sister, who has the psychological acumen to display the covered body of Sigurd, bringing Gudrun to give vent to her sorrow. Gudrun's lament, reminiscent of Sigrun's in the *Second Poem of Helgi Hundingsbani*, vv. 37–8, is vividly poignant—she now feels 'as little as a leaf' and calls down curses on Gunnar and Hogni.

Gudrun sat over Sigurd's dead body. She did not weep like other women and she was on the point of collapsing with grief. Both men and women came to comfort her; it was not easy. People said that Gudrun had eaten some of Fafnir's heart and so she understood the talk of birds. This is also said of Gudrun:

1   It was long ago that Gudrun intended to die,
    when she sat sorrowful over Sigurd;
    she did not weep or strike her hands together,
    or lament like other women.

2   Very wise warriors stepped forward,
    they tried to ease her fierceness of mind;*
    even so Gudrun could not weep,
    she was so impassioned, she might have burst asunder.

3   The gleaming wives of warriors,
    adorned with gold, sat by Gudrun;
    each of them told of their great grief,
    the bitterest which had been visited on them.

4   Then said Giaflaug, Giuki's sister:
    'I know that in the world I'm most deprived of joy,
    the heavy loss of five husbands has come upon me;
    of three daughters, three sisters,
    of eight brothers, I alone am living.'

5 Even so Gudrun could not weep;
   she was so impassioned at the young man's death
   so fierce in mind at the fall of the prince.

6 Then said Herborg, queen of the Huns' land:
   'I have a heavier harm to speak of:
   my seven sons, in the south-lands,
   my husband, as the eighth, all fell in slaughter;

7 father and mother, four brothers,
   the wind played wickedly with them on the waves,
   the waves surged against the gunwale.

8 'I myself had to lay them out, I myself had to bury them,
   I myself had to handle their journey to Hel;
   all that I endured in one half-year,
   thus no man could ever give me any joy.

9 'Then I was taken captive, war-prisoner,
   that same half-year it befell me;
   I had to adorn her, and tie on the shoes
   of the war-leader's wife every morning.

10 'She raged at me in her jealousy
   and struck me with savage blows;
   nowhere have I found a better master,
   nowhere have I found a worse mistress.'

11 Even so Gudrun could not weep;
   she was so impassioned at the young man's death
   and so fierce in mind at the fall of the prince.

12 Then said Gullrond, daughter of Giuki:*
   'You don't really know, foster-mother, though you are wise,
   how to converse with a young wife.'
   She advised against concealing the prince's corpse.

13 She swept the covering from Sigurd
    and pushed a cushion by the woman's knees:
    'Look at your beloved, put your mouth to his moustache,
    as you used to embrace the prince when he was alive.'

14 Gudrun looked at him one time only;
    she saw the prince's hair running with blood,
    the lord's bright eyes grown dim,
    the prince's breast scored by the sword.

15 Then Gudrun knelt, leaning on the cushion;
    her hair came loose and her cheeks grew red,
    and drops like rain ran down over her knees.

16 Then Gudrun wept, the daughter of Giuki,
    so that her tears fell into her hair,
    and the geese in the meadow cackled in reply,
    the splendid birds which belonged to the girl.

17 Then said Gullrond, daughter of Giuki:
    'Yours I know was the greatest love
    of all people across the earth;
    inside or outside, you were never happy
    unless, my sister, you were with Sigurd.'

18 'So was my Sigurd, beside the sons of Giuki,
    as if a leek were grown up out of the grass,
    or a bright jewel threaded onto a string,
    a precious gem, among the nobles.

19 'I seemed also, among the prince's warriors,
    to be higher than any of Odin's ladies;
    I am as little as a leaf
    among the bay-willows now the prince is dead.

20 'I miss in his seat and in my bed
    my friend to talk to, the kin of Giuki caused it;
    the kin of Giuki caused my sorrow,
    wrenching weeping for their sister.

21   'So your people and land will be laid waste,
     on your account, for the oaths you swore;
     Gunnar, you won't get good of the gold,
     the rings will be the death of you,
     for you swore oaths to Sigurd.

22   'In the meadow there was more merriment,
     before my Sigurd saddled Grani,
     and they went off to woo Brynhild,
     that wretched creature, in an ill-fated hour.'

23   Then said Brynhild, Budli's daughter:
     'May that creature lack husband and children,
     who brought you, Gudrun, to weep
     and this morning gave the runes of speaking!'*

24   Then said Gullrond, Giuki's daughter:
     'Be silent, you monstrous woman, cease these words!
     The nemesis of princes you have always been;
     every wave of ill fate drives you along,
     wounding sorrow of seven kings,
     the greatest ruination for women's loved ones!'

25   Then said Brynhild, Budli's daughter:
     'Atli alone caused all the evil,
     born of Budli, brother of mine,

26   when in the Hunnish people's hall
     we saw the fire of the serpent's bed shine on the prince;*
     I have paid for this journey since then,
     for that sight is always before my eyes.'

27   She stood by the pillar, she summoned up all her strength;
     from Brynhild, daughter of Budli,
     fire burned from the eyes, she snorted out poison,
     when she looked at the wounds upon Sigurd.

Gudrun went away from there to a wood in the wasteland, and went as far as Denmark, and stayed there seven half-years with Thora, daughter of Hakon.

Brynhild did not want to go on living after Sigurd. She had eight of her slaves killed and five serving-maids. Then she stabbed herself with a sword, as is told in the 'Short Poem about Sigurd'.

A SHORT POEM ABOUT SIGURD

Like *Gripir's Prophecy*, the *Short Poem about Sigurd* (*Sigurdarkvida in skamma*) is in part a prospective summary of events following the death of Sigurd, integrating the continuing story of Gudrun and her future husbands, and the fate of Gunnar and his doomed affair with Oddrun. The poem also gives in brief the story of how Sigurd came to be killed, although the details of how he came to forget his prior betrothal to Brynhild, and how the change of appearance with Gunnar was effected, are not spelt out. The centre of poetic interest is the characterization of Brynhild, who moves from relentless, monstrous avenger to sorrowing, yet unregretful, bride in death. The contrast with Gudrun's impotence in this poem is striking. At seventy-one stanzas the poem is not especially short; a lost longer poem, explaining events between Sigurd's parting from Sigrdrifa and the brothers' decision to kill Sigurd, has been hypothesized from *Volsunga saga*.

1   Long ago it was that Sigurd visited Giuki,
the young Volsung had already killed;
he took trusty pledges from the two brothers,
oaths exchanged by the men, valiant in great deeds.

2   They offered him a girl and a great deal of treasure,
young Gudrun, Giuki's daughter;
they drank and debated many days together,
young Sigurd and the sons of Giuki,

3   until they went off to woo Brynhild,
so that Sigurd rode along with them;
the young Volsung knew the way*
he would have married her if he could.

4   The man from the south laid a naked sword,*
a slender inlaid blade, between them both;
nor did he seek to kiss the woman,
the southern king did not take her in his arms;
the girl so young he gave to Giuki's son.

5   She had not known of any shame in her life,
nor of any injury in the course of her days,
no disgrace that was or could be imagined.
The terrible fates intervened in this.

6   Outside she sat alone, in the evening,
then quite openly she began to speak:
'I shall have Sigurd—or else he'll die—
that young man I'll have in my arms.

7   'The words I'm speaking now I'll be sorry for later,
Gudrun is his wife, and I am Gunnar's;
the hateful norns decreed this long torment for us.'*

8   Often she went outside, filled with frozen anger,
cold of ice, of glaciers, every evening,*
and he and Gudrun went to bed
and Sigurd wrapped her in the bedclothes,
the southern king caressing his wife.

9   'I go without both happiness and husband,
I'll pleasure myself with my savage thoughts.'

10   Then in her malice she began to goad to slaughter:
'Gunnar, you will altogether lose
my land and lose me myself;
I shall never be satisfied with you, prince!

11   'I shall go back to where I was before,
among my close relatives, my near-born kin;
there I shall sit and sleep away my life,
unless you manage to kill Sigurd
and become superior to other lords.

12   'Let's send the son the same way as the father!*
Don't nurture for long the young wolf;
would vengeance come easier to any man—
later making recompense—than to a son if still alive?'

13 Gunnar was angry and cast down,
     wrapped in thought, and he sat all day;
     he did not know at all clearly
     what would be most honourable for him to do,
     or what would be best for him to do,
     he knew he would have to get rid of the Volsung
     and he knew Sigurd would be a great loss.

14 Different plans he weighed up for hours at a time,
     it was not customary in those days
     for women to abandon the royal rank;
     he had Hogni called to take counsel,
     for he knew him a trusted friend in all.

15 'Brynhild I like better than all other women,
     Budli's girl is a prize among ladies;
     rather would I lose my life,
     than trade away that girl's treasure.

16 'Do you want us both to betray the prince for money?
     It's good to have hold of the Rhine-metal*
     and pleasantly to enjoy wealth
     and to sit revelling in our happiness.'

17 Hogni replied, he had only one answer:
     'It is not fitting for us two to do this,
     cutting asunder with a sword
     the oaths we've sworn, the pledges made.

18 'We don't know of happier men anywhere on earth
     while we four rule the people*
     and the southern leader is alive,
     nor of a mightier kindred in the world
     if we should in time bring up five sons
     of good family to augment our kin.

19 'I know quite well how things stand:
     Brynhild's passions are far too great.'

20   'We should prepare Guthorm for the killing,
     our younger brother, not so experienced;
     he wasn't involved when the oaths were sworn,
     the oaths were sworn and the pledges made.'

21   Easy it was to egg on the undaunted man,
     the sword stood in Sigurd's heart.

22   The battle-eager man sought revenge in the bedchamber*
     and then he hurled at the undaunted one,
     at Guthorm, the powerful sword Gram;
     the wonderfully bright iron flew from the king's hand.

23   His enemy parted into two pieces;
     arms and head dispatched in one direction
     and the leg-half landed backwards.*

24   Sleeping was Gudrun in bed,
     quite carefree, next to Sigurd;
     but she awoke far from joy
     when she found herself swimming in her lover's blood.

25   She clapped together her hands so loudly*
     that the man of mighty spirit heaved himself up in the bed:
     'Do not weep, Gudrun, so fiercely,
     young bride, you have brothers still alive.

26   'I have an heir, too young,
     he doesn't know how to get away from his enemies' house;
     they have decided, fateful and sinister,
     on a new plan which they're carrying out.

27   'No such sister's son, though seven you should nurture,*
     would ride with them afterwards to the Assembly;
     I know quite well what all this means:
     Brynhild alone has caused all this evil.

28 'The girl loves me above all other men,
  but to Gunnar I did no harm;
  I violated neither kinship nor oaths,
  so I should not be called his wife's lover.'

29 The woman gave a sigh, but the king gave up his life,
  she clapped together her hands so loudly
  that the goblets in the corner echoed her
  and the geese in the meadow cackled in reply.

30 Then Brynhild laughed, Budli's daughter,*
  just one time with all her heart,
  when from her bed she was able to hear
  the resounding sobs of Giuki's daughter.

31 Then said Gunnar, the prince of warriors:
  'You're not laughing, woman bent on wickedness,
  merrily in the bedchamber, with any good in mind.
  Why have you lost your pallor,
  engenderer of evil? I think you must be doomed.

32 'More than all women you deserve
  that we should strike down Atli before your eyes,
  so you should see on your brother bloody wounds,
  flowing gashes, that you'd have to bind up.'

33 'No man'll taunt you, Gunnar, you struck home all right!
  Atli won't care about your enmity:
  of the two of you he'll breathe the longer,
  he'll always have the greater strength.

34 'I must tell you, Gunnar, though you know it already,
  how you so quickly fell into guilt;
  I was not too young, nor was I constrained at all,*
  with great supplies of gold in my brother's hall.

35　'Nor did I wish that a husband should have me,
　　before you Giukungs rode into the courtyard,
　　three sovereign kings on horseback—
　　a journey that should never have happened.

39　'To him I'd betrothed myself
　　when he sat with his gold on Grani's back;
　　his eyes were not like those of you brothers,
　　nor did he look like you in any respect,
　　though you seemed to be sovereign kings.

36　'And then Atli said to me only this*
　　that he would never apportion the property,
　　neither gold nor land, unless I let myself be betrothed,
　　nor any ration of my goods and riches,
　　which was given to me so very young,
　　the wealth weighed out for me, so very young in years.

37　'Then my mind was in doubt about this,
　　whether I should fight and fell the slain,
　　a brave woman in a corslet, because of my brother.
　　That would become well known among the nations,
　　bring desire for strife to many a man.

38　'We reconciled our disagreement;
　　but it was more to my mind to accept treasure,
　　red-gold rings from the son of Sigmund,
　　nor did I want any other man's wealth.

40　'I loved only one, I did not love any others:
　　the valkyrie of necklaces was never fickle!*
　　all that will Atli discover,
　　when he knows all about my death-journey,

41　that no light-minded woman should ever
　　keep company with another's man;
　　then there'll be vengeance for all my sorrows.'

42 Up rose Gunnar, prince of the retinue,
  and he put his arms round his wife's neck;
  they all attempted, now one, now another,
  to dissuade the lady with all their hearts.

43 Quickly she pushed away each one from embrace,
  she'd have no man hinder her from the long journey.

44 Then he urged Hogni to offer secret counsel:
  'I want all the men to go into the hall,
  yours and mine together—for now there's great need—,
  to see if we can stop the woman's death-journey,
  else more harm will come of it;
  so let us then devise what's necessary.'

45 Hogni then gave just this answer:
  'Let no man hinder her from the long journey,
  may she never be born again from there!
  From her mother's womb she came out awkward,
  she was ever born to bring misery
  and grief of heart to many a man.'

46 Downcast he turned from the conversation,
  to where the necklace-tree was sharing out her treasure.*

47 She looked at all her property,
  her dead maids and her hall-women;*
  she put on a golden mail-coat—her intention was not good—
  before she pierced herself with the edge of the sword.

48 She fell sideways against the pillow;
  wounded with the sword, she considered what to say:

49 'Now they should come, those who want gold,
  or who want some smaller gift from me;
  I'll give to each woman a fine-worked jewel,
  embroidered coverlets and sheets, bright clothing.'

50 All were silent, they considered what to say,
and very slowly they all gave their answer,
'Enough women have died, we want to live on,
let the hall-women do what's fitting.'

51 Then, thinking it over, the linen-wearing woman,
still so young, added these words:
'I do not want anyone who's reluctant,
or hard to persuade, to die for our sake.

52 'Though the less treasure
will burn with your bones when you come down
—no treasures of Menia—to visit me.*

53 'Sit down, Gunnar! Now I shall tell you,
your radiant bride has no hope of life;
your vessel is not voyaging safely on course
even if I've breathed my last.

54 'You and Gudrun will be reconciled sooner than you think;
the wise woman will have, along with the king,*
sad memories of her dead husband.

55 'A girl will be born, her mother will raise her;
more radiant than the bright day
Svanhild will be, than a ray of the sun.*

56 'You will give Gudrun to some good man,
a harm-bringing arrow to a mass of men;
married against her wishes, she won't be happy in her husband;
Atli will wed her,
my brother, born of Budli.

57 'Much I remember: how they acted against me,
how you bitterly betrayed me, caused me pain;
robbed of what I wished for I was, while I lived.

58   'You'll want to marry Oddrun,*
     but Atli won't permit it;
     you'll have secret embraces,
     she'll love you as I ought to have done,
     if a good fate had been granted to us.

59   'Atli will persecute you, he'll prepare wickedness,
     you'll be lodged in a narrow snake-pit.*

60   'Not much later this will happen,
     that Atli will lose his life,
     lose his happiness and his sons' lives.
     For Gudrun will smear their bed with blood,
     by means of sharp sword-edges, from her wounded heart.

61   'It would be more fitting for our sister Gudrun
     to follow her first husband in death,
     if she were given good advice
     or if she had a spirit like mine.

62   'Slowly I speak now, but she will never
     yield up her life at my urging;
     her the high waves will carry
     over to Ionakr's ancestral land.

63   'They'll be under the protection of Ionakr's sons;
     she'll send Svanhild from that land,
     her daughter and Sigurd's.

64   'Bikki's counsel will bite her down,*
     for Iormunrekk lives to wreak havoc;
     then all Sigurd's line will have passed away:
     Gudrun will have more to weep for.

65   'I must ask you for one thing only,
     this will be my last request in this world:
     let a pyre be built on the meadow
     with enough space for all of us,
     those who died with Sigurd.

66   'Let the pyre be hung with shields and tapestries,
      skilfully patterned foreign weaving, and many foreign slaves;
      burn the southern man beside me.

67   'On the southern man's other side
      burn my maids adorned with jewellery,
      two by his head and two hawks,
      then everything will be orderly.

68   'Lay between us the ring-hilted sword,
      the sharp-edged iron, as it lay before,
      when we two climbed into one bed,
      when we got there the name of man and wife.

69   'The shining hall-door, decorated with a ring,
      must not jangle at his heels;*
      if our retinue is to accompany him from here,
      our journey must not be wretched.

70   'So five serving-girls accompany him,
      eight servants of good family,
      the slaves who grew up with me, my patrimony,
      which Budli gave to his child.

71   'Much I have said, I would say more,
      if fate granted me more time for speech;
      but my voice fails, my wounds are throbbing,
      I told only truth and now I must depart.'

BRYNHILD'S RIDE TO HELL

After her cremation, burnt in a wagon perhaps like that found in the Oseberg ship-burial in Norway, Brynhild sets off to the kingdom of the dead to be reunited with Sigurd. As she approaches the borders of Hel's land, she encounters a dead giantess who challenges her—the meadow by which the giantess lives is her grave-mound. Brynhild, still proud and undaunted, tells the story of her life, making clear the conflation with the valkyrie history of Sigrdrifa, and goes on her way.

After Brynhild's death two pyres were made, one was for Sigurd, and that was kindled first, and Brynhild was burnt on the second one, and she was in a wagon draped with costly woven tapestries. It is said that Brynhild drove the wagon along the road to hell and went past a home-meadow where a certain giantess lived. The giantess said:

1   'You shall not journey through
    my homestead set with stone;
    it would befit you better to be at your weaving*
    than to be going to visit another woman's man.

2   'What should you be visiting, from the southern land,
    with your giddy mind, in my houses?
    Gold-goddess, if you wish to know,
    you, gentle lady, have washed your hands in a man's blood.'

Then Brynhild said:

3   'Don't reproach me, lady living in the rock,
    that I've been on viking expeditions;
    I shall be accepted as of better ancestry than you
    wherever people compare our lineage.'

The giantess said:

4   'Brynhild, Budli's daughter,
    you were born as the worst luck in the world;
    you have ruined the children of Giuki
    and destroyed their good dwelling-places.'

5   'I must tell you, I, the clever woman in the wagon,
    you very stupid woman, if you wish to know,
    how the heirs of Giuki made me love-bereft,
    and made me an oath-breaker.*

6   'The courageous king had our magic garments—
    those of us eight sisters—put under an oak;*
    I was twelve years old, if you wish to know,
    when I gave my promise to the young prince.

7   'They all called me in Hlymdale,
    anyone who knew me, War-lady in the helmet.*

8   'Then I let the old man of the Gothic people,
    Helmet-Gunnar, quickly go off to hell;
    I gave the young man victory, Auda's brother;
    Odin was very angry with me for that.*

9   'With shields he enclosed me in Skata-grove,
    red ones and white ones, shields overlapping;
    he ordered that man to break my sleep
    who in the land knew no fear.

10 'Around my hall with southern aspect,
    the destroyer of all wood he set blazing up high;*
    he decreed only one warrior could ride over it there,
    he who brought me the gold which lay under Fafnir.

11 'The good man rode on Grani, generous gold-giver,
    where my foster-father ruled over his halls;
    he alone seemed better than all men,
    the Danish viking among the retinue.*

12 'We slept and were satisfied in one bed,
    as if he were my brother born;
    nor did we lay one arm over another
    for the eight nights of our lying together.

13 'And yet Gudrun accused me, Giuki's daughter,
   that I had slept in Sigurd's arms;
   then I discovered what I wish I'd never known,
   that they'd betrayed me in my taking a husband.

14 'Men and women, those who are living,
   must spend all too long in terrible sorrow
   but we shall live fully all our time together,
   Sigurd and I—now, ogress, sink!'

THE DEATH OF THE NIFLUNGS

This short prose passage, probably written by the compiler of the Codex Regius in order to pull together the poems which follow, explains how the story of Atli and Gudrun, and the death of her brothers, is related to the killing of Sigurd, and it allows the inclusion of the two poems about Gudrun which follow. Certain details in the passage are not borne out by the poetry: Gudrun does not ask her sons by Atli to plead for the life of Gunnar and Hogni in either of the poems about their deaths, but the compiler seems to be seeking a better motivation for the murder of the two boys than simple revenge upon their father.

Gunnar and Hogni took all the gold, Fafnir's inheritance. There was a feud between the sons of Giuki and Atli. He blamed the Giukungs for the death of Brynhild. In compensation, they were to marry Gudrun to him, and they had to give her a drink of forgetfulness before she agreed to marry Atli. Her sons with Atli were Erp and Eitil, and Svanhild was Gudrun's daughter by Sigurd.

King Atli invited Gunnar and Hogni to visit him and sent Vingi or Knefrod as messenger. Gudrun knew his treacherous plans and sent a message in runes saying that they should not come, and as a sign she sent Hogni the ring, Andvari's Jewel, and twisted round it a wolf's hair.

Gunnar had asked for the hand of Oddrun, Atli's sister, and had not been given it; then he married Glaumvor, and Hogni married Kostbera. Their sons were Solar and Snævar and Giuki. And when the Giukungs came to Atli, then Gudrun asked her sons to plead for the two brothers' lives. But they would not. The heart was cut out of Hogni, and Gunnar was put in a snake-pit. He played his harp and put the serpents to sleep, but an adder bit him in the liver.

THE SECOND POEM OF GUDRUN

Another poem in which Gudrun recounts her sorrows up until the death of her brothers. Her narrative fills in the events between the end of the *First Poem of Gudrun* and the *Poem of Atli*, summarizing the events surrounding the death of Sigurd and explaining how she was compelled to marry Atli against her will. The poem is probably one of the later ones in the collection; *Volsunga saga*, ch. 34 fills out how Gudrun spent her time in the interval between the death of Sigurd and the marriage to Atli.

King Thiodrek* was with Atli and had lost almost all his men there. Thiodrek and Gudrun lamented their woes together. She spoke to him and said:

1   'I was a girl of girls—my mother brought me up
    —radiant in the women's quarters;
    I loved my brothers greatly, until Giuki endowed me with gold,
    endowed me with gold and gave me to Sigurd.

2   'So towered Sigurd over the sons of Giuki
    like a green leek grown up out of the grass,*
    or a long-legged stag above the sharp-eyed beasts,
    or red-glowing gold next to dull silver.

3   'Until my brothers begrudged it me
    that I had a husband more prominent than all;
    they could not sleep, they could not judge cases,
    until they had put Sigurd to death.

4   'Grani ran from the Assembly, the uproar could be heard,*
    and then Sigurd himself did not come;
    all the saddle-horses were dripping with sweat,
    though used to labouring beneath the killers.

5   'Weeping I went to talk to Grani;
    cheeks wet with tears, I asked the horse for news;
    Grani drooped his head then, hid it in the grass,
    the horse knew that his master was no more.

6   'Long I turned it over, long my thoughts ran on,
     until I questioned the warrior-guardian about the prince.

7   'Gunnar looked downwards, Hogni told me
     about Sigurd's painful death:
     "Struck down, he lies beyond the water,
     Guthorm's slayer, given to the wolves.

8   ' "Look for Sigurd there on the roads southwards!
     There you'll hear the ravens shriek,
     the eagles shriek; rejoicing in the carrion,
     the wolves are howling over your husband."

9   ' "How, Hogni, can you bring yourself to tell
     of such terrible harm to me, bereft of joy?
     May ravens tear out your heart
     across more far-flung lands than you can know of."

10   'Hogni answered once only,
     not inclined to be cheerful, out of great grief:
     "More you'd have to weep for, Gudrun, from this:
     if ravens were to tear out my heart."

11   'Away I went from the conversation,
     to the wood, to gather the wolves' leavings;
     I could not weep nor strike my hands together,
     nor lament my man as other women do,
     there I sat close to death over Sigurd.

12   'The night seemed to me as dark as the dark of the moon,
     as I sat grieving over Sigurd;
     the best of all beasts the wolves would have been
     if they took my life
     or if I was burned up like birchwood.

13   'I walked from the mountain, five days together,
     until I recognized the high hall of Half.

14   'I sat with Thora seven half-years,
Hakon's daughter, in Denmark;
she embroidered in gold for my pleasure
southern halls and Danish swans.

15   'We sewed pictures of men's war-play together,
a prince's warriors on our handiwork;
red shields, Hunnish champions,
a sword-band, a helmet-band, a royal retinue.

16   'Sigmund's ships glided from the land,
with golden beast-masks and carved prows;
we showed in our embroidery how they fought
Sigar and Siggeir, south in Fion.

17   'Then Grimhild learned, queen of the Goths,
what my state of mind was;
she threw down her embroidery, summoned her sons,
perversely she asked this:
who would compensate the sister for her son,
who would pay for the slain husband?

18   'Eagerly Gunnar offered gold
to settle the matter, Hogni said the same;
she asked then: that those who wished to go
should saddle the steed, equip a wagon,
ride a horse, let a hawk fly,
shoot arrows from a yew bow.*

19   'Valdar with the Danes, with Iarizleif,
Eymod the third, with Iarizskar—
in they went, all most princely,
the troops of the Langobards; they had red cloaks,
ornamented byrnies, towering helmets,
girded with short-swords, they had dark hair.

20   'Each wanted to pick out treasure for me,
pick out treasure and speak comforting words,
to see if they could, for my many sorrows,
offer trusty pledges: I could not come to trust them.

21   'Grimhild brought me a cup to drink from,
       cool and bitter, so I should not remember the strife;*
       that drink was augmented with fateful power,
       with the cool sea, with sacrificial blood.

22   'In the drinking-horn were all kinds of runes,
       cut and red-coloured—I could not interpret them—
       a long heather-fish, an uncut corn-ear*
       of the Haddings' land, the entrails of beasts.*

23   'Many bad things were mixed into that beer,
       the herbs of all the woodland, and burnt acorns,
       the dew of the hearth, the innards from sacrifice,
       boiled pig's liver, since it blunted the strife.

24   'And then they forgot, those who drank it,
       all the prince's *death* in the hall;*
       three kings came into my presence
       before she addressed herself to me.

25   ' "Gold I will give you, Gudrun, as a gift,
       a great deal of treasure from your dead father,
       red-gold rings, Hlodver's hall,
       precious bed-hangings for the fallen prince;

26   ' "Hunnish girls to do your delicate weaving,
       to work in gold for your pleasure;
       you alone shall control the wealth of Budli,
       be adorned with gold, and given to Atli."

27   ' "I do not want to go to another man
       nor to marry Brynhild's brother;
       it is not fitting for me to increase the family
       of Budli's son, nor to enjoy my life."

28   ' "Don't think of repaying the men's wicked deeds,
       that which we brought about before;
       you'll feel as if they were still alive,
       Sigurd and Sigmund, if you have sons."*

29   ' "I cannot, Grimhild, hurtle onwards into happiness,
       nor nourish hopes of a war-eager warrior,
       since the corpse-greedy one and the raven
       bitterly drank Sigurd's heart-blood." '

30   ' "I have found the most highly-born
       prince of all, the most prominent;
       him you'll be married to, or else till your life's end
       you'll be manless, if you won't take this one." '

31   ' "Stop pressing so perversely
       this unholy kinship upon me!
       He'll make ready ruin for Gunnar,
       tear out the heart from Hogni.
       Then I won't delay until I take
       the life of the vigorous man,
       of the sword-play's-speeder." '

32   'Weeping, Grimhild heard these words
       which portended doom for her sons
       and great balefulness for her boys:

33   ' "Lands I'll give you, troops of men,
       Vinbiorg, Valbiorg, if you'll take them;
       possess them all your days, and be content, daughter!" '

34   ' "I'll choose him from among the kings
       coerced into this by my kin;
       he won't be a husband whom I can love
       nor will my brothers' bad fate save my sons." '

35   'Quickly each man was seen to his horse,
       and the southern women lifted into the wagon;
       seven days we rode over the chilly land,
       and another seven we beat over the waves,
       for a third week we drove over dry land.

36 'There the door-guards opened the gate
     of the high citadel, as we rode into the court.

37 'Atli awoke me, for I seemed to be
     full of evil foreboding of the death of kinsmen.

38 'So just now the norns awakened me,
     he wanted me to interpret prophecies of trouble—
     "I thought that you, Gudrun, daughter of Giuki,
     ran me through with a malice-mixed sword."

39 ' "Dreaming of iron represents fire,
     of the anger of a woman, deception and delusion;
     I'll cauterize your injuries, comfort and heal you
     though it pains me to do it."

40 ' "I thought that in the meadow the saplings had fallen,
     those which I'd wanted to let grow tall,
     they were torn up by the roots, reddened with blood,
     carried to the bench and offered me to eat.

41 ' "I thought that my hawks flew from my hand,
     without their prey to a hall of evil;
     their hearts I chewed up, mixed with honey,
     sorrowful in spirit, gorged with blood.

42 ' "I thought my pups were loosed from my grasp,
     deprived of joy, both of them howled;
     I thought their flesh became carrion,
     corpse-flesh which I was made to enjoy."

43 ' "That means men will discuss sacrifice
     and cut the heads off white beasts;*
     doomed, within a few nights,
     the retinue will consume them just before dawn."

44 'I lay down then, I did not want to sleep,
     obstinate on the bed of pain; that I remember well.'

THE THIRD POEM OF GUDRUN

This poem is set between the death of Gudrun's brothers and her revenge, but is grouped with the *Second Poem* because of the similarity of title; both poems are simply called *Poem of Gudrun* in the manuscript. The story is unknown from anywhere else and probably very late. The combination of possibly contemporary trial by ordeal and archaic Germanic punishment, drowning in a bog, is striking. Thiodrek is well known in both Norse and German heroic legend as the exiled king of Verona. He took refuge at Atli's court where their shared misery brings him and Gudrun together.

Herkia was the name of one of Atli's serving-maids; she had been his mistress. She told Atli that she had seen Gudrun and Thiodrek together. Atli was very upset. Then Gudrun said:

1 'What's the matter, Atli? Always, son of Budli,
   you're downcast; why do you never laugh?
   It would seem better to the warriors
   that you should speak to people and look at me.'

2 'It grieves me, Gudrun, daughter of Giuki,
   what Herkia told me in the hall:
   that you and Thiodrek slept under one coverlet
   and made yourselves comfortable in the bedlinen.'

3 'I'll swear you oaths about all this,
   by the sacred, white stone,
   that with Thiodmar's son I never did anything
   which a lady and man ought not to do together.

4 'Just once only did I embrace
   the battle-leader, the blameless prince;
   but quite other was our conversation,
   when we two, griefstricken,
   spoke privately together.

5   'Thiodrek came here with thirty men,
     not one of them lives now, out of thirty men!
     I am deprived of my brothers, of corslet-wearing men,
     deprived of all my closest kin.*

6   'Summon Saxi, the prince of the southerners!
     He knows how to hallow the boiling cauldron.'

7   Seven hundred men entered the hall
     before the king's lady dipped her hands in the cauldron.

8   'Gunnar will not come now, I do not call for Hogni,
     I shall not ever again see my sweet brothers;
     with a sword Hogni would avenge such an insult,
     now I must purge this accusation myself.'

9   She stretched her bright hands down to the bottom
     and there she seized the precious stones:
     'Look now, warriors—acquitted am I,
     by the sacred test—how this cauldron bubbles!'

10   Then Atli's heart laughed within him
     when he saw Gudrun's hands all whole:
     'Now Herkia shall go to the cauldron,
     she who hoped to slander Gudrun.'

11   Everyone who watched watched wretchedly,
     how Herkia's hands were scalded;
     they led the girl away into a foul bog,*
     Gudrun got recompense for her wrong.

ODDRUN'S LAMENT

This poem is a probably later addition to the story of Gunnar and Atli, providing more motivation than is needed for Atli's killing of his brothers-in-law. It continues the theme of the sorrows and suffering of women which began with the laments of Svava and Sigrun in the Helgi poems and which persists through Gudrun's laments.

About Borgny and Oddrun *There was a king called Heidrek; his daughter was called Borgny. Vilmund was the name of the man who was her lover. She could not give birth to her children until Oddrun, sister of Atli, came; she had been the lover of Gunnar, son of Giuki. This tale is told here.*

1   I heard said in ancient tales,
    how a girl came to Mornaland;
    no one on the face of the earth
    was able to help Heidrek's daughter.

2   Oddrun heard, Atli's sister,
    that the girl was having terrible pains;
    she brought from its stall the bridled horse
    and saddled up the black steed.

3   She let the horse travel over the smooth paths
    until she came where a high hall was standing;
    and in she went along the hall
    —she took the saddle off the hungry horse—
    and these were the first words that she spoke:

4   'What is best known on earth,
    or what is most noteworthy in the land of the Huns?'
    'Here lies Borgny, overcome with labour pains,
    your friend, Oddrun—see if you can help!'

5   'Which prince has brought about this shame?
    Why does Borgny have these sudden pains?'

6   'Vilmund he's called, the hawk-bearer's friend,*
    he kept the girl in a warm coverlet
    for five whole winters, so that she hid it from her father.'

7   I think that they did not speak much more:
    the gentle lady went to sit by the girl's knee;
    strongly Oddrun sang, powerfully Oddrun sang,
    sharp spells for Borgny.*

8   A girl and a boy were able to kick on the earth,
    cheerful children for Hogni's slayer.*
    Then the mortally sick girl began to speak,
    for she had not spoken a word before.

9   'May the kindly beings help you,
    Frigg and Freyia and more of the gods,
    as you warded off that dangerous illness from me.'

10 'I didn't kneel to help you because
    you in any way deserved it;
    I promised, and I've kept it, after I'd said it,
    that I should help any creature
    who shared the inheritance of princes.'

11 'You're mad, Oddrun! you're out of your wits,
    that you say out of spite so many words to me!
    And I used to accompany you on mother earth
    as if we had been born of two brothers!'

12 'I remember what you said one evening,
    when I was preparing the drink for Gunnar:*
    you said such a bad example would never be set
    by women ever after; only I was capable of it!'

13 Then the sorrow-weary woman sat down,
    to recount the evil, from her great grief:

14　'I was brought up in the princes' hall
　　—most people rejoiced at that—according to men's counsel.
　　I enjoyed life and my father's prosperity
　　for just five winters while my father lived.

15　'Then he spoke these very last words,
　　the weary king, before he died:
　　he said I should be endowed with red gold,
　　and given to Grimhild's son in the south;

16　and he commanded Brynhild to take the helmet,
　　he said she'd be Odin's beloved girl.*
　　He said no nobler girl would be reared
　　in the world, unless fate spoilt it—

17　'In the women's chamber Brynhild worked embroidery,
　　she had men and lands under her—
　　the earth resounded and the heaven above,
　　when the slayer of Fafnir saw the stronghold.

18　'Then war was fought with foreign swords
　　and the stronghold seized which Brynhild owned—
　　it was not long thereafter, rather it was pitifully soon,
　　that she knew all those stratagems.

19　'She made harsh vengeance come about for this,
　　we've all had experience enough of that:
　　that news will travel to men in every land,
　　that she killed herself over Sigurd!

20　'And I came to love Gunnar,
　　the giver of rings, as Brynhild should have.

21　'Soon they offered red-gold rings,
　　and no small compensation to my brother;
　　he offered for me fifteen farms,
　　the burden of Grani, if he wanted it.*

22   'But Atli said that he would never
        want a bride-price from the kin of Giuki.
        Nor could we two struggle against our desire,
        so I leaned my head against the ring-breaker.*

23   'Many of my kin said
        that they had discovered us;
        but Atli said that I would not
        act disgracefully or bring myself to shame.

24   'One cannot refuse such a thing to someone,
        where love for another is involved!

25   'Atli sent his messengers
        through the dark wood to test me out;
        and they came where they should not have come,
        where we spread for ourselves a single coverlet.

26   'Red-gold rings we offered to the warriors
        that they should not tell Atli—
        but they excitedly told Atli,
        eagerly they hurried home.

27   'And they completely concealed it from Gudrun,
        something she really ought to have known.

28   'Then the noise was heard of golden-hoofed horses,
        when Giuki's heirs rode into the courtyard;
        out of Hogni they cut the heart,
        and placed the other in the snake-pit.

29   'I'd just gone on that one occasion
        to Geirmund, to brew up some drink;
        the wise king began to play the harp,*
        for he thought, the king of mighty lineage,
        that I would come to help him.

30 'I began to hear it there in Hlesey,
    how the strings were singing of strife;
    I told my serving-maids to get ready,
    I wanted to save the war-leader's life!

31 'We made the ship sail over the sea
    until I saw all the courts of Atli.

32 'Then came the wretched one darting out,
    the mother of Atli—may she shrivel away!—*
    and she dug right into Gunnar's heart
    so that I could not protect the famous prince.

33 'Often I wonder how I can still—
    goddess of the linen-pillow—hold onto my life,*
    when I thought that I loved the terribly brave man,
    the sword-sharer, as I loved myself!

34 'You sat and listened while I told you
    many evil things about my fate and theirs.
    Everyone lives by their desires—
    now the lament of Oddrun is over.'

THE POEM OF ATLI

In this tense, allusively told poem, the heroic deaths of Gunnar and Hogni are related. Atli, anxious to gain the treasure which had belonged to Sigurd, invites Gunnar and Hogni to visit him so he can capture them and force them to hand over the gold. After their deaths Gudrun takes a terrible revenge: like the Greek mythological figure Procne she slaughters her children and feeds them to Atli and his warriors before killing her husband and burning down the hall. In German tradition Gudrun (Kriemhilt) is determined to kill the brothers in revenge for the death of Sigurd; in Norse she is more loyal to her brothers than her husband. The *Poem of Atli* (*Atlakvida*) is likely to be one of the oldest in the *Edda*, the language sometimes elaborate, sometimes studiedly simple.

Gudrun, daughter of Giuki, avenged her brothers, as is very well known: first she killed Atli's sons, then she killed Atli and burned down the hall and all the retinue. This poem was composed about it:

1   Atli sent a messenger to Gunnar,
     a well-travelled man came riding, Knefrod was his name;
     he came to the courts of Giuki and to Gunnar's hall,
     the benches grouped around the hearth, and the sweet-tasting
          beer.

2   The fighting-troop all drank there—still they concealed their
          thoughts in silence—
     wine in the handsome hall, they feared the Huns' hostility;*
     then Knefrod called out in a cold voice,
     the man from the south—he sat on a high bench:

3   'Atli has sent me here, riding with a message,
     on a horse gnashing at its bit, through unknown
          Myrkwood,
     to invite you two, Gunnar, to come to our benches,*
     with helmets grouped about the hearth, to visit Atli's
          home.

4   'There you may both choose shields and smooth-planed ash
        spears,
    golden helmets and a host of the Huns,
    silver-gilt saddle-cloths, scarlet tunics,
    lances with pennants, coursers gnashing at their bits.

5   'He said too that he would give you the plain of wide
        Gnita-heath,
    whistling spears and gilded prows,
    great treasures, farms on the Dnieper,
    that famous forest which men call Myrkwood.'

6   Gunnar turned his head and said to Hogni:
    'What do you advise us, young man, when we hear of such
        things?
    I didn't know of any gold on Gnita-heath*
    that we did not own just as much.

7   'We have seven storehouses full of swords,
    each of them has a golden hilt;
    I know my horse is the best, my blade the sharpest,
    my bow graces the benches, and my corslets are of gold,
    the brightest shield and helmet come from the emperor's hall;
    one of mine is better than all of the Huns' might be.'

8   'What do you think the lady meant when she sent us a ring,
    wrapped in the heath-wanderer's coat? I think she was giving us
        a warning.*
    I found a heath-wanderer's hair twisted round the red-gold
        ring:
    our way is wolf-beset if we go on this errand.'

9   No kinsman urged Gunnar, nor any close relative,
    neither advisers nor counsellors, nor any powerful men;
    Gunnar then said, as a king ought to,
    splendid in his mead-hall, with great spirit:

10 'Rise up now, Fiornir, send the warriors' golden goblets
passing around the hall from hand to hand!

11 'The wolf will reign over the Niflungs' inheritance,
the old grey guardians, if Gunnar is lost,
black-coated bears will bite with tenacious teeth,
make the bitch-pack rejoice if Gunnar does not return.'

12 The valiant troop, the excellent men, weeping,
led the war-eager princes out of the young men's court;*
then said Hogni's young heir:
'Go well now and wisely, where your spirit draws you.'

13 The brave men spurred the bit-gnashing horses to gallop
over the mountains, through unknown Myrkwood;
All the Hun borderlands shook as the resolute ones
passed,
they drove the whip-shy horses over the green plains.

14 They saw Atli's land and watch-towers looking deep down,
Bikki's warriors standing on the high citadel,*
the hall over the southern folk, encompassed with wooden
benches,
with well-bound shields, shining targes,
lances with pennants, there Atli was drinking
wine in the handsome hall; the watchmen sat outside,
guarding against Gunnar and his men, if they should come
visiting
with whistling spears to make war against the prince.

15 Their sister first perceived them come into the hall,
both her brothers, little beer had she drunk:
'Betrayed you are now, Gunnar; what, mighty lord, will you
manage
against the Huns' evil tricks? Quickly, leave the hall!

16 'It would have been better, brother, if you'd come in a corslet,
   with those helmets still grouped round the hearth, to see Atli's
        home;
   if you'd sat in the saddle all through sun-bright days,
   made the norns weep at the pallid corpses,*
   taught Hun shield-maidens how to haul a harrow,
   and Atli himself you could have put in the snake-pit;
   now that snake-pit stands ready for you.'

17 'Too late now, sister, to collect the Niflungs,
   too far to seek a troop of uncowardly men
   from the Rhine's russet mountains.'*

18 They seized Gunnar and put him in fetters,
   the friend of the Burgundians, and bound him fast.

19 Seven Hogni hacked down with a sharp sword,
   and the eighth he hurled into the hot fire;
   so a dauntless man should defend himself against enemies,
   as Hogni defended himself and Gunnar.

20 They asked the brave man, lord of the Goths,*
   if he wanted to buy his life with gold.

21 'Hogni's heart must lie in my hand,
   bleeding, cut from the bold horseman's breast
   with a sharp-biting knife from the prince's son.'

22 They cut the heart out of Hialli's breast,*
   bleeding, laid it on a platter, and brought it to Gunnar.

23 Then said Gunnar, lord of men:
   'Here I have the heart of Hialli the cowardly,
   quite unlike the heart of Hogni the brave;
   it quivers greatly as it lies on the platter;
   it quivered twice as much when it was in the breast.'

24   Then Hogni laughed as they cut to his heart,
        that living smith of scars, he never thought to cry out;
        they laid it bleeding on a platter, and brought it to Gunnar.

25   Then said splendid Gunnar, the Spear-Niflung:
        'Here I have the heart of Hogni the brave,
        quite unlike the heart of Hialli the cowardly;
        it scarcely quivers as it lies on the plate;
        it did not quiver even that much when it lay in his breast.

26   'Atli, now you'll be as far from my eyes*
        as you will be from the treasure.
        Now with me alone the Niflung hoard's
        all hidden, now Hogni is not alive.

27   'I was always in doubt while we were both alive,
        now I am not, now I alone live.
        The swift Rhine shall rule over men's strife-metal,
        the Æsir-given inheritance of the Niflungs,*
        the splendid rings will gleam in running water,
        rather than gold shine on Hun-children's hands.'

28   'Drive out the chariot! now the captive is in chains.'
        And on from there the bit-shaker*
        drew the neckring-guardian to death.

29   Atli the powerful rode the horse with ringing mane,
        sword-armed men surrounded their kinsman;
        Gudrun of the victory-gods
        fought back her tears, bereft in the noisy hall.

30   'May it so befall you, Atli, as you swore to Gunnar,
        oaths you often gave and pledged early:
        by the sun curving to the south and Victory-god's mountain,
        by the marriage-bed horse and by Ull's ring.'

31 The living prince they placed in the pit
    —a crowd of men did it—which was crawling
    inside with snakes; and Gunnar, alone,
    grim-minded struck his harp with his hand.*
    The strings resounded; so should a brave ring-giver
    guard his gold from enemies.

32 Atli turned his gravel-treading horse
    towards his land, back from the murder;
    there was a noise in the courtyard, crowded with horses,
    men's weapon-song, they had come from the heath.

33 Out went Gudrun to meet Atli
    with a golden goblet to render the prince his due:
    'Prince, you may receive in your own hall,
    gladly from Gudrun, little creatures gone into darkness.'*

34 Atli's ale-cups were ringing, heavy with wine,
    as all together in the hall the Huns assembled,
    men with long moustaches, each troop came in.

35 The bright-faced woman darted about, bringing drink,
    the terrible woman, to the nobles; she brought morsels with
        the ale
    for the pale-faced men, reluctantly; then she told Atli his
        shame.

36 'Your own sons'—sharer-out of swords—*
    hearts, corpse-bloody, you are chewing up with honey;
    you are filling your stomach, proud lord, with dead human flesh,
    eating it as ale-appetizers and sending it to the high seat.

37 'You'll never again call to your knee
    Erp or Eitil, two boys merry with ale;
    you'll not see them again amidst the seats,
    those gold-givers, putting shafts on their spears,
    trimming the manes or driving their horses.'

38   There was uproar on the benches, terrible song of men,
      howling in their costly cloaks, the children of the Huns wept;
      all but Gudrun, she who never wept
      for her brothers fierce as bears and her dear sons,
      young, innocent, whom she had with Atli.

39   Gold she scattered, the gosling-bright woman,
      red-gold rings she gave the house-servants;
      she let fate culminate, and the shining metal flow,
      she did not care at all, that lady, about the temple stores!

40   Unaware, Atli had drunk himself to exhaustion,
      he had no weapons, no defence against Gudrun;
      often their sport was better when they lovingly
      would often embrace each other in front of the nobles.

41   With a sword-point she gave the bed blood to drink,
      with a hell-bent hand she loosed the dogs;
      hurled before the hall doors a flaming brand; wakening the
          house-servants,
      the bride made them pay for her brothers.

42   She gave to the fire all who were in there,
      who after the death of Gunnar and Hogni had come from
          Myrkheim;
      the ancient timbers fell, the temples went up in smoke,
      the estates of Budli's descendants, shield-maids inside
      burnt up, their lives stopped, they sank into the hot fire.

43   Now this story is all told; never since has a bride
      in a byrnie acted so to avenge her brothers;
      she brought news of death to three great kings,
      that bright woman, before she died.

The 'Greenlandic Lay of Atli' tells this story more clearly.

THE GREENLANDIC LAY OF ATLI

In comparison with the subtle and allusive style of the *Poem of Atli*, the *Greenlandic Lay of Atli* (*Atlamal in grœnlenzco*) is colloquial and idiomatic, closer to the prose sagas in tone. The protagonists live in farmsteads rather than great halls, and the setting is distinctly unaristocratic. Much of the poem is taken up with bickering between Gudrun and Atli, both reflecting on their marital disappointments. Atli is motivated by sheer enmity towards his brothers-in-law; lust for treasure plays no part. Otherwise, the story unfolds much as in the *Poem of Atli*, with some elaboration of the incident with Hialli into rather effective comedy. What the exact connection with Greenland was is unknown; clearly the compiler of the Codex Regius thought this poem had come from there and it seems quite likely that the harsh frontier conditions in the colony, so distant from the courtly world of Continental European literature, might have prompted the poem's recasting. The *Poem of Atli* is also designated as 'Greenlandic' in the manuscript; it seems probable that the scribe has carried this across from the attribution here. Apart from the reference to the Danish Limfjord in v. 4, the poem could plausibly be set in Greenland: the assumption that the bear in v. 18 must be white provides further evidence. The poem is composed in *malahattr*, a longer line which gives a sense of the story's leisurely unfolding.

1   People have heard of the enmity which happened once,
        when men met in counsel together, of benefit to very few;
        they talked privately together, terror came of it afterward,
        for them and for the sons of Giuki, who were utterly betrayed.

2   They brought the princes' fate to culmination—they should
           not have been doomed—
        Atli was ill-advised, even though he had cunning;
        he brought down a great buttress, injured himself terribly,
        a hasty message he sent that his in-laws should come quickly.

3   The lady of the house was clever; she used her common sense,*
        she heard what they were saying, though they spoke in secret;
        the wise lady was at her wits' end, she wanted to help them;
        they were going to sail over the sea, but she could not reach
           them.

4   She carved some runes, Vingi defaced them
    —hastened on disaster—before he handed them over;
    then they departed, the messengers of Atli,
    over the Limfjord to where the courageous ones lived.

5   They were most welcoming, stoked up the fires,
    they perceived no treachery when those men had come;
    they accepted the gifts which the lovely lady sent them,
    hung them on the hall-pillar, did not think that significant.

6   Then came Kostbera, she was Hogni's wife,
    a most circumspect woman, and greeted them both;*
    and Glaumvor was also glad, who was married to Gunnar,
    the wise lady was not discourteous, busied herself with the
         guests' needs.

7   Hogni they invited home, to see if the other one wished to come;
    the deceptive thought was clear if they'd been on their guard;
    Gunnar said he'd come, if Hogni wished to,
    Hogni didn't refuse if the other thought it best to go.

8   Splendid women brought mead, much hospitality was shown,
    many a horn went round until they had drunk enough.

9   The couple retired then, when they thought it time to do so.*
    Kostbera had been taught, she knew how to interpret runes,
    spelled out the letters in the light of the fire;
    she held her tongue, bit back her words,
    the runes were so confused they could scarcely be made out.

10 They went to bed then, Hogni and his wife;
    the courtly lady dreamed, not at all did she conceal it;
    the wise one told it to the prince as soon as she awoke:

11 'You intend to leave home, Hogni, listen to advice!
    Few are very learned in runes—go some other time!
    I interpreted the runes which your sister cut:
    the radiant lady hasn't summoned you this time.

12 'I'm greatly surprised by one thing—I still can't make it out—
why the clever woman should carve so awry;
for they seemed to indicate an underlying meaning:
the death of both of you if you hastened there now;
the lady's missed out a letter or else others have caused this.'

13 'All women think the worst,' said Hogni, 'I am not so inclined;
I shan't go looking for trouble unless there's something we
    must repay them;
the prince will shower us both with glowing red-gold arm-rings,
I am never afraid, though we hear dire things portended.'

14 'You'll meet your downfall if you set off there,
there's no loving welcome waiting for you this time.
I had a dream, Hogni, I won't delude myself:
an evil fate will come upon you—or am I simply too afraid?

15 'I dreamt your bedclothes were burning up in fire,
high flames were raging all through my buildings.'
'Here are linen garments lying, which have no value,
they'll soon be burnt up, as you saw the bedclothes burn.'*

17 'I thought I saw a bear come in here, smash up the panelling,
swing with his paws so that we were afraid;
many of us he held in his mouth so that we were helpless;
his lumbering made no small amount of noise.'

18 'That must mean a storm coming, it'll soon be raging;
thinking of a white bear, that's a blizzard from the east.'*

19 'I thought I saw an eagle fly in here, all through the house,
something terrible will happen to us, he sprinkled us all with blood;
I thought from its threatenings that it was Atli's spirit.'

20 'We'll soon be slaughtering, then we'll see blood;
often it means oxen—dreaming of eagles;
Atli is well intentioned, whatever you dream.'
They left it at that, every conversation has an end.

21   The well-born ones awoke, they too had this example,
     Glaumvor was anxious, there was disaster in her sleep;
     Gunnar *undertook* that there were two ways to interpret.*

22   'I thought I saw gallows ready for you, you were to be
          hanged,
     serpents gnawed at you, I lost you while you were still alive,
     the doom of the gods came about; tell me what that meant!'

[Here a verse giving Gunnar's interpretation must have been omitted.]

24   'I thought a bloody sword was pulled out of your shirt,
     it's painful to have to tell such a dream to a man so close
          to one;
     I thought I saw a spear pierce right through you,
     wolves were howling at both its ends.'

25   'That will be dogs running, barking a great deal,
     the noise of dogs often stands for spears flying about.'

26   'I saw a river flowing through here, all through the house,
     it roared in its course and crashed over the benches;
     it broke the legs of both you brothers here,
     nothing could calm the water—that must mean something.'

[Gunnar's reply is missing; the paraphrase in *Volsunga saga*, ch. 36, relates
to cornfields.]

28   'I thought that dead women came here tonight,
     they were not badly decked out, they wanted to choose you,
     invite you very soon to their benches;
     I declare that your *disir* are powerless to help you.'*

29   'It's too late to speak thus, all is now arranged;
     I cannot escape these fateful portents, since we intend
          to go;
     everything seems to show that we haven't long to live.'

30 They saw it was getting light, said they were eager to get going,
   though others wanted to detain them;
   five journeyed together—another ten house-retainers
   were there—this was ill-advised.*
   Snævar and Solar, Hogni's sons,
   Orkning the other was called who accompanied them,
   Hogni's wife's brother, a cheerful shield-warrior.

31 The splendidly dressed ladies came too until the fjord
      separated them;
   the beautiful women kept dissuading them; they would not be
      prevented.

32 Glaumvor said, the wife of Gunnar,
   she said to Vingi, since she felt it was warranted:
   'I don't know if our feasting will be rewarded as we would
      wish;
   a guest's coming is a crime if something happens because of it.'

33 Then Vingi swore—he did not spare himself in this—
   'May the giants seize this man if he lies to you,
   may the gallows be all ready for him if he should plot against
      your safety.'

34 Then Bera said, she felt cheerful:*
   'Sail safely and achieve your errand victoriously!
   Let it happen as I wish, let no one contradict it.'

35 Hogni answered—he felt concern for his family—
   'Be in good spirits, wise ladies, whatever happens!
   Many say this—though often it turns out differently—
   for many it makes no matter how they are accompanied from
      home.'

36 A long time they gazed before they turned away from each
      other;
   I think their fates were laid down there when their ways
      parted.

37 Mightily they began to row, split half the keel,
    put their backs into the rowing, they became infuriated;
    the oar-thongs snapped, the rowlocks shattered,
    they didn't tie up the vessel before they left it behind.*

38 A little later—now I shall tell to the story's end—
    they saw the buildings which Budli had owned;
    loudly resounded the gate when Hogni hammered on it.

39 Then said Vingi, what he might have left unsaid,
    'Go away from the house! It is treacherous to go near it,
    soon I'll have destroyed you, shortly they'll hack you down;
    I invited you here warmly but deceit lurked underneath,
    or else you can wait here while I build you your gallows!'

40 Then said Hogni—he didn't weigh his words much—
    not one whit did he hesitate, as was afterwards proved:
    'Don't try to frighten us, don't try that again!
    If you drag out your words it will lengthen your miseries.'

41 They pushed Vingi down and they knocked him into hell,
    set about him with axes while he struggled for breath.

42 Atli and his men gathered, they put on their coats of mail,
    so equipped, they went to the palisade;
    they hurled insults at one another, all straightway stirred to
        fury:
    'For a long time we've intended to take away your lives.'

43 'It doesn't really look as if you had decided any such thing;
    you aren't even ready while we have struck down one,*
    smashed him into hell, one of your number.'

44 Then they were furious when they heard these words,
    moved their hands, caught hold of their javelin-loops,
    they shot accurately, defending themselves with shields.

45 Inside they heard news of what was happening outside;
    in front of the hall they heard a slave speaking loudly.

46 Then Gudrun was terrifying when she heard this grievous
        thing;
    the necklaces weighing on her throat she hurled away entirely,
    flung down the silver chain so the links all broke apart.

47 Then she went outside, flinging open the doors,
    she advanced fearlessly to welcome the arrivals;
    she embraced the Niflungs, it was the last time she greeted
        them,
    this was honourable behaviour, she added words besides:

48 'I tried to remedy this by keeping you at home,
    yet no one defeats fate, and so you still came here.'
    She spoke common sense to try to make peace between them,
    they would not agree at all, both sides said no.

49 Then the high-born lady saw them play a wounding game,
    she resolved on a hard course and flung off her cloak;
    she took a naked sword and fought for her kinsmen's lives,
    she was easy with fighting, wherever she turned her hand.

50 Giuki's daughter brought down two fighters,
    she struck at Atli's brother—he had to be carried off:
    she shaped her strokes so she cut his leg from under him.

51 Another she set to strike so that he did not get up again,
    she had him away into hell; nor did her hands tremble.

52 A battle they fought there for which they were famous;
    that surpassed all others, what the children of Giuki achieved;
    people said of the Niflungs while they were still alive,
    they'd lead their attack with swords, so mail-coats were
        slashed open,
    hack at helmets, as their courage prevailed.

53   They fought most of the morning until midday came and
          went,
      all the dawn and the early day.
      Before they'd fought to the end, the ground was awash with
          blood;
      eighteen, before they fell, they had overcome,
      Kostbera's two boys and her brother.

54   Then the brave man began to speak, even though he was
          enraged:*
      'Terrible it is to look around us, you're to blame for this,
      we were thirty formidable fighters,
      now eleven remain alive, our men are decimated.

55   'There were five of us brothers when we lost Budli,*
      now Hel has half of us, two lie cut down there.

56   'Alliance with splendid men I made—I can't deny it—
      I can get no benefit, monstrous wife, from it.
      We've scarcely had any peace since you came among us,
      you've deprived me of kinsmen, swindled me of property,
      you sent my sister off to hell, that upsets me most.'*

57   'Can you speak of such things, Atli? You did all this first:
      you seized my mother and killed her, to get her treasure,
      my wise cousin you starved to death in a cave;*
      it seems to me laughable when you recount your injuries,
      I thank the gods for it when things go badly for you.'

58   'I urge you, warriors, to greatly increase the grief
      of this redoubtable woman! That I want to see.
      Do all you can to make Gudrun sob,
      so that I might see her without a vestige of joy.

59   'Take Hogni and butcher him with a knife,
      cut out his heart, be ready to do this;
      Gunnar the fierce-spirited, string up on the gallows,*
      get on with this—invite the snakes to come to him!'

Hogni said:

60   'Do as you wish, I'll cheerfully await it,
my courage you can test, I've borne sharper trials before;
you met some resistance when we were unwounded,
now we are so injured that you do as you please.'

61   Beiti spoke—he was Atli's steward—
'Let's seize Hialli and spare Hogni,
let's carry out a deed half done; he's fated for death,*
he won't live very long, he'll always be called useless.'

62   The kettle-minder was terrified, he didn't stay in his place,
he knew how to be pusillanimous, he scrambled into every
      cranny;
said he was a wretched victim of their violence, that he had to
      pay for travail,
said it was a dark day to have to die and leave his pigs,
and all the fine provisions that he'd enjoyed before.

63   They took Budli's scullion and took out their knives,
the wicked slave howled before he felt the point;
said he'd have the time to dung the fields for them,
do the filthiest work, if that would get him out of it;
Hialli said he'd be very glad if he could keep his life.

64   Hogni saw to this—few would act this way—
ensured that the slave would escape:
'I declare that for me it is a small matter to play this game,
why might we want here to listen to his screeching?'

65   Then they seized that great man, there was no chance
for the stout-hearted warriors to delay their action longer.
Hogni laughed then so that the sons of day heard it,*
he knew how to show his mettle and endured the torture
      well.

66   Gunnar took his harp, moved it with his foot-twigs;*
       plucked it as he knew how, so that the ladies wept,
       the men sobbed, those who heard it most clearly;
       he related his fate to the powerful woman so that the rafters split.

67   Then the beloved men died, it was still early in the day;
       they kept alive their prowess right 'til the end

68   Atli thought himself a great man, he had got the better of both
              of them;
       he told the wise woman of her loss and even taunted her with it:
       'Now it's morning, Gudrun, and you've lost the men you love,
       you partly shaped it yourself that this has come about.'

69   'You're exultant now, Atli, you proclaim your murders,
       regret will overcome you when you find out what results;
       there will be a legacy—I can tell you truly of it:
       evil will always befall you unless I die too.'

70   'I can't deny what you say: but I see another alternative,
       twice as pleasant—often we scorn good things:
       I'll comfort you with slave-girls, with splendid treasure,
       snow-gleaming silver, just as you yourself desire.'

71   'There is no hope of this—I shall refuse these things,
       I have broken agreements before for lesser reasons;
       a demon I seemed before, now I'll improve on that,
       I could endure everything while Hogni was still alive.

72   'We were brought up together in the same house,
       we played many games and grew up in the grove;
       Grimhild enriched us both with gold and with neck-rings;
       you can never compensate me for killing my brothers
       nor ever bring me to be content with this.

73   'Women's lot is crushed by the dominion of men—
       the trunk collapses when shorn of its branches,
       a tree begins to topple if the root is cut from under it;
       now you alone, Atli, wield all the power here.'

74 The prince's credulity was enough for him to believe this,
her treachery was clear if he had looked out for it.
Gudrun was impenetrable, she knew how to dissemble,
pretended to be cheerful, played a double game.

75 She ordered a great ale-brewing in memory of her brothers,
Atli agreed the feast should be for his own men also.

76 They left matters so. The drink was brewed—
that was a banquet resulting in great turmoil—
fierce was her strong temperament, she maimed the line of
    Budli,
upon her husband she intended all-encompassing revenge.

77 She enticed the little ones to her and held them against the
    post;
the fierce children were aghast but they did not cry,
they came into their mother's arms and asked what was
    intended.

78 'Don't ask any more! I'm going to destroy you both,
I've long wanted to cure you of old age.'
'Sacrifice, if you wish, your children, no one will prevent you,
but brief will be your respite from rage
when you find out what results.'*

79 She ended then the brothers' childhood, that formidable
    woman,
did what she had to do, cut both their throats.
Then Atli asked whether his boys had gone
playing their games, since he could not see them anywhere.

80 'I intend to go over to tell Atli.*
Grimhild's daughter will not conceal it from you;
it won't gladden you in the slightest, Atli, when you find out
    what's resulted.
A great disaster you stirred up when you killed my brothers.

81   'I've hardly slept since they died,
       I promised you a grim reward, now I'm reminding you of it;
       you said to me it was morning—I remember it so clearly—
       and now it's evening you must hear similar news.

82   'Your boys you have lost, as you ought never to have done;
       their skulls, you know, are used for ale-goblets.*
       I augmented your drink by mixing it with their blood.

83   'I took their hearts and roasted them on a spit,
       gave them to you—told you they were calf-meat;
       you made all this happen, you wouldn't leave any scraps,
       chewed it up greedily, trusting your back teeth.

84   'Now you know about your children—few could ask to hear
          worse—
       I have chosen my course, yet I do not boast of this.'

85   'You were savage, Gudrun, to be able to do such a thing,
       to mix the blood of your children for me to drink;
       you have wiped out your kindred, as you ought never to have
          done,
       you give me little rest between the horrors.'

86   'Had I still one more wish, it would be to kill you,
       few things are too wicked to do to such a prince;
       you've already committed, in a way that's unexampled,
       foolishness and cruelty in this world;
       now you've added to what we'd heard before,
       seized this great crime, prepared your own funeral feast.'

87   'You should be burned on a pyre, and before that be stoned to
          death,
       then you'll have got what you've been begging for.'
       'Recount such sorrows to yourself early tomorrow morning!
       I'll want a more splendid death to journey to another light.'*

88 They sat in the same hall, aiming rancorous thoughts at each
     other,
    threw out hateful words, neither was happy.
    Hatred grew in Hniflung's heart, he was thinking of a great
     stratagem,*
    he let Gudrun know that he felt loathing for Atli.

89 Then came into her mind the dealings with Hogni,
    she said it would be his good fortune if he could bring about
     revenge;
    then Atli was killed, little time did they wait,
    Hogni's son struck him and Gudrun herself.

90 The brave man began to speak, dragged himself out of sleep,
    realized at once his death-wounds, said he had no need of
     bandages:
    'Tell me most truthfully: who has struck down Budli's son?
    No little trick you've played on me, I reckon I've no hope of
     life.'

91 'Grimhild's daughter will not conceal from you:
    I declare I brought it about that your life is over,
    yet Hogni's son had some part in it—that your wounds weary
     you so.'

92 'You have waded deep into killing, though it was not right;
    it is wrong to betray a friend who trusted you well.
    I left home, urged to woo you, Gudrun;

93 you were an esteemed widow, they said you were demanding,
    there was no hope of a lie in that—as we discovered.
    You came home here, an army of men came with us,
    our appearances were entirely brilliant.

94 'All the honour was here that distinguished men should have,
    plenty of cattle, we made great use of them;
    great wealth, given out to many.

95 'I paid a bride-price for a splendid lady, gave a great deal of
  treasure,
  thirty slaves and seven good slave-women
  —it was honourable to do so—there was even more silver.

96 'You said that all this seemed as nothing to you,
  while those lands lay unclaimed, my inheritance from Budli;
  you undermined us so, no one got a share;
  your mother-in-law you often made sit and weep,
  I found no good-heartedness ever again among our
    household.'

97 'You are lying now, Atli, though I don't really care;
  I was hardly ever docile but you lorded it greatly.
  You young brothers fought each other, sent strife round
    amongst yourselves,
  half your line were sent off to Hel.
  Everything tottered which should have been to our advantage.

98 'We were three brothers and a sister, we seemed
    unconquerable,
  we left our country and went with Sigurd;
  we hastened our ships onwards, each of us captained one,*
  we roamed where our fate led us, until we came to the east.

99 'First we killed a king there, chose land in that place;
  earls submitted to us—this demonstrated their fear;
  by fighting we brought from outlawry those we wished to
    rescue,
  we gave any man a fortune who had no wealth of his own.

100 'The southern prince died, my luck was speedily destroyed;
  bitter torment it was for a young girl to be given the name of
    a widow;
  it seemed anguish for a survivor to come to Atli's house;
  she was married to a hero before—that was a cruel loss.

101 'You never came back from the Assembly—or so we heard—
having prosecuted a case or crushed an adversary's;
you always wanted to yield, you'd never stand firm in any
       matter,
you'd quietly let things be.'

102 'Now you're lying, Gudrun: that won't much improve
the fate of either of us—we have both suffered injury.
Now, Gudrun, out of kindness,
act in keeping with our honour when they carry me out.'

103 'I will buy a ship and a painted coffin,*
I shall wax the shroud well to enclose your corpse,
I'll consider all that's needful as if we cared for one another.'

104 Atli became a corpse, made his kin's anguish grow.
The splendidly born lady did all as promised;
Gudrun the wise tried to kill herself—
but her days were long drawn out; another day she died.

105 Fortunate is any man who afterwards can father
such heroic children as Giuki fathered.
After them in every land
their defiance lives on wherever people hear of it.

THE WHETTING OF GUDRUN

There are clearly close affinities between the *Whetting of Gudrun* (*Gudrunarhvot*) and the *Lay of Hamdir*, which follows it. They open with the same scene: Gudrun urging her sons by Ionakr to set out to the court of Iormunrekk to avenge the death of their half-sister Svanhild. While the *Lay of Hamdir* follows the brothers' adventure, the *Whetting of Gudrun* stays with the heroine while she laments her past woes. At the close of the poem, once again, she seems intent on death.

When Gudrun had killed Atli she went to the sea, she waded out into the water and wanted to drown herself but she could not sink. She drifted across the fjord to the land of King Ionakr who married her.

Their sons were Sorli and Erp* and Hamdir. Svanhild, Sigurd's daughter, was brought up there. She was married to Iormunrekk the powerful. Bikki was at his court. He advised that Randver, the king's son, ought to marry her, and then he told the king this.* The king had Randver hanged and Svanhild trampled under the feet of horses. And when Gudrun heard this, she spoke to her sons.

1   Then I heard of quarrelling of the most ill-fated sort,*
    faltering words uttered out of great grief,
    when the fierce-spirited Gudrun whetted for the fight,
    with grim words, her sons.

2   'Why do you sit, why do you sleep away your life?
    Why does it not grieve you to speak of cheerful things?
    —since Iormunrekk had your sister,
    still so young, trampled with horses,
    white and black, on the paved road,
    with the grey horses of the Goths, trained to pace slowly.

3   'You haven't become like Gunnar and his brother,
    nor any the more been brave as Hogni was—
    you would have tried to avenge her,
    if you had the temperament of my brothers
    or the fierce spirit of the Hunnish kings.'

4   Then said Hamdir, the strong-minded one:
    'Little did you praise the achievement of Hogni,
    when they awakened Sigurd from his sleep.
    Your embroidered coverlets, the blue and white ones,
    were red with your husband's blood, drenched in
        slaughter-blood.

5   'Vengeance for your brothers was wounding and painful
    to you when you murdered your sons.
    We could all have avenged on Iormunrekk*
    our sister, all of the same mind.

6   'Bring out the treasures of the kings of the Huns!
    You have stirred us up to a sword-meeting.'

7   Laughing, Gudrun went to the store-room,
    she chose from the coffers the helmets of kings,
    long mail-coats, and brought them to her sons.
    The brave men leapt on horseback.

8   Then said Hamdir, the strong-minded one:
    'So comes home to visit his mother*
    the spear-lord brought low in the land of the Goths,
    so that you may drink the funeral ale for us all,
    for Svanhild and for your sons.'

9   Weeping, Gudrun, the daughter of Giuki,
    went sorrowfully to sit on the threshold
    and to recount, with tear-wet cheeks,
    grievous stories, in many ways:

10 'Three fires have I known, three hearths have I known,
    to three husbands' houses I was brought.
    Sigurd alone for me was better than all,
    he whom my brothers brought to his death.

11   'Heavier wounds I have not seen,
      nor did they know of such;*
      yet they intended to hurt me more
      when the noble men gave me to Atli.

12   'My sharp young boys I called to secret counsel.
      I could not get remedy for my wrongs
      before I lopped off the heads of the Hniflungs.

13   'I went to the sea-strand, I was enraged with the norns;
      I wanted to reject their unyielding protection.
      Great waves lifted me, did not drown me—
      so I came to land, I had to go on living.

14   'I entered the bed—I thought it best for me—
      for the third time of a nation's king.
      I had children, legal heirs,
      legal heirs in Ionakr's sons.

15   'Then still with Svanhild sat her maids,
      the one of my children whom I loved best in my heart,
      so was Svanhild in my hall
      like a splendidly glowing sun-ray.

16   'I endowed her with gold and gorgeous garments
      before I gave her to the people of the Goths.
      That was the cruellest of all my injuries,
      when the white-blonde hair of Svanhild
      they trampled in mud under horses' hooves.

17   'And the most searing when they killed my Sigurd,
      robbed him of victory, in our bed;
      and the grimmest when the gleaming snakes
      crept towards Gunnar's life;
      and the sharpest when they cut to the heart
      of the unafraid king; they sliced into the living man.

18   'I remember many wrongs . . .

19 'Bridle, Sigurd, the dark-coloured, shining horse,
    the swift-footed charger—let it gallop here.
    Here sits neither daughter-in-law nor daughter
    who might give treasure to Gudrun.

20 'Do you recall, Sigurd, what we promised,
    when we two lay in bed together,
    that, brave warrior, you would visit me from hell,
    and I would come to you from the world?

21 'Nobles, build high the oak-wood pyre!*
    Let it be the highest among the princes.
    May fire burn up the breast so full of wrongs,
    may sorrows melt about my heart.

22 'To all warriors—may your lot be made better;
    to all ladies—may your sorrows grow less,
    now this chain of griefs has been recounted.'

THE LAY OF HAMDIR

This poem completes the story of the descendants of Gudrun with the two brothers Hamdir and Sorli dispatched by their mother to avenge the death of their sister. Thought to be amongst the oldest poems in the *Edda*, the *Lay of Hamdir* (*Hamdismal*) is defective in places; some verses are out of order, and in places the diction is strange and archaic. The story is allusively told; the brothers meet their half-brother on the way to Iormunrekk's court. He offers them help in riddling terms which they misunderstand, and they kill him. Thanks to their magical invulnerability, the brothers have surprising success in their revenge, maiming Iormunrekk and burning his severed limbs. It is only when Iormunrekk screams out the answer to their invulnerability—stoning them—that they realize why they needed their brother. He would have known to cut off the head and have silenced the king. The theme of hands and feet, the metaphor used in Erp's proverbial riddle, is taken up again in the torture scene.

1   There sprang up on the threshold grievous actions,
   to make elves weep, their joy dammed up;*
   early in the morning the wicked deeds of men,
   all kinds of miseries, kindle sorrow.

2   It was not today nor yesterday,
   a long time has passed since then,
   —few things are so long ago that this is not twice as long—
   when Gudrun born of Giuki urged
   her young sons to avenge Svanhild:

3   'She was your sister—Svanhild was her name—
   whom Iormunrekk trampled with horses,
   white and black, on the paved road,
   with the grey horses of the Goths, trained to pace slowly.

4   'You are thrust back, you great kings,
   the last living strands of my lineage.

5   'I have come to stand alone like an aspen in the forest,
    my kinsmen cut away as a fir's branches,
    bereft of happiness, as a tree of its leaves,
    when the branch-breaker comes on a warm day.'*

6   Then said Hamdir the strong-minded one:*
    'Little would you praise the achievement of Hogni,
    when they awakened Sigurd from sleep,
    you sat in the bed and the killers laughed.

7   'Your embroidered coverlets, blue and white,
    woven by craftsmen, were bathed in your husband's blood.
    There Sigurd died, you sat over the dead man,
    had no heart for happiness. That's what Gunnar thought up for
        you.

8   'Atli you intended to hurt by Erp's death
    and by the loss of Eitil, but it was even worse for you;
    every one should bring about death for others,
    with a painfully biting sword, so that he does not harm
        himself.'

9   Sorli said—he had good sense—
    'I do not want to bandy words with mother;
    each of you two thinks there's more to be said:
    what do you plead for now, Gudrun, what lack makes you weep?

10 'Weep for your brothers and your dear sons,
    close-born kinsmen, brought to strife;
    for us both, Gudrun, you shall weep too,
    we who sit here, doomed men on our horses; far from here
        we'll die.'

11 They went out of the courtyard, roaring in rage;
    the young men then travelled over the wet mountains,
    on the Hun-bred horses, to avenge the murder.

14 They met on the road a man full of clever stratagems:
   'How can this dark-haired little lad give us any help?'

12 The son of a different mother answered, said he would give
       help*
   to his kinsmen, as one foot does another.
   'How can a foot help a foot,
   or a hand grown from flesh help a hand?'

13 Then Erp said—he spoke once only—
   splendidly he pranced on the horse's back:
   'It's no good showing the way to a cowardly man.'
   They said the bastard was very bold.

15 They pulled from their sheaths the sheathed iron,
   the edges of the sword, to the joy of the troll-woman;*
   they diminished their might by a third,
   they made the young lad sink to the ground.

16 They shook their fur cloaks, fastened on their swords,
   the descendants of the gods put on splendid garments.

17 The roads stretched ahead, they found the sinister path
   and their sister's son wounded on the gallows,*
   the wind-cold wolf-tree west of the settlement;
   the incitement to cranes was bobbing about; it was not pleasant
       to remain there.

18 There was cheerful noise in the hall, men made merry with ale,
   and they did not hear the horses at all,
   until an attentive man blew his horn.

19 They went to tell Iormunrekk
   that men in helmets had been sighted:
   'Think of some plan! Mighty lords have come,
   you defied powerful men when you trampled the girl.'

20 Iormunrekk laughed then, he smoothed his moustache,
   looked forward to the violence, made battle-bold by wine;
   he tossed back his dark hair, glanced at his shining shield,
   he dangled in his hand the golden cup.

21 'Happy I'd think myself, if I were to see
   Hamdir and Sorli in my hall;
   I should tie up the boys with bow-sinews,
   string the good sons of Giuki up on the gallows.'

22 Then spoke Hrodrglod, who stood by the doors,*
   the slender-fingered woman said to that young man:
   'Now they promise what can't be achieved—
   can two men alone bind ten hundred Goths
   or fight against them in the high fortress?'

23 There was tumult in the hall, beer-cups rebounded,
   men lay in blood, shed from Goths' breasts.

24 Then said Hamdir the strong-minded:
   'You were longing, Iormunrekk, for our arrival,
   brothers born of the same mother, within your citadel.
   You see your own feet, you see your own hands,
   Iormunrekk, hurled into the hot fire.'

25 Then the man growled, he who knew powerful magic,
   the brave man in his mail-coat, growled as a bear might growl:
   'Stone the men, since spears will not bite on them,*
   neither edges nor iron, on Ionakr's sons.'

[*This said Hamdir the strong-minded*]:*

26 'Evil you brought about, brother, when you opened up that
      bag,*
   for often from the bag comes bad advice.'

27 'You'd have had a mind, Hamdir, if you had some wits;
   much is lacking in a man when he lacks common sense.'

28 'Off his head would be now, if Erp were alive,*
    our brother bold in battle, whom we killed on the road,
    the man so fierce in war—the *disir* drove us to do it—*
    the man inviolate in fighting—they spurred us to slaughter.'

29 'I don't think it is for us to follow the wolves' example
    and fight among ourselves, like the norns' bitches,
    greedy beasts, brought up in the wilderness.

30 'We have fought well, we stand on Goth corpses,
    weary from the sword-edge like eagles on a branch;
    we have won great glory if we die now or yesterday,
    no man outlasts the evening after the norns have given their
        verdict.'

31 Then Sorli fell at the hall-gable
    and Hamdir sank behind the house.

That is called the ancient 'Lay of Hamdir'.

BALDR'S DREAMS

Alarmed by Baldr's bad dreams the Æsir send Odin down to Hel to seek an explanation. At the edge of Hel's kingdom Odin awakens a dead seeress who tells him what he needs to know, that Baldr will soon be killed by his brother Hod. Odin ends the conversation by asking for a piece of mythological information which reveals his true identity to the seeress. *Baldr's Dreams* (*Baldrs draumar*), like the poems which follow it, is not found in the Codex Regius; it is preserved in manuscript A (AM 748 4to) which contains a number of fragmentary poems in eddic style.

1   All together the Æsir came in council*
    and all the Asynior in consultation,
    and what they debated, those dauntless gods,
    was why Baldr was having baleful dreams.

2   Up rose Odin, Gaut of men,*
    and on Sleipnir he laid a saddle;
    down from there he rode to Mist-hell,
    there he met a whelp coming from hell.*

3   Bloody it was on the front of its chest
    and long it barked at the father of magic;
    on rode Odin, the earth-road resounded,
    he approached the high hall of Hel.

4   Then Odin rode east of the doors,
    where he knew the seeress's grave to be;
    he began to speak a corpse-reviving spell for the magic-wise
      woman,*
    until reluctantly she rose, spoke these corpse-words:

5   'Which man is that, unknown to me,
    who makes me travel this difficult road?
    I was snowed upon, I was rained upon,
    dew fell on me, dead I've been a long time.'

6　'Way-tame is my name, I'm the son of Slaughter-tame;
　　tell me news from hell—I bring it from the world:
　　for whom are the benches decked with arm-rings,
　　is the dais so fairly strewn with gold?'

7　'Here mead stands, brewed for Baldr,
　　clear liquor; a shield hangs above,
　　and the Æsir are in dread anticipation.
　　Reluctantly I told you, now I'll be silent.'

8　'Don't be silent, seeress! I want to question you,
　　until all is known, I want to know more:
　　who will be Baldr's killer
　　and who'll rob Odin's son of life?'

9　'Hod will dispatch the high glory-tree to this place;*
　　he will be Baldr's killer
　　and rob Odin's son of his life.
　　Reluctantly I told you, now I'll be silent.'

10　'Don't be silent, seeress! I want to question you,
　　until all is known, I want to know more:
　　who'll achieve vengeance on Hod for this wickedness,
　　who'll bring Baldr's killer to the funeral pyre?'

11　'Rind will give birth to Vali in western halls,*
　　Odin's son will fight when one night old;
　　he won't wash his hands nor comb his hair
　　until he's brought to the pyre Baldr's enemy.
　　Reluctantly I told you, now I'll be silent.'

12　'Don't be silent, seeress! I want to question you,
　　until all is known, I want to know more:
　　who are those girls who weep for their pleasure*
　　and who throw up to the sky the corners of their neckerchiefs?'

13   'You are not Way-tame, as I thought,
rather you are Odin, the old Gaut.'
'You are not a seeress nor a wise woman,
rather you're the mother of three ogres.'

14   'Ride home, Odin, and be proud of yourself!
May no more men come to visit me,
until Loki is loose, escaped from his bonds,
and the Doom of the Gods, tearing all asunder, approaches.'*

THE LIST OF RIG

The *List of Rig* (*Rigsthula*) tells how the god Heimdall sets out to create the structures of human society. He calls at three houses, observes the way of life there—dull and peasant-like, skilled and practical, noble and courtly, respectively—and receives the hospitality of the couple in each house. Heimdall (Rig) sleeps between them in their bed for three nights. Later a child is born to the parents: to the first couple, Thrall, the lowest labourer; to the second couple, Farmer; to the third, Lord. These are the progenitors of each class, each marrying a suitable wife and producing a bevy of children with symbolic names to continue the line. The poem is incomplete, but the line of Lord seems to culminate in the birth of 'King', the youngest son. Where the poem breaks off, the boy destined for kingship is about to embark on conquering other territories, at the urging of a wise bird. The poem is preserved in one of the manuscripts of Snorri's *Edda* (AM 242 fol, the Codex Wormianus).

People say in old stories that one of the Æsir, the one called Heimdall, went on a journey, and as he went along the sea-shore somewhere he came to a household and he called himself Rig.* This poem is about that story.

1   Long ago they say that along the green paths
    a powerful, mature, and knowledgeable god went walking,
    mighty and vigorous, Rig stepping along.

2   Then he walked on in the middle of the road,
    he came to a house, the door was in the mortice.
    In he stepped, there was a fire on the floor;
    a couple sat there, grey-haired, by the hearth,
    Great-grandfather, and Great-grandmother
    in an old-fashioned head-dress.

3   Rig was able to give them some advice;
    then he sat in the middle of the bench,
    with the couple of the household on either side.

4   Then Great-grandmother brought a coarse loaf,*
    thick and heavy, stuffed with husks;
    and she set it among the bowls;
    broth was in the jug, she put it on the table;
    calf had been boiled in it, the best of delicacies;
    he got up from there, made ready to sleep.

5   Rig was able to give them some advice;
    then he lay in the middle of the bed,
    with the couple of the household on either side.

6   There he was for three nights together;
    then away he went in the middle of the path,
    nine months passed after that.

7   Great-grandmother had a baby, sprinkled him with water;*
    dark-skinned, they called him Thrall.

8   He began to grow and to thrive well;
    on his hands there was wrinkled skin,
    knotted knuckles, . . .
    thick fingers, he had an ugly face,
    a crooked back, long heels.*

9   Then he began to use his strength,
    to bind bast-rope to make bundles;
    brushwood he carried home the whole day long.

10 Then there came to the farm a bandy-legged girl;
    she had mud on her soles, her arms were sunburned,
    her nose bent downwards, her name was Thrall-girl.

11 Then she sat in the middle of the bench;
    the son of the house sat next to her;
    they talked and they whispered, they went to bed together,
    Thrall and Thrall-girl, day after day.

12 Children they had, they lived together and were happy;
  I think they were called Noisy and Cowshed-boy,
  Stout and Horsefly, Shagger, Smelly,
  Stumper, Fatty, Sluggard and Greyish,
  Lowbent and Longlegs; they built fences,
  put dung on the fields, looked after pigs,
  herded goats, dug the turf.

13 Their daughters were Stumpy and Dumpy,
  Bulgy-calves and Ash-nose,
  Rackety and Bondwoman, Great-gabbler,
  Raggedy-clothes and Crane-legs.
  From them are descended all the race of thralls.

14 Rig went on along the straight paths;
  he came to a hall, the door was on the latch.
  In he stepped, a fire was on the floor,
  a couple sat there; they kept on working.

15 The man was carving wood for a loom-beam.
  His beard was trimmed, his hair above his brows,
  his shirt close-fitting, a chest was on the floor.

16 There sat a woman, spinning with a distaff,
  stretching out her arms, ready to make cloth;
  a curved cap was on her head, a shirt on her breast,
  a kerchief round her neck, brooches at her shoulders.
  Grandfather and Grandmother owned the house.

17 Rig was able to give them advice;*
   . . . . .

(19) He rose from the table, made ready to sleep;
  then he lay in the middle of the bed,
  with the couple of the household on either side.

20 There he was for three nights together;
  then away he went in the middle of the path,
  nine months passed after that.

21　Grandmother had a baby, sprinkled him with water,
　　they called him Farmer, the woman swaddled him,
　　red-haired and rosy, with lively eyes.

22　He began to grow and to thrive well;
　　he tamed oxen, made a plough,
　　he built houses and threw up barns,
　　made carts and drove the plough.

23　Then they drove home the woman with keys at her belt,
　　in a goatskin kirtle, married her to Farmer,
　　Daughter-in-law she was called, she sat down in a bridal veil;
　　the couple settled down, exchanged rings,*
　　spread the bed-coverlets, made a household together.

24　Children they had, they lived together and were happy,
　　called Man and Tough-Guy, Landlord, Thane and Smith,
　　Broad, Yeoman, Boundbeard,
　　Dweller, Boddi, Smoothbeard and Fellow.

25　And these were called by other names:
　　Lass, Bride, Lady, Maiden, Damsel,
　　Dame, Miss, Mistress, Shy-girl, Sparky-girl;
　　from them descend all the race of farmers.

26　Rig went on along the straight paths;
　　he came to a hall, the doors looked south,
　　the door was half-open, the door-ring in the mortice.

27　In he stepped, the floor was strewn with straw;
　　a couple sat, gazing into one another's eyes,*
　　Father and Mother, playing with their fingers.

28　There sat the householder and twisted bow-strings,
　　strung the elm-bow, put shafts on arrows,
　　and the lady of the house was admiring her arms,
　　stroking the linen, smoothing the sleeves.

29   She straightened her head-dress, there was a coin-pendant on
          her breast,
      a trailing dress and a blue-coloured blouse;
      her brow was brighter, her breast more shining,
      her neck was whiter than pure fresh-fallen snow.

30   Rig was able to give them some advice;
      then he sat in the middle of the bench,
      with the couple of the household on either side.

31   Then Mother took a patterned cloth,
      a white one, of linen, covered the table,
      then she brought fine loaves
      white ones, of wheat-flour, and laid them on the cloth.

32   She brought in full dishes,
      chased with silver, put them on the table,
      dark and light pork-meat and roasted birds;
      wine was in the flagon, ornamented the goblets;
      they drank and they conversed, the day drew to a close.

33   Rig was able to give them some advice;
      up he rose, made ready the bed;
      there he was for three nights together;
      then away he went in the middle of the path
      nine months passed after that.

34   Mother gave birth to a boy, wrapped him in silk,
      they sprinkled him with water, had him named Lord;
      blond was his hair, bright his cheeks,
      piercing were his eyes like a young snake's.

35   Lord grew up there on the benches;
      he began to swing linden shields, fit bow-strings,
      bend the elm-bow, put shafts on arrows,
      hurl a javelin, brandish Frankish spears,
      ride horses, urge on hounds,
      wield swords, practise swimming.

36   Then out of the thicket came Rig walking,
     Rig came walking, taught him runes;
     gave him his own name, said he had a son;
     he told him to take possession of ancestral plains,
     ancestral plains, long-established settlements.

37   Then he rode from there through the dark wood,
     over frost-covered mountains, until he came to a hall,
     he brandished the shafted spear, swung his linden shield,
     made his horse gallop, wielded his sword;
     he wakened a war, began to redden the plain,
     began to fell dead men, he fought to gain lands.

38   Then he alone ruled eighteen settlements;
     he started to share his wealth, offered to everyone
     treasures and precious things, slim-ribbed horses;
     he scattered rings, hacked up arm-rings.

39   Messengers travelled over the dewy roads,
     came to the hall where Chieftain lived;
     he met there a slender-fingered girl,
     radiant and wise, they called her Erna.

40   They asked for her hand and home they drove her,
     married her to Lord, she walked under a bridal veil,
     they lived together, and were happy,
     increased the family and enjoyed their life.

41   Boy was the eldest and Child the second,
     Baby and Noble, Heir and Offspring,
     Descendant and Relative—they learned games—
     Sonny and Lad—swimming and chequers—
     Kinsman one was called, Kin was the youngest.

42   Those born to Lord grew up there,
     tamed horses, bound rims to shields,
     smoothed arrow-shafts, brandished ash spears.

43 But young Kin knew runes,*
life-runes and lifespan-runes;
and he knew how to help people,
to deaden sword-blades, quiet the ocean.

44 He learned birds' speech, to quench fires,
to pacify waters, to make sorrows disappear,
he had the strength and vigour of eight men.

45 He contended in rune-wisdom with Lord Rig,
he played more tricks, knew more than he did;
then he gained and got the right
to be called Rig and to deploy runes.*

46 Young Kin rode through woods and thickets,
he let fly a bird-bolt, charmed the birds.

47 Then a crow said—it sat alone on a branch—
'Why, young Kin, are you charming birds?*
Rather you could be riding horses,
laying low an army.

48 'Dan and Danp own splendid halls,
a better patrimony than you possess;
they know very well how to sail ships,
to test a sword blade, to rip open wounds.'

THE SONG OF HYNDLA

The *Song of Hyndla* (*Hyndluliod*) is two poems in one. The main story concerns the goddess Freyia, who is anxious to assist her protégé Ottar in gaining his inheritance against the competing claims of someone called Angantyr. In order to do this Ottar needs to know all about his ancestry. Freyia disguises him as the pig with golden bristles, Battle-hog, on which she rides and brings him to the giantess Hyndla to elicit the information he seeks. Freyia tries to flatter the giantess, calling her 'sister'; after some initial sparring the giantess settles down to recount the ancestors of Ottar, though she refuses to ride to Valhall with Freyia. At verse 29 an interpolation, often known as the *Short Prophecy of the Seeress* (*Voluspa in skamma*), begins, listing the Æsir and referring very unclearly to 'one who is greater than all' who will come after Odin, conceivably an allusion to Christ. The poem concludes with further bickering between the goddess and the giantess. Little is known about most of the figures mentioned in the *Song of Hyndla*; where more information exists it is given in the notes. The poem is preserved only in Flateyjarbók (GkS 1005 fol), a large late fourteenth-century Icelandic codex.

*This is the beginning of the 'Song of Hyndla', told about Ottar the simpleton.**

1 'Wake up, girl of girls, wake up, my friend,
   Hyndla, sister, who lives in the rock cave!
   Now it's the darkness of darknesses, we two shall ride
   to Valhall, to the sacred sanctuary.

2 'Let's ask Odin, lord of hosts, to be kindly,
   he gives and pays out gold to the deserving;
   he gave Hermod a helmet and corslet,
   and to Sigmund a sword to keep.

3 'He gives victory to some, to some riches,
   eloquence to many, and common sense to the living;
   he gives following winds to sailors, turns of phrase to poets,
   he gives manliness to many a fighter.

4 'She will sacrifice to Thor, she will ask for this,*
    that he should always behave staunchly towards you;
    though he doesn't much care for giant women.

5 'Now take one of your wolves out of the stable,*
    let him race beside my boar!'
    'Your boar is slow at treading the gods' paths;
    I don't want to overload my excellent steed.

6 'You're deceitful, Freyia, when you test me so,
    when you look at us that way,
    when you're taking your man on the road to Valhall,
    young Ottar, son of Innstein.'

7 'You're confused, Hyndla, I think you're dreaming,
    when you say my man is on the road to Valhall;
    there where my boar is glowing with his golden bristles,
    Battle-hog, whom those skilful ones,
    Dain and Nabbi, two dwarfs, made for me.*

8 'Let's contend from our saddles! We should sit down,
    and talk of princes' lineages,
    about those men who are descended from the gods.

9 'They have wagered foreign gold,
    young Ottar and Angantyr;
    it's vital to help, so that the young warrior
    should get his paternal inheritance after his kinsmen's death.

10 'He's made a sanctuary for me, faced with stone,
    now that stone has turned to glass;*
    he's reddened it with fresh ox blood,
    Ottar has always trusted in the goddesses.

11 'Now let ancient kinsmen be counted up
    and men's lineages be declared:
    who is of the Skioldungs, who is of the Skilfings,
    who is of the Odlings, who is of the Ylfings,*
    who is born of landowning stock, who is born of lordly stock,
    the greatest choice of men on the face of the earth?'

12 'You, Ottar, were son of Innstein,
and Innstein of Alf the old,
Alf of Ulf, Ulf of Sæfari,
and Sæfari from Svan the red.

13 'Your father had a mother adorned with rings,
Hledis the priestess, I think she was called;
Frodi was her father, and Friaut her mother;
all that line is thought to be most superior.

14 'Ali was previously the mightiest of men;
Halfdan before was the highest among the Skioldungs;
famous were the battles which the excellent men fought;
his deeds known far and wide under heaven's vault.

15 'He strengthened himself with Eymund, best of men,
and he killed Sigtrygg with chill sword-edges;
he married Almveig, best of women,
they had, they raised, eighteen sons.

16 'From them come the Skioldungs, from them the Skilfings,
from them the Odlings, from them the Ynglings,
from them the landowning stock, from them the lordly stock,
the greatest choice of men on the face of the earth;
all these are your kin, Ottar the simpleton.

17 'Hildigunn was her mother,*
child of Svava and the sea-king;
all these are your kin, Ottar the simpleton;
it's important that you know it, do you want to know more?

18 'Dag married Thora, mother of tough men;
the best champions were born into that lineage:
Fradmar and Gyrd and both the Frekis,
Am and Iosurmar, Alf the old;
it's important that you know it,
do you want to know more?

19 'Ketil their friend was called, Klypp's heir,
   he was your mother's maternal grandfather;
   there Frodi came before Kari,
   Alf was born as the elder son.

20 'Nanna came next, Nokkvi's daughter,
   her son was your father's in-law;
   forgotten is that inlaw-bond; I can recite further.
   I knew both Brodd and Horvir;
   all these are your kin, Ottar the simpleton.

21 'Isolf and Asolf, sons of Olmod
   and of Skurhild, Skekkil's daughter;
   you must count them among the many warriors;
   all these are your kin, Ottar the simpleton.

22 'Gunnar the bulwark, Grim the plough-maker,*
   Thorir Ironshield, Ulf the gaper.

23 'Bui and Brami, Barri and Reifnir,
   Tind and Tyrfing and the two Haddings;*
   all these are your kin, Ottar the simpleton.

24 'Ani, Omi were both born
   sons of Arngrim and Eyfura;*
   the din of all kinds of berserker-wickedness
   on land and on sea sped like flame;
   all these are your kin, Ottar the simpleton.

25 'I knew both Brodd and Horvir,
   they were retainers of Hrolf the old,
   all Iormunrekk's descendants,
   son-in-law of Sigurd—listen to my account—
   of the man fierce to enemies, who slew Fafnir.

26 'He was a prince descended from Volsung
   and Hiordis from Hraudung,*
   and Eylimi of the Odlings;
   all these are your kin, Ottar the simpleton.

27　'Gunnar and Hogni, heirs of Giuki,
　　and likewise Gudrun, their sister;
　　Guthorm was not of the line of Giuki,*
　　though he was brother of both of them;
　　all these are your kin, Ottar the simpleton.

28　'Harald Battletooth, born to Hrœrek,
　　ring-scatterer, he was son of Aud,*
　　Aud the deep-minded, daughter of Ivar,
　　and Radbard was Randver's father;
　　they were men blessed by the gods;
　　all these are your kin, Ottar the simpleton.'

29　['Eleven were the Æsir when all counted up,*
　　Baldr who slumped against a death-hummock;
　　Vali was worthy to avenge this,
　　he slew his brother's hand-killer;*
　　all these are your kin, Ottar the simpleton.

30　'Baldr's father was heir to Bur,*
　　Freyr gained Gerd, she was Gymir's daughter,
　　of the giant race, and Aurboda's,*
　　though Thiazi was their kinsman,
　　the disguise-loving giant; Skadi was his daughter.

31　'Much we tell you, we will tell you more,
　　I think that you should know it, do you want to know more?

32　'Haki was the best by far of the sons of Hvædna,
　　and Hvædna's father was Hiorvard,
　　Heid and Horse-thief were Hrimnir's children.

33　'All the seeresses are descended from Vidolf,
　　all the wizards from Vilmeid,
　　and the *seid*-practisers from Svarthofdi,*
　　all the giants come from Ymir.

34 'Much we tell you, we will tell you more,
I think that you should know it, do you want to know more?

35 'One was born in bygone days,
with mightily enhanced strength from the divine powers;
nine women bore him, the spear-magnificent man,*
giant-girls, at the edge of the earth.

36 'Much we tell you, we will tell you more,
I think that you should know it, do you want to know more?

37 'Gialp bore him, Greip bore him,
Eistla bore him and Eyrgiafa;
Ulfrun and Angeyia,
Imd and Atla and Iarnsaxa.*

38 'He was empowered with the strength of earth,
the coolness of the sea, and pigs' blood.

39 'Much we tell you, we will tell you more,
I think that you should know it, do you want to know more?

40 'Loki got the wolf on Angrboda,
and he conceived Sleipnir by Svadilfari;*
one witch seemed the most sinister of all,
she was descended from Byleist's brother.*

41 'Loki ate some heart, roasted on a linden-wood fire
a woman's thought-stone, that he found half-singed;
Lopt was impregnated by a wicked woman,*
from whom every ogress on earth is descended.

42 'The ocean rises in storms against heaven itself,
washes over the land, and the air yields;
from there come snowstorms and biting winds;
then it is decreed that the gods come to their end.

43 'One was born greater than all,
    he was empowered with the strength of earth;
    this prince is said to be the wealthiest,
    closely related to all the great houses.

44 'Then will come another, even mightier,
    though I dare not name his name;*
    few can now see further than when
    - Odin has to meet the wolf.']

45 'Give some memory-ale to my boar,*
    so that he can recount all these words,
    this conversation, on the third morning,
    when he and Angantyr reckon up their lineages.'

46 'Go away from here! I wish to sleep,
    little you get from me, few pleasant things;
    you run about, noble lady, out in the night,
    as Heidrun runs in heat among the he-goats.*

47 'You ran after Od, always full of desire,*
    many have thrust themselves under your over-skirt;
    you run about, noble lady, out in the night,
    as Heidrun runs in heat among the he-goats.'

48 'I'll surround this place with fire from the troll-woman,*
    so that you can never get away from here.'

49 'Fire I see burning and the earth aflame,
    most will submit to ransoming their lives;
    put this beer into Ottar's hand,
    mixed with a great deal of poison, to his ill fortune.'

50 'Your curse will have no effect,
    though, giant's-bride, you intend to call down evil;
    he shall drink precious liquors,
    I pray all the gods to aid Ottar.'

THE SONG OF GROTTI

The Danish king Frodi acquires on a visit to Sweden two female slaves whom he takes home to grind with the magic millstone Grotti. This would grind out whatever the grinder asked for. At first the stone ground out riches and treasure, peace and happiness, but so relentless was Frodi as an employer, refusing to allow the women any rest, that by the end of the poem they are grinding out an army to fight against him. According to Snorri, *Edda* (p. 107), a sea-king called Mysing came and overthrew Frodi. Fenia, Menia, and Grotti were taken away on his ship and made to grind out salt. They ground so much that the ship sank under the weight and that is why the sea is salt to this day—a common European fairy-tale motif. The *Song of Grotti* (*Grottasongr*) is the work-song of the two girls as they grind under Frodi's orders.

1   Now there have come to the king's dwellings
    two fore-knowing women, Fenia and Menia;
    the mighty girls were with Frodi,
    Fridleif's son, kept as slave-girls.

2   They were led to the mill-box
    and they ordered the grey stones to grind into motion;
    to neither girl did he promise rest or pleasure
    until he had heard the slave-girls' clatter.

3   They kept up the noise of the no-longer-silent mill:
    'Let's set up the mill-box, let's lift up the stones!'
    He ordered the girls again to get grinding.

4   They sang and they swung the fast-turning stone,
    while Frodi's household mostly fell asleep;
    then said Menia, who'd got down to the milling:

5   'Wealth let's mill for Frodi, mill an all-blessed state,
    mill a mass of money in the joyful millbox!
    May he sit on his wealth, may he sleep on a down-quilt,
    may he wake to happiness! Then the grinding's gone well!

6 'Here no one shall harm another,
   nor plan evil, nor plot against a life,
   nor strike with a sharp sword,
   even if he finds his brother's killer—trussed up!'

7 He said nothing, until he said this:*
   'You shan't sleep any more than the cuckoos over the hall
   nor longer than I take to sing a single song.'

8 'Frodi, you weren't entirely wise about your own interest,
   eloquent friend to men, when you bought the slave-girls;
   you chose them for their strength and their appearance,
   but you didn't ask about their lineage.

9 'Hrungnir was stern, as was his father,
   though Thiazi was mightier than they;
   Idi and Aurnir, our close kinsmen,
   mountain-giants' brothers, we're descended from them.

10 'Grotti would not have come out of the grey mountain,
   nor the hard boulder out of the earth,
   nor would the mountain-giant girl keep grinding so,
   if we had known nothing about it.

11 'Nine winters we were playmates,
    strong girls, brought up under the earth;
    the girls were doers of mighty deeds,
    we ourselves moved the mountain-seat from its place.

12 'We rolled the boulder over the giants' dwelling
    so that the earth in front of it began shaking;
    we swung the fast-turning stone,
    the heavy boulder, so that men seized it.*

13 'And afterwards in Sweden,
    we two fore-sighted ones advanced in the army;
    we challenged bearlike warriors, we smashed shields,
    we marched through the grey-corsleted army.

14 'We overthrew one prince, we supported another one,
we gave good Gothorm help;
there was no sitting quiet until Knui fell.

15 'So we went on for some seasons,
so that we were acclaimed as champions;
there we scored with sharp spears
blood out of wounds and reddened the sword.

16 'Now we have come to the king's dwellings
we two without mercy, and are kept as slaves,
mud eats away at our feet, chilled through is the rest of us,
we drag the strife-calmer; it's dull at Frodi's.*

17 'Hands shall rest, the stone stand still,
I have ground out my full share.'
'Now our hands will be given no proper rest
until it seems to Frodi we've milled it all out.'

18 'Hands shall grip hard shafts,
slaughter-stained weapons; wake up, Frodi!
Wake up, Frodi, if you want to hear
our songs and our ancient tales.

19 'I see fire burning east of the fortress,
news of war awakening, that's known as a beacon;
an army will come here very shortly,
and burn down the settlement despite the prince.

20 'You shan't hold onto the throne of Lejre,
nor the red-gold rings, nor this magical millstone.
Let's grasp the handle, girl, more tightly!
We're not frozen stiff in slaughtered men's blood.

21 'My father's daughter ground fiercely
for she saw a warrior-multitude's doom;
the great supports snapped away from the mill-box,
enclosed in iron, let's grind further!

22   'Let's grind further! Yrsa's son
     takes vengeance on Frodi with the Half-Danes;
     he'll be famed as both her son
     and brother; as we two know.'*

23   The girls ground, they tested out their strength,
     the young girls were in a giant rage;
     the wooden mill-shafts shuddered, the mill-box collapsed,
     the heavy grindstone broke in two.

24   And the mountain-giant woman spoke these words:
     'We've ground, Frodi, to the point where we must stop,
     the women have done a full stint of milling!'

GROA'S CHANT

This poem and the one which follows together constitute the story of Svipdagr (*Svipdagsmal*). The two poems are found together in at least forty-six late manuscripts, and they seem to represent a later medieval attempt at composing a new eddic poem, independent of the myths and legends found in the Codex Regius, though making use of motifs and names found there. In the first poem, Svipdag visits the grave-mound of his dead mother Groa to ask her for help. His stepmother laid a curse upon him when he lost to her at a board-game they were playing and he must now go on a dangerous wooing journey. Compare the dialogues of Freyia and Hyndla in the *Song of Hyndla*, and of *Brynhild's Ride to Hell* for other encounters between the living and the dead.

Svipdag:

1 'Wake up Groa! wake excellent lady!
I awaken you at the doors of the dead.
If you remember, you invited your son
to come to the grave-mound.'

Groa:

2 'What is it now troubles my only son?
What evil has come upon you
when you call on your mother who has turned to dust
and has passed away from the homes of men?'

Svipdag:

3 'An ugly game the malicious woman has pushed me into—*
that one who put her arms around my father—
she has ordered me to go where she knows there's no going,
to see Menglod.'

Groa:

4 'Long is the journey, long are the pathways,
long are men's desires—
if it happens that you gain your wish,
then Skuld will dispose in accord with the fates.'*

Svipdag:

5 'Chant me some chants—those which are good ones,
mother, save your son!
It will be all up with me on the journey,
I think I am too young a lad for this.'

Groa:

6 'This first one I will chant for you: they say this one is very
useful,
this one Rind sang for Rani:*
so you may shrug off from your shoulder anything that seems
fearful to you—
you must be your own guide.

7 'This second one I will chant for you: if you must go on this
errand,
whether you like it or not;
may Urd's charms keep you safe on all sides*
when you are on your way!

8 'This third one I will chant for you: if mighty rivers
threaten your life as they fall—
may Horn and Rud turn back towards hell*
and always diminish up before you.

9 'This fourth one I will chant for you: if your enemies lie in wait
on the gallows-path,
may their spirits swerve into your keeping
and their minds turn to reconciliation.

10 'This fifth one I will chant for you:* if a fetter is bound about
your limbs—
A loosing-spell I'll have called out
over your calves so the manacle drops from your arms
and the fetter from your feet.

11 'This sixth one I will chant for you: if you come to the sea,
running higher than men can stand,
    may calm and quiet ocean run together for you in the mill-box*
    and may more peaceful voyages lie ahead for you.

12 'This seventh one I will chant for you: if frost assails you
up on the mountain height,
    may no corpse-cold come to ravage your flesh
    nor bind your body in its joints.

13 'This eighth one I will chant for you: lest night overtake you in
the open
    out on a misty path,
    so that it's inconceivable that she might do you harm—
    a dead Christian woman.*

14 'This ninth one I will chant for you:
in case you have to bandy words
    with the spear-magnificent giant:*
    may eloquence and good sense
    come into mouth and heart,
    and you be granted enough of both.

15 'Never now go where peril seems poised ahead;
may no wickedness bar you from your desires!
    I stood within the doors by an earth-fast stone,
    while I chanted these chants for you.

16 'Your mother's words, take, son, from here,
and let them settle in your breast;
    endless good fortune you'll have all your life long,
    while you keep my words in mind.'

THE SAYINGS OF FIOLSVINN

Having gained supernatural protection from his dead mother, Svipdag successfully makes his way to Menglod's hall. Outside he meets the giant Fiolsvinn who bars his way and sets a series of conditions for him to enter. These have a neat circularity: Svipdag can only get past the gates if he can pacify the guard-dogs with meat from the cock Vidofnir, but the only weapon which can kill the bird is in the possession of a giantess. And she in turn will only yield that weapon in exchange for a scythe which lies inside the cock's body. Svipdag's quest looks to be frustrated, but the revelation of his identity allows him to overcome the impasse and he is admitted to Menglod's presence.

1   From outside the walls he saw rising up
     the ogre-people's dwelling-place.

Svipdag:

    'What kind of monster is that who stands before the outer courts,
    and lurks at the dangerous flame?'

Fiolsvinn:

2   'Who are you looking for, for whom are you questing?
     What, friendless man, do you want to know?
     Over the dewy roads make your way back,
     you can't stay here, defenceless man!'

Svipdag:

3   'What kind of monster is that who stands before the outer court
     and offers no welcome to travellers?'

Fiolsvinn:

    'Bereft of fitting speech you've lived, man,
    go on home from here!'*

Fiolsvinn:

4   'Much-wise I'm called and I've a wise mind indeed,*
    though I'm not over-generous with food;
    within these walls you will never come—
    so be off now, wolf, on your way!'

Svipdag:

5   'For the eyes' delight scarcely a man is not eager,
    wherever he can see what's lovely;
    these courts glow, it seems to me, round the golden halls—
    I would love to make my home here.'

Fiolsvinn:

6   'Tell me, boy, of whom you are born,*
    which man's son are you?'

Svipdag:

    'Wind-cold I'm called, Spring-cold was my father,
    and Very-cold was his.'

Svipdag:

7   'Tell me, Much-wise, because I'm asking you,
    and because I want to know;
    who rules here—who has power—
    over the property and its wealth-filled halls?'

Fiolsvinn:

8   'Menglod she's called, her mother conceived her
    by Svafrthorin's son;
    she rules here—she has power—
    over the property and its wealth-filled halls.'

Svipdag:

9 'Tell me, Much-wise, because I'm asking you,
   and because I want to know;
   what is that gate called? Amidst the gods no men ever saw
   a greater peril than this.'

Fiolsvinn:

10 'Noise-clang it's called, and three men made it,
   the sons of Sun-blind;
   a strong fetter chains every journeying man
   who lifts it out from its place.'*

Svipdag:

11 'Tell me, Much-wise, because I'm asking you,
   and because I want to know;
   what is that wall called? Amidst the gods no men ever saw
   a greater peril than this.'

Fiolsvinn:

12 'Gastropnir it is called, and I made it
   out of Clay-surf's limbs;*
   I have buttressed it so that it will stand for ever
   as long as men exist.'

Svipdag:

13 'Tell me, Much-wise, because I'm asking you,
   and because I want to know;
   what are these dogs called who prowl ravenously about?'
   . . .*

Fiolsvinn:

14 'One is called Gifr, and the other Geri*
   if you would know;
   they will guard for eternity that which they guard
   until the Powers are torn apart.'

Svipdag:

15 'Tell me, Much-wise, because I'm asking you,
and because I want to know;
is there any man who could come in here
while the battle-brave ones are sleeping?'*

Fiolsvinn:

16 'Very different sleep-shifts were strictly established for them,
once guard-duty was assigned them;
one sleeps by night, and the other by day,
and nothing that comes there comes in.'

Svipdag:

17 'Tell me, Much-wise, because I'm asking you,
and because I want to know;
is there any food which men might give them
so they could run right in while they're eating?'

Fiolsvinn:

18 'Two bits of wing-meat there are in Vidofnir's limbs,*
if you want to know;
that's the only food which men might give them
so they could run right in while they're eating.'

Svipdag:

19 'Tell me, Much-wise, because I'm asking you,
and because I want to know;
what that tree is called which stretches out its boughs
over every land?'

Fiolsvinn:

20 'The wood of Mimi it is called and no man knows*
from where its roots run;
it will fall by something which very few expect:
neither fire nor iron will destroy it.'

Svipdag:

21 'Tell me, Much-wise, because I'm asking you,
    and because I want to know;
    what stems from the nature of this famous tree,
    which neither fire nor iron will destroy?'

Fiolsvinn:

22 'Some of its fruit should be thrown into the flames
    when suffering women are there;*
    outward will appear what they may inwards conceal—
    this is the Measuring-Tree among men.'

Svipdag:

23 'Tell me, Much-wise, because I'm asking you,
    and because I want to know;
    what is the cockerel called who roosts in the tall tree?
    He glows all with gold.'

Fiolsvinn:

24 'Vidofnir he's called and he roosts in Weatherglass,
    on the branches of Mimi's tree;
    with one sorrow alone he crushes unbearably
    Sinmara, with agony.'*

Svipdag:

25 'Tell me, Much-wise, because I'm asking you,
    and because I want to know;
    is there some weapon which could make Vidofnir plunge
    into the dwellings of Hel?'

Fiolsvinn:

26 'Malice-twig it's called, Loki uprooted it
    down below the corpse-gates;
    it lies in Segjarn's cauldron, at Sinmara's
    sealed with nine mighty locks.'

Svipdag:

27   'Tell me, Much-wise, because I'm asking you,
       and because I want to know;
       will that man come back who goes in search of it
       and intends to seize that twig?'

Fiolsvinn:

28   'Back he'll come—the one who goes in search of it,
       and intends to seize that twig—
       if he can bring that thing which few possess
       to Aurglasir's goddess.'*

Svipdag:

29   'Tell me, Much-wise, because I'm asking you,
       and because I want to know;
       is there some splendid thing which men could obtain
       and which would gladden the pale giantess?'

Fiolsvinn:

30   'A gleaming scythe, you must bear into the container,*
       the one lying in Vidofnir's joints,
       you must give it Sinmara before she's ready to consent
       to bestow on you a weapon for slaughter.'

Svipdag:

31   'Tell me, Much-wise, because I'm asking you,
       and because I want to know;
       what that hall is called which is encompassed
       with knowing, flickering flame?'*

Fiolsvinn:

32   'Lyr it's called, and a long time it will
       quake on a spike's tip;*
       this treasure-store is one which through all the ages
       men will only know by repute.'

Svipdag:

33 'Tell me, Much-wise, because I'm asking you,
and because I want to know;
who of the sons of the Æsir made that thing I can see
within the enclosure?'

Fiolsvinn:

34 'Uni and Iri, Iari and Bari,
Var and Vegdrasil,
Dori and Ori—and Delling was there too,
the completer of the lookout.'*

Svipdag:

35 'Tell me, Much-wise, because I'm asking you,
and because I want to know;
what that rock is called where I see an unmoving woman,
a most-glorious lady?'

Fiolsvinn:

36 'Healing-mountain it's called—for a long time the joy
of a poorly and pain-ridden woman;
every woman becomes well, even if she's barren,
if she can clamber up it.'*

Svipdag:

37 'Tell me, Much-wise, because I'm asking you,
and because I want to know;
what are those girls called who sit peaceably together
at Menglod's knees?'

Fiolsvinn:

38 'Hlif is one, a second one is Hlifthrasa,
Thiodvar is the third;
Bright and Look, Happy and Peaceful,
Eir and Aurboda.'*

Svipdag:

39 'Tell me, Much-wise, because I'm asking you,
    and because I want to know;
    whether they protect those who sacrifice to them
    if there is need of this?'

Fiolsvinn:

40 'The wise women give protection, wherever men sacrifice to them,
    in an altar-hallowed place;
    no matter how dire the peril that comes upon men's sons,
    they save them from their straits.'

Svipdag:

41 'Tell me, Much-wise, because I'm asking you,
    and because I want to know;
    whether there might be any man who may slumber
    in the sweet arms of Menglod?'

Fiolsvinn:

42 'No man at all may slumber in the sweet arms of Menglod,
    except for Svipdag alone;
    for him the sun-bright lady is
    destined as his bride.'

Svipdag:

43 'Fling open the doors! Open wide the gates!
    For here you see Svipdag indeed!
    But go and discover if Menglod may desire
    my happiness.'

Fiolsvinn:

44 'Hear, Menglod! A man has come here,
    come and see the guest!
    The dogs fawn around him, the house has opened of its own
        accord;
    I think that this is Svipdag!'

Menglod:

45 'Wise ravens will pick out your eyes
    on the high gallows,
    if you lie about this: that a young man has journeyed
    the long distance to my halls.

46 'From where have you come, from where begun your journey,
    what do your kinfolk call you?
    Of your lineage and name I must see true token
    if I was destined to be your wife.'

Svipdag:

47 'Svipdag I'm called, Sun-bright is my father;
    I've wandered wind-cold ways from there;
    no man can overcome Urd's decree—
    even if it's been shamefully laid down.'*

Menglod:

48 'Welcome now to you! I have gained my desire—
    and my kiss must go with my greeting;
    a surpassing sight will gladden everyone
    who is in love with another.

49 'A long time I sat on Healing-rock,
    waiting day after day for you;
    but now it's come to pass, what I hoped for,
    that you've come, young man, to my halls.

50 'Torments I've endured to make love with you,
    just as you've had in desiring me;
    now it is truly so that together we will
    live fully out life and time.'*

THE WAKING OF ANGANTYR

Preserved in *Heidreks saga*, this poem tells how Hervor, Angantyr's daughter, braves the ghost-filled burial-mound of her father and his eleven brothers. The brothers were berserks who had been slain on the Danish island of Samsø by the heroes Hialmarr and Arrow-Odd, despite Angantyr's possession of Tyrfing, a magical sword. Hervor dresses as a man and calls herself by a man's name, Hervard. Leading a band of vikings she anchors off Samsø, but the men refuse to set foot on the haunted island after sun-set. Hervor/Hervard determines to visit her father's mound alone. Angantyr surrenders the sword only grudgingly, warning that the weapon bears a curse which will play out in future generations.

1   The young girl met at Munar-bay,
      at sun-set a man with his flock.

The shepherd said:

2   'Who has come alone to the island?
      Quickly! Look for some lodging!'

Hervor said:

3   'I shan't go to any lodging,
      because I know none of the island-dwellers;
      tell me swiftly before you go from here:
      where are the burial mounds named for Hiorvard?'

The shepherd said:

4   'Don't ask about this, you are not wise!
      Vikings' friend, you've gone badly astray;
      let's flee as fast as our feet will take us—
      all out here is horrible to humans!'

Hervor said:

5   'A neck-ring I'll give you to pay for your speech,
      the warriors' friend won't easily be dissuaded:
      no one could give me such splendid treasures,
      rings so lovely, that I would not go there.'

The shepherd said:

6 'Foolish seems to me anyone who journeys here,
   a person alone, in the dark shadows of night;
   flames are flickering, the mounds are opening,
   solid ground and marshland burning—let's go more swiftly
      still!'

Hervor said:

7 'Let's not tremble at such snorting,
   even if all the isle's aflame!
   Let's not—on account of dead men—
   soon start shaking; we must talk about it.'

8 The shepherd speedily went off to the woods,
   left his conversation with the girl.
   But Hervor's hard-forged spirit
   swelled in her breast at such happenings.

*Now she saw the mound-flames and a mound-dweller standing outside;
she walked up to the mounds and was not at all frightened; she slipped
through the fire as if it were smoke. Then she said:*

9 'Wake up, Angantyr! Hervor awakens you,
   Svafa's only daughter and yours.
   Give me from the grave the cutting blade,
   the one dwarfs forged for Svafrlami.*

10 'Hervard, Hiorvard, Hrani, Angantyr!
    I awaken you all, under the roots of the tree,
    with helmet and corslet, with sharp sword,
    shield and war-gear, with blood-reddened spear.

11 'Sons of Arngrim, violent-minded young men,
    you've really become nothing but dust,
    if not one of Eyfura's sons*
    will talk to me here in Munar-bay.

12   'May you all be devoured from within your ribs
      as if you were shrivelling up in an ant-heap!
      Unless you give me the sword that Dvalin forged;
      it's not good for ghosts to hide away worthy weapons.'

Then Angantyr answered:

13   'Hervor, daughter, why do you call out so?
      Risking danger-runes, you are heading for disaster!
      You are mad, you are out of your wits,
      your thinking's awry, to awaken dead men!

14   'My father did not bury me, nor other kinsmen.
      Two men still living, they had Tyrfing,
      though one alone later became the owner.'*

She said:

15   'You do not tell me the truth: so may the God then leave you*
      safe inside the mound, if you don't have
      Tyrfing with you! Unwilling you are
      to offer one boon to your heir.'

*Then it seemed as if a spurt of flame flashed all round the mounds which
stood open. Then Angantyr said:*

16   'Hel-gate is lowered, the graves have opened,
      the island's surface is seen all aflame;
      it is terrible to be outside, to see this thing.
      Hurry, girl, if you can, back to your ships!'

She said:

17   'You cannot so kindle pyres by night,
      that I will be frightened by your flames;
      this girl's spirit-enclosure isn't shuddering*
      though she sees an undead man stand by the doors.'

Then Angantyr said:

18   'I tell you, Hervor, listen for a while to what I say,
        prince's daughter, for it will come true;
        Tyrfing will, if you may believe it,
        destroy your kindred, girl, utterly.

19   'You'll bear a son and he will afterwards
        wield Tyrfing and trust in its strength;
        Heidrek people will call him—
        reared the mightiest man under the sky's tent.'*

She said:

20   'I determine it thus, worthy dead men,
        that you will never manage to lie quietly
        dead with the ghosts, decaying in the mound;
        unless you give me out of the grave
        the danger to shields, Hialmar's killer!'

Angantyr said:

21   'Young girl, I declare you are not like most men,
        hanging around mounds by night,
        with an engraved spear and in metal of the Goths,*
        a helmet and corslet before the hall-doors.'

She said:

22   'I thought myself man enough for this,
        before I decided to come and visit your hall;
        Give me from the mound that hater of mail-shirts,*
        the dwarf-crafted weapon! It won't help if you hide it!'

Angantyr said:

23   'Hialmar's killer lies under my shoulders,
        it's all encompassed with flame,
        I know of no girl anywhere on earth,
        who'd dare take that sword in her hand.'

She said:

24 'I will keep it and take it in my hands,
     that biting blade, if I could have it;
     I'm not afraid of the blazing fire—
     for the flame dies down when I look at it.'

He said:

25 'Foolish you are, Hervor, though you surely have spirit,
     that you rush into the fire with eyes wide open;
     rather I'll give you the sword from the mound,
     young girl, I cannot refuse you.'

She said:

26 'You did well, descendant of vikings,
     when you gave me the sword from the mound;
     it seems better to me, brave lord, to have it,
     than if I were to seize all Norway.'

He said:

27 'You don't know—sorry is what you say,
     most disastrous woman—why you should rejoice.
     That sword Tyrfing will, if you can believe it,
     destroy your kindred, girl, utterly.'

She said:

28 'I will go to my gulf-horses;*
     now the princely girl is in good spirits:
     it doesn't much frighten me, great lords' descendant,
     how later my sons will strive against one another.'

He said:

29 'You will own it and enjoy it a long time,
     keep Hialmar's killer in its sheath;
     don't touch its edges, there's poison in both of them;
     that's a man's fate-measurer, sharper than sickness.

30 'Farewell, daughter! willingly I'd give you
    twelve men's lives, if you can believe it,
    strength and determination, all the good things
    that Arngrim's sons left behind them.'

She said:

31 'May you all dwell —I'm off away now—
    safe in the mound! I'll go quickly.
    For now I thought most of all that I was between worlds
    when these flames blazed all about me.'

APPENDIX

THE SEERESS'S PROPHECY (HAUKSBÓK TEXT)

In addition to the version found in the Codex Regius manuscript and printed first in this volume, the *Seeress's Prophecy* (*Voluspa*) is also found in a variant version in Hauksbók, a large, early fourteenth-century compendium of prose and verse written for Haukr Erlendsson, a prominent Icelandic official. The *Seeress's Prophecy* has many verses in common with the Codex Regius version, but it also differs significantly, both in order and in content. The manuscript is difficult to read in places, particularly in the verses describing the gods' final battles. The major differences between the texts are signalled in the Explanatory Notes.

1   Hearing I ask from all the holy tribes,
      greater and lesser, the offspring of Heimdall;
      do you wish me to declare Woe-father's deception,*
      living beings' ancient stories, those I remember
      from furthest back?

2   I remember giants born early in time,
      those nurtured me long ago;
      I remember nine worlds, I remember nine giant women,
      the mighty Measuring-Tree below the earth.

3   Early in time Ymir made his settlement,
      there was no sand nor sea nor cool waves;
      earth was nowhere nor the sky above,
      a void of yawning chaos, grass was there nowhere

4   before the sons of Bur brought up the land-surface,
      who shaped glorious Midgard;
      the sun shone from the south on the stone-hall,
      then the ground was grown over with the green leek.

5   From the south, Sun, companion of the moon,
      threw her right hand round the sky's edge;
      Sun did not know where she had her hall,
      the stars did not know where they had their stations,
      the moon did not know what might he had.

6   Then all the Powers went to the thrones of fate,
the sacrosanct gods, and considered this:
to night and her children they gave names,
morning they named and midday,
afternoon and evening, to reckon up in years.

7   The Æsir met on Idavoll Plain,
they tried their strength, they tested everything;
they set up their forges, smithed precious things,
shaped tongs and made tools.

8   They played chequers in the meadow, they were merry,
they did not lack for gold at all,
until three ogre-girls came,
all-powerful women, out of Giant-land.

9   Then all the Powers went to the thrones of fate,
the sacrosanct gods, and considered this:
who should create the dwarf-folk
out of Brimir's blood and from Blain's limbs?

10   Then Motsognir became most famous of
all dwarfs, and Durin next;
They made many manlike figures,*
dwarfs out of the earth, as Durin recounted.

11   New-moon and Dark-of-moon, North and South,
East and West, Master-thief, Dvalin,
Corpse and Nain, Niping and Dain,
Liquor and Staff-elf, Wind-elf and Thorin.

12   Bivor, Bavor, Bombur, and Nori,
An and Anar, Great-grandfather and Mead-wolf,
Thrar and Thrainn, Thror, Colour and Wise,
New and New-advice: now I have rightly
—Regin and Counsel-clever—reckoned up the warriors.

13 Fili and Kili, Foundling and Nali,
    Haft and Vili, Hanar and Svid,
    Corpse and Nain, Niping and Dain,
    Billing, Bruni, Bild and Buri,
    Frar and Forn-bogi, Fræg and Sea-pool.

14 Loam-field, Iari, Oakenshield.
    Time it is to tally up the dwarfs in Dvalin's troop,
    for the children of men, to trace them back to Lofar;
    for those who sought out from Hall-Stone,
    the dwelling of Loam-field on Ior-vellir.

15 There were Draupnir and Dolgthrasir,
    Greyhair, Mound-river, Lee-wolf, Glow,
    Skirvir, Virvir, Skafid, and Great-grandfather,
    Elf and Yngvi, Oakenshield.

16 They'll be remembered while the world endures,
    the long list of ancestors, going back to Lofar.

17 Until three ogre-girls came . . .*
    loving and strong Æsir to that house;
    they found on land, capable of little,
    Ash and Embla, lacking in fate.

18 Breath they had not, spirit they had not,
    blood nor bearing nor fresh complexions;
    breath gave Odin, spirit gave Hænir,
    blood gave Lodur, and fresh complexions.

19 An ash I know that stands, Yggdrasill it's called,
    a tall tree, drenched with shining loam;
    from there come the dews which fall in the valley,
    green, it stands always over Urd's well.

20 From there come girls, knowing a great deal,
    three from the hall standing under the tree;*
    Urd one is called, Verdandi another—
    they carved on a wooden slip—Skuld the third.

21   They laid down laws, they chose lives
for the sons of men, fates to be told.

22   Then all the Powers went to the thrones of fate,
the sacrosanct gods, and considered this:
which one had troubled the air with treachery,
or given Od's girl to the giant race.

23   Thor alone struck a blow there, swollen with rage,
he seldom sits still when he hears such a thing;
the oaths broke apart, words and promises,
all the solemn pledges which had passed between them.

24   She knows that Heimdall's hearing is hidden
under the bright-grown, sacred tree;
she sees, flowing down, the loam-filled flood
from Father of the Slain's pledge—do you want to
know more: and what?*

25   In the east dwells the old woman in Iron-wood
and gives birth there to Fenrir's offspring;
one of them in trollish shape
shall be snatcher of the moon.

26   It gluts itself on doomed men's lives,
reddens the gods' dwellings with crimson blood;
sunshine becomes black all the next summers,
weather all vicious—do you want to know more: and what?*

27   She remembers the first war in the world,*
when Gullveig was stuck with spears
and in the High One's hall they burned her;
three times they burned her, three times burned her,
three times she was reborn,
over and over, yet she lives still.

28   Bright One they called her, wherever she came to houses,
and the seer with pleasing prophecies, she practised spirit-magic;
she performed *seid* where she could,
seid she performed, the entranced one,
she was always a wicked woman's favourite.

29 Then all the Powers went to the thrones of fate,
    the sacrosanct gods, and considered this:
    whether the Æsir should yield the tribute
    or whether all the gods should share sacrificial feasts.

30 Odin hurled a spear, sped it into the host;
    that was war still, the first in the world;
    the wooden rampart of the Æsir's stronghold was wrecked;
    the Vanir, with a war-spell, kept on trampling the plain.

31 Then oppressive bonds of Vali could be twisted,*
    rather severe fetters, made of entrails.
    There sits Sigyn, getting very little
    joy from her husband—do you want to know more: and what?

32 Garm bays loudly before Gnipa-cave,
    the fetter will break and the ravener run free,
    I see further ahead, much wisdom I can utter*
    about the mighty Doom of the Gods, of the victory-gods.

33 He sat on the mound and struck his harp,
    the giantess's herdsman, cheerful Eggther;
    there crowed above in Gallows-wood,
    that bright-red rooster who is called Fialar.

34 Golden-comb crowed over the Æsir,
    he wakens the warriors at Father of Hosts' hall;
    and another crows below the earth,
    a sooty-red cock in the halls of Hel.

35 A hall she sees standing far from the sun,
    on Corpse-strand; its doors look north;
    poison-drops fall in through the roof-vents,
    the hall is woven of serpents' spines.

36 There she sees wading in turbid streams
    false-oath swearers and murderers,
    and the seducer of another man's close confidante;
    there Nidhogg sucks the corpses of the dead—
    a wolf tears at men—do you want to know more: and what?

37   Now Garm bays loudly before Gnipa-cave,
     the fetter will break and the ravener run free.

38   Brother will fight brother and become each other's slayer,
     sister's sons will violate the kinship-bond;
     hard it is in the world, whoredom abounds,
     axe-age, sword-age, shields are cleft asunder,

39   wind-age, wolf-age, before the world plunges headlong;
     the depths resound, the troll-woman goes flying;
     no man will spare another.

40   The sons of Mim are at play and the Measuring-Tree is
       kindled;
     on the ancient Giallar-horn
     Heimdall blows loudly, his horn is in the air.
     Odin speaks with Mim's head.

41   Yggdrasill's ash shudders, standing upright,
     the ancient tree groans and the giant gets loose;
     terrified are all on the roads to hell,
     before Surt's kinsman swallows that one up.*

42   What disturbs the Æsir? What disturbs the elves?
     All Giant-land is roaring. The Æsir are in council.
     The dwarfs groan before their rocky doors,
     wise ones of the mountain wall—do you want to know more:
       and what?

43   Garm bays loudly before Gnipa-cave,
     the fetter will break and the ravener run free.

44   Hrym drives from the east, heaves his shield before him,
     the great serpent writhes in giant rage;
     the serpent churns the waves, the eagle shrieks in anticipation,
     pale-beaked he rips the corpse, Naglfar breaks free.

45   A ship journeys from the east, Muspell's troops are coming
     over the ocean, and Loki steers.
     All the giant-sons advance along with the ravener,
     Byleist's brother goes in company with them.

46 Surt comes from the south with branches-ruin,
the slaughter-gods' sun glances from his sword;
rocky cliffs clash together and the troll-women are abroad,
heroes tread the hell-road and the sky splits apart.

47 Then Frigg's second sorrow comes about
when Odin advances to fight against the wolf,
and Beli's bright slayer against Surt;
then Frigg's dear-beloved must fall.

48 Now Garm bays loudly before Gnipa-cave,
the fetter will break and the ravener run free.

49 Above in the air yawns the Earth-serpent,
the terrible serpent's jaws gape in the heights.
Odin's son will meet the serpent
after the [death] of the wolf and Vidar's kinsman.*

50 . . . *

51 The sun turns black, land sinks into the sea,
the bright stars vanish from the sky;
steam rises up and the conflagration,
hot flame plays high against heaven itself.

52 Now Garm bays loudly before Gnipa-cave,
the fetter will break and the ravener run free.

53 She sees, coming up a second time,
earth from the ocean, eternally green;
the waterfalls plunge, an eagle soars above them,
over the mountain hunting fish.

54 The Æsir meet on Idavoll
and they converse about the mighty Earth-girdler,
and they remember there the great events
and Fimbultyr's ancient runes.

55 Then the Æsir will find the wonderful
golden chequers in the grass,
those which they possessed in the bygone days.

56 Without sowing the fields will grow,
   all evil will be healed, Baldr will come;
   Hod and Baldr settle in Hropt's victory-homesteads
   the golden-gods are well—do you want to know more: and
   what?*

57 Then Hænir will choose a wooden slip for prophecy,
   and two brothers' sons build a settlement
   in the wide wind-realm—do you want to know more: and what?

58 A hall she sees standing, fairer than the sun,
   thatched with gold, at Gimle;
   there the noble fighting-bands will dwell
   and enjoy the days of their lives in pleasure.

59 Then comes the mighty one*
   to the judgment of the Powers,
   full of strength, from above,
   he who rules over all.

60 The shadow-dark dragon comes flying,
   the gleaming serpent, up from kinsmen;
   Nidhogg flies over the plain, in his pinions
   he carries corpses; now she will sink down.

EXPLANATORY NOTES

Readers are also referred to the Annotated Index of Names, pp. 323–47. The numbers in the left-hand column refer to the verse numbers in the text.

THE SEERESS'S PROPHECY

1 *offspring of Heimdall*: the offspring of Heimdall are the different classes of humankind (see the *List of Rig* below). The 'sacred people' in l. 1 are the gods.

2 *nine giant women*: who these may be is not certain, though nine giantesses are listed as mothers of a 'spear-magnificent man' in *Song of Hyndla*, vv. 35–7. This is probably Heimdall, who is said to have had nine mothers in Snorri, *Edda*, pp. 25–6.

3 *Ymir*: the primeval being, according to this poem. In *Grimnir's Sayings*, vv. 40–1, Odin describes how the universe was created out of Ymir's dismembered body.

4 *the sons of Bur*: Odin and his brothers, Vili and Ve. Bur was the son of Buri, a being licked out of the primeval ice by Audhumla, the first cow, according to Snorri, *Edda*, p. 11.

8 *three ogre-girls*: who these girls might be is not at all clear. They seem to be inimical to the gods and their appearance marks the end of the Golden Age. Some critics have identified them as the fates who appear in v. 20.

9 *Brimir*: probably identical with Ymir. *Brim* normally means 'ocean', *blain* the 'dark or black one'.

10 *the dwarfs made*: once Motsognir and Durin are created, they make further dwarfs. In the Hauksbók version, the gods are responsible for the genesis of all dwarfs.

11 *New-moon and Dark-of-moon*: this list of dwarf-names cannot be original to the poem; the dwarfs have no further role in the *Seeress's Prophecy* and the catalogue is disproportionately long.

17 *until three gods*: one or more verses must be missing from before v. 17. The three gods are Odin, Hænir, and Lodur. Little is known of Hænir, though he returns after Ragnarok, and still less about Lodur, who is mentioned only here and in a couple of kennings. Odin and Hænir are found journeying together, accompanied by Loki, at the beginning of the gods' contest with Thiazi, Skadi's father (Snorri, *Edda*, p. 59). Earlier in Snorri's account of the creation of humanity, it is the sons of Bur (Odin, Vili, and Ve) who give life to mankind (Snorri, *Edda*, p. 13). Nor is it clear whose house it is that the gods come to.

Ash and Embla: Ash and Embla (elm? vine?) are two pieces of driftwood washed up on the shore.

19 *Urd's well*: the well of fate; Snorri, *Edda*, p. 17, assigns a well to each of Yggdrasill's three roots. Urd's well is located in Asgard.

22 *She*: throughout the poem the pronoun used to denote the speaker varies between 'I' and 'she'. It seems most likely that they refer to a single seeress.

High-One: Odin.

23 *Bright One*: (*Heid*) is usually thought to be a hypostasis of Freyia, like Gullveig in the previous verse. Freyia is said to be skilled in *seid* (a particular shape-changing form of magic). Heid also has shaman-like powers, employing spirits (*gandar*), the other important ritual practice mentioned in Old Norse sources. The raising of spirits is associated with the kinds of shamanistic ritual usually ascribed to the Lapps. The Vanir thus manifest themselves both in the divine and the human worlds, demanding a share of sacrifice (v. 24). The Æsir at first go to war over this but eventually concede the tribute.

26 *Od's girl*: Freyia, who is married to Od.

28 *Father of the Slain's pledge*: both Heimdall, watchman of the gods, and Odin have left some body part in the well. Odin exchanged one of his eyes for wisdom from Mimir, guardian of the well, while Heimdall seems to have forfeited his ear.

31 *She saw valkyries*: Odin's warrior-maidens whose duties include choosing those doomed to die in battle, and serving the horns of mead in Valhall. See also Introduction, pp. xvi–xvii.

33 *Baldr's brother*: Vali, son of Odin by Rind, begotten solely to avenge Baldr's death. The story of his conception is told more fully in Saxo, *History of the Danish People*, Book III, pp. 69–79.

36 *Sindri's lineage*: the hall, then, must belong to the dwarfs.

40 *the next summers*: the poet may be thinking here of the effects of a volcanic eruption and consequent ash cloud, perhaps pointing to an Icelandic origin for the poem.

42 *Father of Hosts' hall*: Valhall.

43 *Garm*: Garm seems to be a hound of hell, destined, according to Snorri, *Edda*, p. 54, to fight with Tyr at Ragnarok. Originally he may have been identical with Fenrir the wolf.

she knows, I see: here the poem seems to reach the mythic present: the seeress describes the chaotic conditions which prevail in the world and then looks forward to Ragnarok.

45 *Mim*: the sons of Mim are unknown. Mim in l. 4 seems to be identical with Mimir, who, according to *Ynglinga saga*, ch. 4, was sent as a hostage to the Vanir, where he displayed remarkable wisdom. The Vanir beheaded him, preserved his head, and sent it back to the Æsir along with Hænir.

47 *Hrym*: a frost-giant.

Naglfar: a ship made of the uncut nails of the dead (Snorri, *Edda*, p. 53).

48 *Muspell's troops*: although in Old High German and Old Saxon *Muspilli*
    simply means 'the end of the world', the Norse poet understands it as a
    giant's name.

    Byleist's brother: nothing is known about Byleist; his name only appears in
    kennings like this one, referring to Loki, whose brother he seems to be (cf.
    also *Song of Hyndla*, v. 40.4).

50 *Surt comes from the south*: Surt is a fire-giant, so his kinsman may be fire
    itself. What is swallowed is unclear—whether the hell-road or Yggdrasill
    (the Measuring-Tree)— already alight in v. 45.

    branches-ruin: a kenning for fire.

    heroes tread the hell-road: these may be the Einheriar, coming to fight, or
    the human victims of Ragnarok.

51 *Frigg's second sorrow*: the death of Odin. Her first was the death of Baldr.

    Beli's bright slayer: Freyr killed the giant Beli with a deer horn as he had
    given away his sword to Skirnir. See *Skirnir's Journey*.

52 *Loki's son*: the wolf, borne to Loki by the giantess Angrboda.

53 *Odin's son*: Thor is Odin's son by Earth. Instead of 'serpent' the R text has
    'wolf' here, an error imported from v. 51.

    Midgard's-protector: one might expect this to be Thor: *véorr*, 'protector',
    is used to denote him in *Hymir's Poem*. Logically however, 'he' must refer
    to Thor, and the serpent who encircles the earth—thus paradoxically its
    protector—is the object of the verb 'to strike'.

57 *Earth-girdler*: the Midgard-serpent.

59 *slaughter-gods*: Hod and Baldr continue to be associated with those who die
    in battle even in this new world—or perhaps this designation refers back
    to their role in the present divine order.

SAYINGS OF THE HIGH ONE

13 *Gunnlod*: this alludes to the story of the winning of the mead of poetry,
    told in full in Snorri, *Edda*, pp. 61–4. The mead originally belonged to two
    dwarfs, Fialar and Gialar, and was stolen by the giants. Odin had worked
    for a year as a thrall for the brother of Suttung, the giant who had the
    mead. When the year was up he went to Suttung (confusingly called Fialar
    in v. 14) to claim his reward of mead. By seducing Gunnlod, Suttung's
    daughter, he gained her help and escaped with the mead back to Asgard.
    Odin alludes to his adventure in fuller detail in vv. 104–10 below.

25 *Assembly*: in both mainland Scandinavia and Iceland people would regu-
    larly meet at regional assemblies (Things) to resolve law cases.

41 *those which can be seen on them*: the sense seems to be that presents which
    can be shown off by wearing them on the body will be best received.

49 *two wooden men*: these may be scarecrows, or they may be wooden idols,

mentioned in some sagas. In the *Saga of Ragnar Lodbrok*, ch. 20, some vikings come to a Baltic island where they find a huge wooden idol. The idol speaks some verses complaining that once he used to be given food and clothing but now he is neglected.

50 *stands on the farmstead*: the word 'þorp' may mean a number of things (such as 'village'). The sense here may be that the farm-dwellers have stripped off the tree's bark and needles to use about the house.

62 *the eagle*: opinion is divided as to whether this is a sea-eagle on the lookout for fish as prey, or a land eagle who has flown away from his accustomed habitat and so is disoriented.

65 *paid back*: this verse is missing some lines.

73 *a hand*: the metre changes suddenly in this verse and the meaning is obscure. Possibly a rich outer garment may conceal a hand ready to strike.

76 *Cattle die, kinsmen die*: a parallel has been detected in the Old English poem *The Wanderer*: 'here cattle are transient | here property is transient, here a friend is transient' (1. 108). If there is a direct connection it most likely stems from the formulaic use of the words 'cattle' and 'kinsmen', an alliterating pair both in Old Norse, *fé* and *frœndr*, and in Old English, *feoh* and *freond*.

78 *Fitiung's sons*: although they sound proverbial, Fitiung's sons are otherwise unknown.

80 *mighty sage coloured*: the sage is probably Odin. Carved runic letters appear originally to have been filled in with some kind of paint.

84 *whirling wheel*: the image is of a potter's wheel or of a turning lathe; in its turning the wheel incorporates changeability into women's hearts. Some have seen the medieval image of the Wheel of Fortune here, but that deals with a human's external fate, not his internal character. These lines are also cited in *Fostbrœðra saga* (Saga of the Foster-Brothers), ch. 21, where a thrall in Greenland begins to suspect that his sweetheart is spending rather too long with the saga's hero in the evenings.

97 *Billing's girl*: this story is unknown from other sources, though the sequence of events is not difficult to follow. Odin importunes the wife or daughter of Billing (probably a giant). She puts him off until the evening; when he first comes to her hall everyone is still awake, the second time she has gone, leaving a bitch in her place. It seems likely that Billing's girl fears to reject Odin openly lest he bewitch her as he does Rind, who was fated to be the mother of Vali, avenger of Baldr. Her story is told in Saxo's *History of the Danish People*, Book III, pp. 69–79.

104 *the old giant*: a further elaboration of the story of the mead of poetry begun in vv. 13–14.

106 *auger*: according to Snorri, *Edda*, p. 63, Odin makes use of an auger called Rati to bore his way into the mountain where Gunnlod is to be found, and, turning himself into a snake, wriggles in through the hole.

107 *Odrerir*: according to Snorri this is the name of one of the vats in which the mead of poetry was kept, though the name 'Stirrer of Inspiration' seems more likely to refer to the mead itself.

109 *Bolverk*: the name Odin had used when disguised as a thrall, and in his dealings with Gunnlod.

110 *ring-oath*: in Iceland oaths were sworn on large silver rings kept at the local temple and reddened with sacrificial blood.

112 *Loddfafnir*: the name is unknown from other sources. *Lodd* seems to mean 'rags', while Fafnir is the name of the dragon Sigurd killed. The combination 'Ragged-dragon' may be a mocking term for someone who is not yet fully initiated into arcane knowledge.

somewhere outside: probably a euphemistic reference to the privy.

129 *look upwards in battle*: the phenomenon warned against here is a kind of mass panic, frequently found in Irish sources, and for which an Irish loan-word is used in the Norse.

137 *earth's power*: the substances mentioned may be invoked or be incorporated into some kind of ritual.

138 *I hung on a windswept tree*: Odin performs a sacrifice by hanging for nine nights on the tree Yggdrasill, pierced with a spear in order to gain knowledge of the runes. The parallels with the Crucifixion are marked, though interpretation is controversial. The motif of the Hanged God is widespread in Indo-European and ancient Near Eastern religion, however, so direct Christian influence need not be present here.

140 *Bolthor*: Odin's maternal grandfather; Bolthor's son is therefore Odin's mother's brother, a particularly close relationship in Germanic society.

145 *Thund*: an Odinic name.

146 *spells*: the spells which Odin alludes to here broadly match those magical skills listed for him in *Ynglinga saga*, chs. 2 and 6.

164 *quite useless*: so reads the R manuscript; just as Odin teases Loddfafnir in v. 162 that he will never learn the spells which the god knows, so here Odin intimates the paradoxical nature of his spells. They will not benefit the sons of men if they are not told them. In the manuscript margins a younger hand emends to 'the sons of giants'; a number of editors follow this suggestion.

VAFTHRUDNIR'S SAYINGS

5 *Im's father*: i.e. Vafthrudnir. Im is otherwise unknown.

12 *Hreid-Goths*: though the Goths lived in southern Sweden, this phrase probably means simply 'among men'.

21 *Ymir*: Ymir was the primeval giant, the earliest creature. This account of the creation of the world differs markedly from that in the *Seeress's Prophecy*. Snorri's *Edda*, pp. 11–12, elaborates the creation myth.

30 *Aurgelmir*: according to Snorri, *Edda*, p. 10, Aurgelmir was the name given to Ymir by the frost-giants.

31 *Elivagar*: the name seems to mean 'mighty waves', some sort of icy primeval matter. In his *Edda* (p. 10) Snorri says that they are a number of rivers.

from there . . . terrifying: lines 3–4 of this stanza are missing in R and are supplied from Snorri's *Edda*.

35 *coffin*: the Norse word *lúðr* means primarily 'box, chest'; some scholars have suggested that it might equally be interpreted as 'cradle'. Vafthrudnir's boast is that he is so old that he recalls the death of the most ancient of giants. Snorri, *Edda*, p. 11, identifies it as an 'ark', and introduces a Flood-narrative, borrowed from Christian tradition. Cf. *Song of Grotti*, vv. 2 ff., where it is part of the milling apparatus (translated as 'mill-box'). In *Groa's Chant*, v. 12, *lúðr* seems to refer to a ship.

39 *home among the wise Vanir*: no other source tells of Niord's return to the Vanir, nor anything about his fate at Ragnarok.

41 *Einheriar*: the warrior dead who live in Valhall, and who will fight on the side of the gods at Ragnarok.

45 *Hoddmimir*: from the connection between Mimir and Yggdrasill noted in the *Seeress's Prophecy*, it is possible that Hoddmimir is another name for Mimir, and that the two survivors hide in Yggdrasill. We are not expressly told whether Yggdrasill survives Ragnarok or not, though it certainly catches fire.

48 *girls who glide*: neither the question nor its answer is easy to construe; they may well be human, or they may be, or have some connection with, female fate-figures, such as the norns. See also the *Lay of Fafnir*, v. 13.

49 *Three mighty rivers*: the verse describes conditions after Ragnarok, where the world remains flooded.

Mogthrasir's girls: Mogthrasir himself is unknown; his name may mean 'Striver for Sons' and thus connect with the idea of human continuity after Ragnarok. Cf. Lifthrasir in v. 45 above.

protective spirits: this interpretation follows the syntax of the R manuscript. The girls have effective protecting spirits (*hamingiur*), hence they have survived the cataclysm by taking refuge with the giants.

51 *Vidar and Vali . . . Modi and Magni*: sons of Odin and Thor respectively. Miollnir is Thor's weapon, his mighty hammer.

54 *son's ear*: this refers to Baldr. No one but Odin knows what was whispered in Baldr's ear; it is assumed that it was a promise of resurrection. Compare *Heidreks saga*, ch. 10.

GRIMNIR'S SAYINGS

Hlidskialf: Odin's high-seat, from which he can see into all the worlds.

5 *Ull*: god of the bow. Since bows were normally made of yew, it is appropriate that the god should have his palace in Yewdale.

tooth-payment: a gift given to a child when it gets its first tooth. Freyr is the only god who seems to have had a childhood; Skirnir notes in *Skir* v. 5 that they were young together in bygone days.

6 *the God*: according to Snorri, *Edda*, p. 20, this is Odin himself.

7 *Saga*: Snorri, *Edda*, p. 29, lists Saga as a separate goddess, based on this passage. Saga is likely to be another name for Frigg, however.

10 *wolf . . . eagle*: these, along with the raven, are Germanic beasts of battle; their appearance signals that a fight is impending.

11 *Thiazi*: a giant who kidnapped Idunn, keeper of the apples of youthfulness, and was subsequently killed by the gods. See Snorri, *Edda*, p. 60.

Skadi: Thiazi's giantess daughter who gained Niord as a husband in compensation for her father's death. They were divorced, hence her separate habitation. See Snorri, *Edda*, pp. 23–4, 61.

15 *Forseti*: Baldr's otherwise obscure son. The name means 'Ruler', and is the title used by the president of Iceland.

18 *Andhrimnir . . . Eldhrimnir*: Andhrimnir is the cook in Valhall, Eldhrimnir the cooking-pot, and Sæhrimnir the boar whom the Einheriar (heroes who died in combat, chosen to live in Valhall) eat every day; the boar is rejuvenated every night.

19 *Geri and Freki*: Odin's wolves, whom he keeps as dogs.

20 *Hugin and Munin*: Odin's ravens. Their names mean 'Thought' and 'Memory' and they are also mentioned in *Ynglinga saga*, ch. 7.

21 *Thund*: this verse is very obscure. Thund is probably a river in which the 'Great Wolf' (Þjóðvitnir's fish), possibly the World-serpent, swims. The 'slaughter-horse' (valglaumr) perhaps brings the dead from the battlefield to Valhall. *Glaumr* is an attested horse-name.

23 *hundred*: this is the so-called 'long hundred' = 120.

24 *Bilskirnir*: a hall belonging to Thor.

25 *Heidrun . . . Lærad*: Heidrun provides enough mead for all the Einheriar from her udder. Cf. Snorri, *Edda*, p. 33. The tree, Lærad, may be another name for Yggdrasill, but Snorri does not make the connection.

27 *Sid and Vid*: this list of river-names contains some real rivers such as the Rhine and Dvina, but the rest are mythical.

32 *Nidhogg*: a dragon, cf. the *Seeress's Prophecy*. Snorri, *Edda*, pp. 17–20, elaborates the description of Yggdrasill and Valhall.

36 *Hrist and Mist*: these, and the other names in the verse, are valkyries. Cf. Snorri, *Edda*, p. 31, and the list of valkyries in *Seeress's Prophecy*, v. 31.

37 *Arvak and Alsvid . . . cooling-iron*: horses who pull the sun. Snorri, *Edda*, p. 14, interprets the cooling-iron as bellows which both cool the horses and perhaps function to keep the sun ablaze. The sense here however seems to imply a protective shield for the horses.

39 *Skoll . . . Hrodvitnir*: the wolf Skoll and his companion Hati are chasing the sun and moon. They will swallow them at Ragnarok (Snorri, *Edda*, pp. 14–15). Hrodvitnir (like the 'Great Wolf' *Thiodvitnir* in v. 21) is likely to be another name for Fenrir.

40 *Ymir's flesh*: this allusion to the making of the world conflicts with the version we have in the *Seeress's Prophecy*, but agrees with *Vafthrudnir's Sayings*. See also Snorri, *Edda*, pp. 11–12.

42 *seize the flames*: the import of this verse is obscure. The speaker's focus returns to Odin's opening situation, tormented by the heat from the fires. Whether seizing the flames implies extinguishing them (perhaps with the contents of the kettles) is unclear.

    kettles: the removal of the kettles permits the sons of the Æsir (likely humans) to see what is happening in all the worlds. If Agnarr relieves Odin's torment he will gain the insight that the god has achieved through his suffering. The reference may be to some kind of shamanistic rite involving heat and steam, perhaps with hallucinogenic herbs, to allow initiates to see into another world.

43 *Ivaldi's sons*: these were dwarfs who not only made Skidbladnir, a ship which Freyr can fold up and put in his pocket, but also various other treasures, including Gungnir, Odin's spear, and Miollnir, Thor's hammer. For the full story, see Snorri, *Edda*, pp. 96–7.

44 *Sleipnir . . . Bilrost . . . Garm*: Odin's eight-legged horse is the offspring of Loki and the Giant-builder's stallion: Snorri, *Edda*, pp. 35–6. Bilrost is the rainbow bridge also known as Bifrost, Garm the hound whose baying portends Ragnarok.

45 *Fleeting visions*: another verse which is difficult to interpret. Odin now brings his recitation of mythological facts for the humans ('victory-gods' sons', cf. *Lay of Fafnir*, v. 24) in the hall to an end as he prepares to reveal his identity through the list of Odinic names which follow. The 'wished-for protection' is thus the god's favour, now transferred from Geirrod to his son Agnarr, and notified to all the gods, partaking in a feast at Ægir's.

    Ægir's feast: a personification of the sea, possibly a giant. Ægir is ordered to host a feast for the gods in *Hymir's Poem*; the feast actually takes place in *Loki's Quarrel*. Agnar's horn, given to Odin, functions as a sacrifice, connecting the human hall with the divine assembly.

46 *Mask*: Odin reckons up a long list of names by which he is known. Some have meanings, others are obscure. Snorri draws on this list, among others, both for the names of his triple protagonists in the *Gylfaginning* section of his *Edda* and for his list of Odinic names in *Edda*, pp. 8–9 and 21–2.

50 *Sokkmimir's*: this story is otherwise unknown.

53 *disir*: fateful female figures who often contrive the death of heroes, notably in the Norwegian genealogical poem *Ynglingatal* (cited in Snorri's *Ynglinga saga*) and in the *Lay of Hamdir*.

SKIRNIR'S JOURNEY

Skadi: the giantess is not said to be Freyr's mother elsewhere; Loki claims that Freyr and Freyia were born of the union between Niord and his sister in *Loki's Quarrel*, v. 36, an allegation which Snorri does not address.

4 *elf-radiance*: the sun.

11 *herdsman*: the watchman sitting on the mound, warning of danger, is a familiar motif. Originally this figure—who may be identical with the brother Gerd mentions in v. 16—may have had to be overcome by Skirnir in battle.

16 *my brother's slayer*: what Gerd means by this remark is obscure. The only mythological figure who embraces her brother's slayer is Idunn, according to Loki in *Loki's Quarrel*, v. 17. It may be that in some version of the story, the herdsman on the mound was Gerd's brother whom the hero had to kill to gain access to the bride.

19 *Eleven apples*: apples are normally the attribute of Idunn, who prevented the Æsir from ageing with her apples of youth. Eleven is not normally a significant number in Norse, and it may be there has been confusion between *ellifo*, 'eleven', as the manuscript reads, and *ellilyf*, 'old-age drug', which would confirm the connection with Idunn.

21 *every ninth night*: this must be the famous ring Draupnir which belonged to Odin and which has the self-replicating property mentioned. Odin placed it on Baldr's funeral pyre and Baldr sent it back to him from Hel with the messenger, Hermod: Snorri, *Edda*, p. 50. How, or indeed whether, Skirnir has it within his gift is not clear.

28 *watchman among the gods*: Heimdall. Gerd, perched at the edge of hell on the eagle's mound, would become a kind of demonic Heimdall since he watches for Ragnarok at the edge of heaven.

35 *goat's piss*: the goat Heidrun supplies mead from her udders for the warriors in Valhall. Gerd would be enduring the very opposite of the splendid life lived among the gods.

36 *three runes*: runes were the pre-Christian writing system in Scandinavia. Each rune represented both a sound (e.g. 'h') and a concept (e.g. 'hail' for the 'h' rune); they could be used for magical purposes, both for good and evil. See the *Lay of Sigrdrifa*, vv. 6–13. The first rune 'ogre' (*þurs*) is normally called 'thorn', but *þurs* is given as the name of this rune in the *Norwegian Rune Poem*, v. 3.

HARBARD'S SONG

1 *lad of lads*: Odin is usually imagined as an old man, and in this poem his assumed name 'Harbard' means 'Greybeard'. Thus Thor's ironic address, 'lad of lads', sparks off the quarrel.

4 *your mother's dead*: this is not true, but is part of Odin's psychological strategy; Thor's mother is Earth.

13 *prick*: what Thor declines to wet is unclear, but etymologically it seems to be something staff-shaped (and thus phallic).

14 *Hrungnir*: a giant with a head of stone. Knowing that Thor was coming to attack him, but persuaded that he was approaching from underground, he stood on his shield and thus was an easy target. Hrungnir was armed with a whetstone, a fragment of which is still stuck in Thor's head. See Snorri, *Edda*, pp. 77–81.

18 *seven sisters*: who these women are is not clear, but Odin's riddling style and the references to sand and digging out valleys suggest that they may perhaps be the unpredictable waves, daughters of Ran, the sea-goddess.

19 *Thiazi*: the account of the death of Thiazi, recounted in Snorri, *Edda*, pp. 60, 86–8, citing Thiodolf of Hvinir's poem *Haustlong*, gives Thor no particular role in killing Thiazi. Loki claims the credit for it in *Loki's Quarrel*, v. 50.

Allvaldi's son: Thiazi. Snorri, *Edda*, p. 61, says that it was Odin who transformed Thiazi's eyes into stars as part of the Æsir's compensation to his daughter, Skadi. It is not known whether they were identified with any particular constellation.

26 *stuffed in a glove*: this is the well-known story of Thor's trip to Utgarda-Loki, recounted in Snorri, *Edda*, pp. 37–46. En route Thor and his companions stay overnight in, as they think, an oddly designed hall. They spend an anxious night, kept awake by a terrifying rumbling. The next morning they meet the giant Skrymir (here called Fialar, a common giant-name) whose snoring was the source of the rumbling. He points out that they have been using his glove as accommodation. Thor is worsted by the giants' magic in this tale, and his enemies delight in reminding him of it—cf. Loki in *Loki's Quarrel*, vv. 60, 62.

29 *Svarang's sons*: this story is unknown from other sources.

42 *an arm-ring*: this offer visibly upsets Thor. More than one scholar has suggested that the ring may refer to the anus, and the offer thus be an invitation to homosexual activity. A simple explanation may be that a single ring is poor compensation for the insults directed at Thor, or that to accept compensation instead of taking violent revenge on his persecutor is shameful for a fighting-god.

44 *their home in the woods*: the connection with burial cairns is obscure, but the phrase appears in both manuscripts of the poem. The 'ancient men' are presumably the dead, a frequent source of wisdom in Norse.

48 *Sif*: Thor's wife. There is no record of Sif being unfaithful to Thor, though Loki claims in *Loki's Quarrel*, v. 54, that he has been her lover.

56 *Fiorgyn*: another name for Earth, Thor's mother.

HYMIR'S POEM

1 *shook the twigs*: twigs or wooden slips seem to be involved in Norse prognostications, though how they are used is not clear. In the *Seeress's Prophecy*, v. 60, Hænir chooses a slip of wood for divination. Probably a number of sticks carved with runic symbols were thrown.

2 *mash-blender*: this line is obscure, but the mountain-dweller (giant) seems to be Ægir, since he makes the stipulation about the cauldron and he is presumably a skilled brewer. Odin's son is Thor.

4 *Hlorridi*: a name for Thor.

5 *my father*: it would be surprising if the giant Hymir really were Tyr's father, but we know little about Tyr. Possibly Loki, whose father certainly was a giant, was the original companion on this adventure, as in *Thrym's Poem*. Thialfi, Thor's companion in other adventures, son of the giant Egil, may also have been the other protagonist.

7 *Egil . . . goats*: Egil is the father of Thialfi and Roskva. Thor's goats, which draw his chariot, could be cooked and eaten each night and reconstituted from the bones every morning. Contrary to instructions, Thialfi splits open a bone to get at the marrow and next day the goat is lame. The furious Thor demands the children as his servants in recompense. The story is told fully in Snorri, *Edda*, pp. 37–8, and alluded to in vv. 37–8 of this poem.

8 *The lad*: presumably Tyr.

10 *cheek-forest*: beard.

11 *Hrod*: an otherwise unknown giant.

14 *the one who makes the giantess weep*: Thor, killer of giants.

16 *Hrungnir's grey-haired friend*: Hrungnir was a well-known giant; 'Hrungnir's friend' is a kenning for 'giant'.

19 *head*: the ox's head is used for bait for the Midgard-serpent, and can be quite clearly seen in the illustration of this scene on the Gosforth Fishing Stone, a large standing stone from the late tenth or early eleventh century in Cumbria, England. The scene is also illustrated on a number of other Scandinavian picture-stones. Following is a narrative gap. The missing details can be summarized from Snorri, *Edda*, pp. 46–7: Thor went on board the boat, and began to row very quickly. Then Hymir said that they had come to the waters where he usually sat and caught flatfish, but Thor said he wanted to row out much further; Hymir said that now they had gone so far out it was dangerous because of the Midgard-serpent. Thor continued, but Hymir was very unhappy.

20 *lord of goats . . . launchway-horse*: a series of zoological kennings. The lord of goats is Thor, since they pull his chariot; the monkey's offspring is an unusual designation for a giant, while the wave-horse is the boat.

22 *serpent's sole slayer*: prolepsis. Thor and the Midgard-serpent will kill

one another at Ragnarok. The All-Lands-Girdler (1. 3) is the Midgard-serpent, who encircles the world.

23 *the wolf's intimate-brother's head*: the Midgard-serpent is the brother of Fenrir the wolf. His head is described with the kenning 'the high hair-mountain'.

24 *collapsing*: another narrative omission follows. Snorri, *Edda*, p. 47, says that Hymir was terrified when he saw the serpent, and the sea washing in and out of the boat. As Thor raised his hammer, the giant grabbed the bait-knife and cut Thor's line; the serpent sank into the sea. In Snorri's account, Thor throws Hymir overboard in disgust; here he survives in order to conclude the 'Fetching the Cauldron' story.

26 *floating-goat*: boat.

27 *sea-pigs*: these are the whales.

31 *helmet-stump*: Hymir's head.

34 *stamped down through the floor*: on some picture-stones, for example the Altuna and Hørdum stones, Thor puts his foot through the bottom of the boat during the fishing-expedition; the scene is also in Snorri's account, *Edda*, p. 47.

36 *lava-whales*: a term for giants.

37 *malevolent Loki*: Loki's responsibility for the goat's lameness is unclear. Possibly, if Loki rather than Tyr was Thor's original companion, he advised Thialfi to crack open the goat's leg-bone to get at the marrow. Certainly, in Snorri's account of the laming, Loki is present, *Edda*, pp. 38–9.

38 *both his children*: this refers back to the story of the lamed goat (see note to v. 7, above). It is likely these verses belong earlier in the poem, and thus that Thor's companion in the cauldron adventure might originally have been Thialfi, rather than Tyr.

LOKI'S QUARREL

9 *blended our blood*: Odin and Loki had thus sworn blood-brotherhood in the past.

10 *wolf's father*: Loki is father of the wolf Fenrir.

11 *further in*: that is, in a more honourable seat.

16 *those who are adopted*: an obscure term perhaps meaning 'the Vanir' as opposed to the Æsir.

17 *brother's killer*: the story is not known from elsewhere. However, the motif of the wooer who has to kill his bride's male relations to gain her is a common one—see the *Second Poem of Helgi Hundingsbani*.

20 *thigh*: the story is unknown: however, we do know from Snorri that Gefion bartered sex for territory in her dealings with Gylfi, the king of Sweden (Snorri, *Edda*, p. 7, and *Ynglinga saga*, ch. 5).

22 *the faint-hearted*: Odin was notorious for deserting his protégés in battle and giving victory to the other side so that his favourites could join him in Valhall.

23 *pervert*: this story is not otherwise known, though Loki gives birth to Sleipnir, the eight-legged horse of Odin, after having sex with the Giant-builder's stallion, Svadilfari (Snorri, *Edda*, p. 36).

24 *seid on Samsey*: the use of drums and cross-dressing seems to be typical of *seid*, a type of magic said to be practised by the Vanir, especially Freyia (*Seeress's Prophecy*, v. 23), and by the Lapps.

26 *Ve and Vili*: Odin's brothers. Once when Odin was away on a journey, Vili and Ve shared Frigg, Snorri reports in *Ynglinga saga*, ch. 3. Snorri's account seems to be based on this passage, so it adds nothing to our understanding. Saxo, *History of the Danish People*, Book I, p. 26, tells how Othinus (= Odin) went away into exile at one point, because of his wife's disgraceful behaviour, and did not return until she was dead. There is no mention of the two brothers in Saxo, however.

28 *Baldr*: for Loki's part in the killing of Baldr, see Snorri, *Edda*, pp. 48–51.

32 *Freyia*: Freyia's affair with her brother is not mentioned elsewhere, but the fact that Niord seems to have fathered her and Freyr on his sister (v. 36 below) suggests that brother–sister sexual relations were a distinguishing characteristic of the Vanir.

34 *pissed in your mouth*: Niord is a god of the sea; the daughters of the giant Hymir are conceivably the rivers which flow down into the sea.

38 *Fenrir tore*: when the gods tried to bind Fenrir with a magic unbreakable rope, the wolf suspected them and would only submit to binding if one of them would put his hand in the wolf's mouth as a pledge of good faith. When the rope proved unbreakable Fenrir bit off Tyr's hand (Snorri, *Edda*, pp. 25, 28–9).

40 *wife*: nothing is known of Tyr's wife, nor whether Loki's allegation is true.

42 *Gymir's daughter*: Gerd, see *Skirnir's Journey*.

Muspell: i.e. at Ragnarok.

Byggvir: Byggvir's name means 'Barley': hence his small size, his fate to be milled between grindstones, and his pride in his role in the brewing of beer.

48 *mucky back*: from *Seeress's Prophecy*, v. 28, we know that white loam pours down Yggdrasill to where Heimdall's hearing is hidden. As the watchman of the gods, perhaps Heimdall has to sit under Yggdrasill, waiting for the first signs of Ragnarok, though he is often depicted as sitting at the edge of heaven.

49 *gods shall bind you*: this story is told in the prose which follows this poem.

50 *Thiazi*: Skadi's father, who kidnapped Idunn. Loki rescued her and thus was instrumental in Thiazi's death. The story is related in Snorri, *Edda*, pp. 59–61. Thor claims the credit for killing Thiazi in *Harbard's Song*, v. 19.

52 *bed*: this claim is not corroborated elsewhere.

54 *Loki*: Sif is not recorded elsewhere as unfaithful, although Odin suggests as much to Thor in *Harbard's Song*, v. 48. In one story (Snorri, *Edda*, p. 96) Loki cuts off all of Sif's hair: how he got close enough to carry this out may be explained by this verse.

57 *your shoulder-rock*: i.e. head.

59 *roads to the east*: Thor threw Thiazi's eyes up into the sky to become stars after killing him (*Harbard's Song*, v. 19), and also the toe of Aurvandil, another giant (Snorri, *Edda*, pp. 79–80).

60 *glove*: see note on *Harbard's Song*, v. 26 (p. 292 above), for the story of Thor's trip to Utgarda-Loki.

61 *Hrungnir's killer*: i.e. Miollnir. See note on *Harbard's Song*, v. 14.2 (p. 292 above).

62 *starved*: this is a reference to Thor's adventure with Skrymir. Thor proved unable to get food out of the giant's pack because it was secretly fastened with trick wire (Snorri, *Edda*, pp. 39, 45).

Narfi: Snorri rationalizes the rather confusing details given here: one son is changed into a wolf and tears open the other to provide the guts for the binding (Snorri, *Edda*, p. 52).

THRYM'S POEM

3 *feather-shirt*: an attribute of Freyia which allows her to fly.

8 *Hlorridi:* a name for Thor.

13 *necklace of the Brisings*: this is frequently mentioned in connection with Freyia, but we know little more about it. On one occasion Loki stole it. It was recovered by Heimdall, who fought with him for it at a place called Singastein. Both gods were in the form of seals (Snorri, *Edda*, p. 76).

16 *keys*: keys to the pantry, storehouses, and chests were the house-wife's responsibility. The bunch of keys is a mark of her status as married woman.

21 *goats*: Thor always drives a chariot drawn by his magic goats.

30 *Var*: the goddess of pledges between men and women, according to Snorri, *Edda*, p. 30.

THE POEM OF VOLUND

valkyries: the women are swan-maidens, women who can fly with the aid of cloaks of swan feathers. Valkyries are not normally imagined as swan-maidens; perhaps the two kinds of beings have been conflated here since both can fly, and both eschew domesticity. The three have ordinary human names but two—Swanwhite and Strange-Creature (Alvit)—have bynames which indicate their supernatural qualities.

4 *weather-eyed shooter*: Volund.

skied off: this detail (also included in the poem's introduction), and Volund's later meal of bear-flesh (v. 9) seems to confirm the brothers' association with the far north.

5 *serpent-rings*: the rings may be snake-shaped arm-rings, or they may be closed up around a bast-rope (cf. v. 7); the text is ambiguous.

14 *Grani's road*: Grani is the hero Sigurd's horse, on whose back he bore off Fafnir's treasure-hoard, the Rhinegold, alluded to in the next line. Volund seems to be claiming that the gold is neither Nidud's property, nor part of the legendary hoard, but is rightfully his.

16 *She*: Nidud's malicious queen.

17 *Cut . . . the might of his sinews*: i.e. hamstring him so that he cannot run away.

28 *overcame her with beer*: this scene is illustrated on the eighth-century whalebone box known as the Franks Casket, which can be seen in the British Museum.

29 *webbed feet*: this phrase, and the crippled smith's method of escape from the island, remains obscure. It is possible that the ring which he has now recovered has some transformative power, changing Volund into a swan (hence the webbed feet), like the swan-maiden for whom it was made. The later prose account of the story, *Thidreks saga*, has Volund's brother Egil come to his rescue, shooting down geese with his bow so that the smith can make himself wings. This scene may also be illustrated on the Franks Casket.

30 *perched to rest himself*: Volund, who has flown to Nidud's palace.

36 *with child*: in *Thidreks saga* Volund returns with an army, kills Nidud, and marries Bodvild. Their son, Vidga, becomes a great Germanic hero.

ALL-WISE'S SAYINGS

3 *lord of wagons*: probably a reference to Thor's goat-drawn chariot.

6 *Sidgrani*: Odin.

16 *Dvalin's plaything*: Dvalin is a frequent dwarf-name. This name must be ironic, for it is the sun that plays with the dwarf by turning him into stone, just as All-wise is at the end of the poem.

24 *liquid-fundament*: this translation is uncertain. The same word (*lagastaf*) is used to denote grain in v. 32.

THE FIRST POEM OF HELGI HUNDINGSBANI

2 *norns*: female fate figures who determine the lives of men. They are associated with textile work; here they twist separate strands of fate into a strong rope.

3 *as strongholds were breaking*: the syntax is odd here, but it seems likely that battle rages as Helgi is born. Cf. v. 7.3.

3 *moon's hall*: i.e. the sky.

4 *Neri's kinswoman*: Neri is unknown, but the reference must be to one of the norns.

5 *kinsman of the Ylfings*: Sigmund, Helgi's father. What concerns Helgi's parents is unclear: possibly his precocious warrior-behaviour presages an early death.

6 *stands in his mail-coat . . . friend of wolves*: like Vali, the son begotten by Odin to avenge Baldr, Helgi is ready to fight when one day old. The conversation between the ravens points to the hero's future prowess in battle. He will be a friend to wolves and ravens by providing corpses for them to eat.

7 *splendid leek*: a sword.

8 *blood-snake*: a sword.

Sinfiotli: son of Sigmund by his sister Signy. Sinfiotli was born to help the brother and sister avenge the death of their father, Volsung, at the hands of Signy's husband, Siggeir. Sigmund and Sinfiotli spent some time in the forest living as werewolves before the revenge was achieved (see *Volsunga saga*, ch. 8, and the accusations in vv. 36 and 41 below).

9 *splendidly-born elm*: humans are often metaphorically designated as trees, no doubt because the story of Ash and Embla (*Seeress's Prophecy*, vv. 17–18) tells of mankind's origin, shaped from trees. Women are 'trees of jewellery', men 'trees of battle' or some variant of this.

13 *peace of Frodi*: Frodi was a mythical Danish king (see *Song of Grotti*, below); his reign was famous for its peacefulness.

Odin's hounds: wolves.

14 *spear-Mimir*: a wise fighter, here referring to Hunding.

17 *breaker of rings*: generous man. A successful leader would break up the big arm-rings captured as booty and distribute the fragments of gold or silver to his men.

18 *kitten of a cat*: at the equivalent point in *Volsunga saga* (ch. 9), Sigrun says that she would rather marry a young crow than Hodbrodd.

21 *river-fire*: gold, an allusion to the legend of the Rhinegold.

28 *the sister of Kolga*: Kolga is one of the nine daughters of Ægir, who rules over the sea, and she and her sisters represent the waves; v. 29.3 refers to the same belief.

30 *Ran*: the goddess of the sea, who seeks to catch and drown men in her net.

31 *the others*: allies of Hodbrodd, led by Gudmund.

34 *pigs . . . bitches*: an insult: feeding such low creatures was the work of slaves.

36 *slunk into a stone-tip*: the verse refers to Sinfiotli's former exploits as a werewolf, accusing him of sleeping out in the forest instead of living in

a hall like an ordinary man. Sinfiotli also killed his half-brothers when they betrayed Sigmund and Sinfiotli as they waited to take revenge on Siggeir.

37 *except Sinfiotli*: the suggestion that two men have had sexual relations is a disgraceful one. In such taunts shame attaches to the one who takes the female role; hence Sinfiotli asserts that he was the dominant sexual partner in this encounter.

38 *Einheriar had to fight . . . headstrong woman*: Gudmund is characterized as a trouble-making valkyrie.

41 *home under haystacks*: this seems to be another taunt based on Sinfiotli's time as a werewolf. Lying about under the haystacks may suggest an idle youth, in which Sinfiotli achieved no heroic deeds. Sinfiotli also killed his half-brothers as part of the vengeance taken on Siggeir by Sigmund and his son.

42 *You were Grani's bride*: Grani was Sigurd's stallion. To accuse someone of being a mare was particularly insulting, implying both sexual deviancy and bestial appetite. The verse is a variation on the insult of v. 37.

43 *as Imd's daughter*: Imd seems to be a giant-name. The story is unknown, but the accusation combines transvestism and doing the tasks of slaves.

   [Helgi said:]: it is not clear from the manuscript who speaks verses 45 and 46, and the corresponding ones in *A Second Poem of Helgi Hundingsbani*, vv. 23–4. The tone seems to be that of a commander, advising Sinfiotli to get ready for battle and judiciously summing up the nature of the opposition, so I have, like a number of editors, assigned the speech to Helgi.

47 *Svipud and Sveggiud*: horse-names.

51 *wound-flames*: swords.

54 *troll-woman's mount*: traditionally, troll-women ride on wolves. Here the wolf is feasting on corpses—the fodder of the raven.

THE POEM OF HELGI HIORVARDSSON

3 *Don't choose*: Atli wisely avoids making an open-ended bargain with the talking bird.

   no name would stick to him: some Germanic heroes are unpromising in their youth, and their fathers do not bother to give them a name. Often called 'coal-biters' because of their habit of idling by the hearth, it takes an unusual occurrence to make them show their mettle.

   burial-mound: as liminal places, on the threshold between the living and the dead, burial-mounds are places where supernatural incursions often occur.

6 *apple-tree of strife*: warrior.

7 *with the name*: traditionally, the giving of a name or nickname had to be accompanied by a gift if the name was to stick to its new owner.

13 *Helgi is his name . . .* : at v. 13 the change in style from narrative to flyting
    produces a change in metre from *fornyrdislag* to *ljodahattr*.

15 *Atli . . . atrocious*: this pun is in the original: *Atli* and *atall* meaning
    'terrifying'.

18 *give to Ran*: to give someone to the sea-goddess is to drown them.

20 *gelded*: female–male flytings often use sexual insult; Hrimgerd suggests
    that Atli is sexually incapable. A comparable exchange of sexual insults can
    be found in Saxo, *History of the Danish People*, Book V, pp. 132–3.

33 *a prince*: Alf, the son of Hrodmar. A *holmgang*, literally 'going to an island',
    was a single combat which might be fought to settle matters of honour.

    fetches: in Norse, *fylgjur*, kinds of guardian spirit, usually female, who
    appear when the death of the hero is near. Both the wolf and the troll-
    woman are manifestations of Helgi's doom.

A SECOND POEM OF HELGI HUNDINGSBANI

2   *Piercing*: the belief that the hero has especially piercing eyes which can-
    not be disguised occurs often in Old Norse; compare Volund's eyes in the
    Poem of Volund, v. 17.

7   *goslings of Gunn's sisters*: Gunn is a valkyrie, as are her sisters. The goslings
    of the valkyrie are ravens, given carrion to eat by the warrior.

8   *bears in Bragalund*: Helgi talks in riddles, still disguising his identity.

    '*Old Poem of the Volsungs*': this has not survived.

25 *the troll-woman's grey horse-herd*: wolves.

26 *strange creature*: the same term is used for Volund's swan-maiden wife
    Hervor and her sisters in the *Poem of Volund*.

    norns: spirit women who determine fate; cf. *First Poem of Helgi Hund-
    ingsbani*, v. 2.

32 *not go forward*: the elements of Sigrun's curse may be compared with the
    curses in the *Poem of Atli*, v. 30.

39 *fetch the foot-bath*: Hunding is humiliated in Valhall by being made to do
    the work of slaves.

43 *hawks of Odin*: ravens.

44 *slaughter-dew*: blood.

46 *precious liquors*: presumably Sigrun has brought some mead or ale into the
    mound with her.

49 *Salgofnir*: the cock who awakens the inhabitants of Valhall.

50 *dream-assembly*: sleep.

    '*Song of Kara*': this has not survived.

THE DEATH OF SINFIOTLI

[?]: the manuscript leaves a space for the missing name.

disappeared: the old man is most likely Odin, come to take Sinfiotli to Valhall.

GRIPIR'S PROPHECY

3 *Hiordis*: the relationship between a man and his sister's son is a privileged one in Germanic culture.

5 *Grani*: Sigurd's famous horse; how Sigurd chose him from his grand-father's stud is recounted in the prose following the poem. *Volsunga saga*, ch. 13, relates that Odin guided Sigurd to choose Grani, who is a descendant of Sleipnir, Odin's eight-legged steed.

9 *Eylimi's sorrow*: Eylimi, Sigmund's father-in-law, fell fighting the sons of Hunding when Sigmund was killed. Thus Hiordis, Sigurd's mother, lost husband and father in a single battle. *Volsunga saga*, chs. 11–12, gives full details.

13 *ride to Giuki's*: this is out of sequence. Sigurd does not visit Giuki until he has freed the valkyrie on the mountain top; v. 31 has the visit in its proper place.

15 *the killing of Helgi*: this seems to link Sigrdrifa/Brynhild with Sigrun. She represents another variant of the 'valkyrie bride' motif; as in the *Poem of Helgi Hiorvardsson* and the *Second Poem of Helgi Hundingsbani*, marriage with the valkyrie ultimately causes the hero's death, though in the story of Sigurd it is the valkyrie herself who brings it about. The prose after v. 4 of the *Lay of Sigrdrifa* records that it was the death of a certain Helmet-Gunnar which prompted Odin to banish Sigrdrifa to the mountain top.

17 *and now farewell, king!*: Gripir seeks to end the conversation before he has to relate Sigurd's later misfortunes.

27 *Brynhild*: the poet of *Gripir's Prophecy* follows the succeeding poems in distinguishing between the valkyrie Sigrdrifa, whom Sigurd encounters on the mountain, and Brynhild, whom he first meets on this visit to Heimir. For further discussion of the complications of the doubling of Sigrdrifa and Brynhild, see p. 168 above.

41–3 the verses are numbered in the order of the manuscript. However, logically, 42 cannot follow 41, since it is a reaction to the news (given in 43) that Gunnar will marry Brynhild despite the nights she and Sigurd have spent together. The verses have been transposed to make narrative sense.

THE LAY OF REGIN

Sigurd . . . Grani: the events recounted here are also narrated in *Volsunga saga*, chs. 13 and 14.

1 *serpent's flame*: gold, because serpents, especially dragons, like to bask on heaps of gold.

2 *a wretched norn*: norns, dispensers of fate, are not normally imagined singly, but this one seems to have put a curse on Andvari.

3 *wound . . . with words*: Loki's question seems to be a *non sequitur*, but various figures in the *Edda*, notably Sigurd in the *Lay of Fafnir*, vv. 12–15, take the opportunity when they have a supernatural being at their mercy to question him about knowledge normally hidden from gods and humans.

4 *Vadgelmir*: an underworld river, probably similar to Slid ('Fearful') in the *Seeress's Prophecy*, v. 36.

   ring: according to Snorri, *Edda*, p. 100, the ring had a replicative function, generating more gold from itself. Hence Andvari is particularly reluctant to give it up.

5 *cause of strife*: Andvari puts a curse on the gold. The death of two brothers refers to Regin and Fafnir, who will both be destroyed through their lust for the gold. The strife between eight princes is less easy to assimilate to the later stages of Sigurd's life—the phrase may be a general one.

8 *princes . . . not yet born*: possibly Gunnar and Hogni, who will be killed for the gold-hoard by Atli in the *Poem of Atli*.

11 *son will avenge*: one might expect Lyngheid's descendants to be significant in the rest of the Sigurd story, but in fact this is a blind motif. Hreidmar takes the view that vengeance is the duty of a great-grandson, if it cannot be achieved any earlier.

   helmet of dread: exactly what this magical device is, is not clear, but Fafnir relies on it to maintain his power—see the *Lay of Fafnir*, vv. 16–17.

18 *Hnikar they called me*: Odin in disguise has come to Sigurd's rescue; *Volsunga saga*, ch. 17, tells of Odin's continuing patronage of the Volsungs.

23 *late-shining sister of the moon*: i.e. the sun. Not to face into the sun in the late afternoon is common-sense advice.

   wedge-shaped battle-array: this battle-formation is particularly associated with Odin, who teaches it to the hero Haddingus, under similar circumstances, according to Saxo, *History of the Danish People*, Book I, p. 31.

24 *disir*: female spirits, either fertility spirits or ancestors, who concern themselves with the fates of fighting men.

26 *a bloody eagle*: there is considerable controversy among scholars as to whether this phrase simply means that the eagle perches on the back of the corpse, or whether it is a reference to the (probably not historical) practice of sacrificing a defeated enemy to Odin by breaking open the ribs and drawing the lungs out onto the back in the shape of an eagle's wings. The 'blood-eagle' rite is mentioned in the purportedly historical *Orkneyinga saga*, here, and in the legendary *Saga of Ragnar Lodbrok*.

THE LAY OF FAFNIR

2 *"Pre-eminent beast"*: this riddling allusion still has not been satisfactorily explained, nor why Sigurd then voluntarily reveals his identity in v. 4.

5 *innate qualities*: the Norse text makes little sense at this point. I follow the suggestion of La Farge and Tucker here.

11 *The norns' judgement*: the norns are fate-figures—their judgement is the hero's doom. However, though Fafnir seems to be threatening Sigurd with drowning, this is a blind motif.

12 *Tell me, Fafnir*: as in the *Lay of Regin* the hero presses the supernatural figure to share his wisdom with him, mythological knowledge which will fit Sigurd for future kingship.

   bring children forth from their mothers: some norns preside over childbirth, determining the fate of the newborn.

13 *daughters of Dvalin*: i.e. descended from the dwarfs, a fact not found elsewhere in Norse myth.

14 *sword-liquid*: i.e. blood.

16 *helm of terror*: the nature of Fafnir's magical protection is unclear.

29 *the old giant*: see note to v. 38 below.

32 *destroyer of rings*: generous man, who breaks up arm-rings to distribute to his followers.

35 *I expect a wolf*: a proverbial saying, meaning that savagery is to be expected from a savage person, referring either to Regin's nature or Sigurd's courage.

38 *frost-cold giant*: Regin is described as a dwarf in the prose introduction to the *Lay of Regin*, but he himself calls Fafnir a giant above at v. 29. Probably the tradition that the brothers were giants is the older one; Regin's dwarfishness is likely to have developed in connection with his skills as a smith.

42 *radiant river-light*: a kenning for gold.

43 *terror of the linden*: fire, for the tree is consumed by it.

   thorn: a sleep-thorn as a punishment for giving victory to the wrong fighter.

   goddess of flax: conventional term for a woman, who wears linen garments.

THE LAY OF SIGRDRIFA

acquainted with fear: this is the condition of marriage which Brynhild makes, pointing to an original identity between Sigrdrifa and Brynhild. Certainly Sigrdrifa is not known to Snorri, nor does this name appear in *Volsunga saga*.

5 *apple-tree of battle*: warrior.

7 *"Naud"*: 'need', the name of the rune denoting the sound 'n'. Sinfiotli, Sigurd's half-brother, had been killed by just such a poisoned horn (see the *Death of Sinfiotli* above).

9 *disir*: female ancestors or fertility spirits. Here they are said to help women in childbirth, a function ascribed to norns in the *Lay of Fafnir*, v. 12.

13 *Hoddrofnir's horn*: this verse is obscure; the liquid referred to here may be identical in some way with the mead of poetry (see *Sayings of the High One* above). Heiddraupnir ('Bright-dropper') and Hoddrofnir ('Hoard-tearer') are unknown. Hropt is a name for Odin; compare Hroptatyr in *Grimnir's Sayings*, v. 54.

14 *Brimir's sword*: the reference is unknown.

Mim's head: presumably identical with Mimir, who was sent as a hostage to the Vanir, according to Snorri in *Ynglinga saga*, ch. 4. The Vanir cut off his head, preserved it, and returned it to the Æsir. Odin consults it for advice, cf. *Seeress's Prophecy*, v. 45.

15 *shield . . . Alsvinn's hoof*: the shield must be Svalin, the shield in front of the sun, mentioned in *Grimnir's Sayings*, v. 38. Arvak and Alsvinn must be identical with Arvak and Alsvid who, in *Grimnir's Sayings*, v. 37, are named as the horses who draw the sun.

19 *book-runes*: or possibly beech-runes, but most likely an error for 'healing-runes' (*bótrúnar*).

20 *maple of sharp weapons*: warrior.

29 *becomes offensive*: this is where the lacuna in the Codex Regius begins. The remainder of the verses in the poem are supplied from later paper manuscripts.

30 *Songs*: these seem an unlikely cause of sorrow—the great manuscript collector Árni Magnússon suggested *sennur* 'quarrels' instead.

31 *burnt inside*: burnt alive in your house, a tactic used sometimes in the sagas, most notably in *Njals saga*.

34 *coffin*: the reference seems closer to Christian burial rites than the usual pagan practice of cremation.

FRAGMENT OF A POEM ABOUT SIGURD

2 *all are broken*: Brynhild has persuaded Gunnar that, during the three nights (according to *Volsunga saga*, ch. 29) or eight nights (*Brynhild's Ride to Hell*, v. 12) when she and Sigurd slept side-by-side after Sigurd, disguised as Gunnar, had ridden through the magic flame-wall and won her, Sigurd took her virginity. This is not true; the two, as Brynhild later admits in v. 19, were separated by a sword.

4 *Guthorm*: the youngest brother did not swear oaths of loyalty to Sigurd.

He needs to be fed on magical food which will increase his courage in order to become brave enough to attack Sigurd.

9 *the inheritance of Giuki*: Brynhild seems to imply that Sigurd would in time have displaced Gunnar and Hogni from their territory. Whether Sigurd would in time have fathered five sons or whether the five sons are the offspring of Giuki is unclear. Only three are mentioned in the Poetic Edda and *Volsunga saga*, but *Thidreks saga*, drawing on the Middle High German tradition in the *Nibelungenlied*, knows of two others, Gernoz and Gisler.

13 *the raven and the eagle*: presumably the two birds of battle portended doom to Gunnar after the murder; no more is revealed about this.

17 *blood run into a trench*: Sigurd and Gunnar had sworn blood-brotherhood to one another. The ceremony involved scraping a trench in the earth and pouring the mingled blood of the oathtakers into it. Similar rituals are referred to in the *Saga of Gisli* and in the *Saga of the Foster-brothers*.

18 *destroyer of armies*: Sigurd; the young prince of the next line is Gunnar. Brynhild reveals that, contrary to what she had previously told Gunnar, she and Sigurd had slept chastely together.

19 *wound-wand*: sword.

'*Old Poem of Gudrun*': this seems to correspond to the *Second Poem of Gudrun*, below.

THE FIRST POEM OF GUDRUN

2 *fierceness of mind*: the poem leaves open the question of whether Gudrun is so traumatized that she cannot weep for her husband or whether she deliberately withholds the normal signs of female mourning, alarming the onlookers, who fear her rage and perhaps vengeance.

12 *Gullrond*: Gudrun's sister, although she appears only here.

23 *runes of speaking*: i.e. unlocked, as if by magic, Gudrun's power of speech. Once her lament begins, Gudrun displays proper female grieving behaviour. Brynhild's curse indicates that her hostility to her sister-in-law has not ended with Sigurd's death.

26 *fire of the serpent's bed*: gold, as dragons (serpents) like to lie on top of gold. Atli's greed for gold, a theme developed later in the *Poetic Edda*, caused him to force Brynhild into marriage.

A SHORT POEM ABOUT SIGURD

3 *knew the way*: this verse gives the clearest indication of Sigurd's prior relationship with Brynhild, whom he would have married if fate had allowed it.

4 *man from the south*: in this poem the epithet refers to Sigurd, perhaps because of his mother's connections with the land of the Franks.

7 *norns*: female figures who determine fate.

8 *cold of ice, of glaciers*: since the events of the Sigurd story take place near the Rhine, the reference to glaciers suggests icy resolution rather than a realistic description of the landscape.

12 *the son*: i.e. the son of Sigurd and Gudrun, named elsewhere as Sigmund, who would be a likely future avenger for his father.

16 *the Rhine-metal*: i.e. Fafnir's hoard, now in Sigurd's possession. The history of the hoard is told in the *Lay of Regin*. Its designation as 'Rhine-metal' is prospective; it will only become associated with that river when Gunnar orders it to be thrown in the Rhine rather than yielded to Atli.

18 *we four*: Gunnar, Hogni, Guthorm, and Sigurd.

22 *battle-eager man*: i.e. Sigurd.

23 *backwards*: the slightly comic effect here underlines the cowardly nature of Guthorm's attack on the sleeping Sigurd.

25 *clapped together her hands*: this gesture seems to be a sign of grief: compare the *First Poem of Gudrun*, v. 1.

27 *No such sister's son*: the sense is that Sigurd's oldest son is the finest boy that Gudrun could ever give birth to, even if she were to have many sons by future husbands. Her brothers will not tolerate the boy's survival. The logic is spelt out in *Volsunga saga*, ch. 32.

30 *Then Brynhild laughed*: compare *Fragment of a Poem about Sigurd*, v. 10.

34 *constrained at all*: Brynhild points out her happiness and independence before she was forced to marry.

36 *Atli said*: Brynhild's full inheritance of her father's treasure, in particular the portion set aside for her dowry, depends upon her getting married to a suitor Atli approves of. Brynhild can either fight him over this or capitulate, as the following verse makes clear. In *Volsunga saga*, ch. 31, it is Budli who compels Brynhild to marry.

40 *valkyrie of necklaces*: i.e. woman, Brynhild herself.

46 *necklace-tree*: a kenning for woman, thus Brynhild.

47 *her dead maids*: Brynhild's close female companions seem to have committed suicide to join their mistress in death, though in v. 50 some—less heroic—women decline to follow the same path, despite Brynhild's promises of rewards and honour.

52 *treasures of Menia*: Menia is one of the giantesses in the *Song of Grotti* who was employed as a slave to grind out gold for King Frodi from a magic millstone.

54 *along with the king*: this probably refers to Gunnar, remembering his lost friendship with Sigurd.

55 *Svanhild*: Sigurd's posthumously born daughter; her fate is related in the *Whetting of Gudrun* and the *Lay of Hamdir* as well as later in Brynhild's prophecy.

58   *Oddrun*: the love of Oddrun and Gunnar is a late addition to the cycle, developed in *Oddrun's Lament*. Oddrun is unknown to the German tradition. In Norse she is a sister of Atli and Brynhild. Gunnar's seduction of Oddrun thus provides a further motive for Atli's killing of Gunnar, though it is clear that his desire to get Sigurd's treasure is the more original and important motive.

59 *snake-pit*: this exotic method of execution is to be found in several places in Old Norse, notably in the *Saga of Ragnar Lodbrok*. The idea is most probably imported from the Near East.

64 *Bikki's counsel*: the reference is to the events which precede the *Lay of Hamdir*. Svanhild is sent to marry the cruel emperor of the Goths, Iormunrekk, but his wicked counsellor, Bikki, advises the emperor that Svanhild is the lover of the emperor's son, Randver. Furious, Iormunrekk has his son hanged and Svanhild trampled to death by horses. See Snorri, *Edda*, pp. 104–6.

69 *jangle at his heels*: i.e. I must not delay following Sigurd much longer. The funeral is described in *Volsunga saga*, ch. 33.

BRYNHILD'S RIDE TO HELL

 1 *befit you . . . weaving*: the giantess takes a conservative view of women's behaviour; compare the Old English *Exeter Maxims*, l. 63, which observes that it befits a woman to be at her embroidery.

 5 *made me an oath-breaker*: in the preceding poem Brynhild has accused her husband and his brother of breaking their oaths to Sigurd. Here she recognizes that their deception of her has caused her to break her own oath: that she would marry only the man capable of crossing the flame-wall, that is, Sigurd.

 6 *put under an oak*: this part of Brynhild's story is unclear and not mentioned elsewhere. Most likely the motif is borrowed from swan-maiden stories, like the one in the *Poem of Volund*. Brynhild and her sisters were able to change their shape by means of the magic garments, probably into some kind of bird, in connection with their life as valkyries. A king— perhaps Gunnar, perhaps Atli—brings this life to an end by taking the shape-changing garment and forcing her into marriage. Or conceivably this is a reference to the beginning of the valkyrie's career, acquiring the magic garments from beneath the tree.

 7 *War-lady in the helmet*: a kenning for a valkyrie.

 8 *Odin was very angry*: Brynhild's story is identical with that of Sigrdrifa in the *Lay of Sigrdrifa*, showing that the two figures have coalesced.

10 *destroyer of all wood*: i.e. fire.

11 *Danish viking*: i.e. Sigurd. Although he is often characterized in the Volsung poems as the man from the south, Sigurd was brought up in Denmark and it is there that Gudrun takes refuge after his death in the poem that follows this one. The Volsungs' ancestral territories are said in *Volsunga saga* to be in *Húnaland*, the land of the Huns.

THE SECOND POEM OF GUDRUN

Thiodrek: a legendary Germanic ruler, only loosely connected with the historic Theodoric the Great. Thiodrek spent thirty years in exile from his kingdom of Verona, in flight from Iormunrekkr (Ermanaric), his maternal uncle. During his exile at Atli's court he becomes Gudrun's confidante; this leads to the accusation central to the *Third Poem of Gudrun*.

2 *green leek*: cf. the *First Poem of Gudrun*, v. 18.2.

4 *from the Assembly*: the manuscript reads 'to' here. This poem follows the tradition pointed out at the end of the *Fragment* (p. 171), that the brothers killed Sigurd at the Assembly rather than in his bed.

18 *yew bow*: Grimhild arranges a splendid formal procession to make peace with Gudrun.

21 *I should not remember*: Grimhild's drink of forgetting contrasts with the memory-drinks which Sigrdrifa gives to Sigurd in the *Lay of Sigrdrifa*, and which Freyia asks for to give to Ottar in *Hyndla's Song*, v. 45.

22 *heather-fish*: a snake.

corn-ear of the Haddings' land: obscure. The 'land of the Haddings' is the sea—an uncut corn-ear of the sea is perhaps seaweed.

24 *death*: a conjecture; the word *iorbjug* in R is unexplained.

28 *Sigmund*: the son of Sigurd and Gudrun, murdered at Sigurd's death and named after Sigurd's father.

43 *white beasts*: the meaning of the Norse *hviting* ('white thing') is obscure; it is possible that these are animals intended for sacrifice, anticipating the killing of Erp and Eitil. Gudrun deliberately misinterprets Atli's doom-laden dreams, which presage the events of the *Poem of Atli*. In *Volsunga saga*, ch. 35, in contrast, Gudrun tells Atli the truth about the import of the dreams.

THE THIRD POEM OF GUDRUN

5 *deprived of all my closest kin*: along with v. 8 this suggests that, despite the position of the poem in the manuscript before the *Poem of Atli*, Gudrun's brothers Gunnar and Hogni are already dead.

11 *foul bog*: drowning criminals under a lattice in a bog was a well-attested Germanic punishment, mentioned by Tacitus in *Germania*, ch. 12.

ODDRUN'S LAMENT

6　*the hawk-bearer's friend*: warrior.

7　*sharp spells*: the idea that problematic labour can be helped with spells or runes is a common one in the *Edda*. See also the *Lay of Sigrdrifa*, v. 9, and the role of the norns in the *Lay of Fafnir*, vv. 12–13.

8　*Hogni's slayer*: Vilmund, father of the children, is not named as the killer of Hogni anywhere else. That Borgny's lover murdered Oddrun's lover's brother may explain some of the hostility between the former friends.

12　*drink for Gunnar*: the significance seems to be that for a woman to prepare a drink for a man is a sign of intimacy; since the betrothal between Oddrun and Gunnar had not yet been arranged, Borgny was scandalized by Oddrun's action. Her moral stance is ironic given her own later liaison with Vilmund. Editors have often rearranged vv. 11–16, but sense can be made of them in their manuscript order.

16　*Odin's beloved girl*: the dying Budli arranges a marriage to Gunnar for Oddrun and the life of a valkyrie for Brynhild, but their fates go awry.

21　*burden of Grani*: this is a common kenning for 'gold', but in this context it may literally refer to the treasure-hoard Sigurd won from the dragon and which he loaded on his horse's back to take away. The hoard had passed into the hands of Gunnar and Hogni.

22　*ring-breaker*: a generous man who breaks up gold rings to distribute to his followers.

29　*wise king*: i.e. Gunnar.

32　*the mother of Atli*: here Oddrun says that Atli's (and thus her own) mother is responsible for Gunnar's death; in other sources, one particularly large serpent, resistant to Gunnar's harp-playing, strikes the death-blow (Snorri, *Edda*, p. 104; *Volsunga saga*, ch. 39). Scholars have reconciled the two accounts by assuming that Atli's mother magically turns herself into a snake and hence is immune to Gunnar's serpent-charming.

33　*goddess of the linen-pillow*: i.e. lady, Borgny, whom Oddrun is addressing.

THE POEM OF ATLI

2　*handsome hall*: the original *valhollo* may refer to Valhall, the home of warriors after death, and perhaps implies that Gunnar and his brother are as good as dead. *Val-* can also mean 'exotic', 'splendid', however.

3　*you two*: though Knefrod at first addresses Gunnar, as the elder brother, he makes it clear that Hogni is included in the invitation by the use of a dual form.

6 *gold on Gnita-heath*: Gnita-heath was the home of the dragon Fafnir; the gold there had been taken by Sigurd and has now passed to Gunnar. So the brothers literally already own the gold of Gnita-heath, though they have no jurisdiction over the territory of Fafnir's former home.

8 *heath-wanderer*: the wolf. Gudrun sends the ring with a wolf-hair twisted round it as a secret message which Hogni correctly interprets. The motif is subtler than the altered runes which have a similar function in the *Greenlandic Lay of Atli*.

12 *young men's court*: the manuscript has 'court of the Huns', which cannot be right. Normally the poem keeps the two tribes scrupulously separate.

14 *Bikki*: the evil counsellor of Iormunrekk of the Goths, who belongs in the *Lay of Hamdir*. Possibly Budli, Atli's father, is meant; although according to the chronology of the heroic poems he is dead, he may still have recruited the warriors who keep watch.

16 *norns weep*: even the implacable determiners of fate would have been moved to pity by the greatness of the slaughter if Gunnar and Hogni had come armed.

17 *the Rhine's russet mountains*: this is a crux in the Norse and may refer to Worms on the Rhine, the Niflung headquarters.

20 *lord of the Goths*: i.e. Gunnar.

22 *Hialli*: a cowardly retainer of Atli.

26 *far from my eyes*: Gunnar prophesies Atli's death.

27 *the Æsir-given inheritance*: the Norse is obscure here. This interpretation, coming at the climax of the Rhinegold theme, recalls how it came to play a part in the history of the Volsung and Niflung dynasties.

28 *bit-shaker*: the 'bit-shaker' is a horse. The 'neckring-guardian' in the following line is a possessor of treasure. The elaborate metaphors work to conceal the slow horror of Gunnar's death-journey. Editors, for example Neckel-Kuhn, sometimes split v. 28 and put the second half after v. 30, but this is not necessary: the action switches between the procession to the pit, Atli on his horse, and Gudrun left behind in the hall.

31 *harp*: Gunnar harps to show his aristocratic fearlessness, but the harping is also imagined to have a charming effect on the snakes in some sources.

33 *little creatures gone into darkness*: Gudrun is deliberately riddling here. In Norse the word signifying 'gone into darkness', *niflfarna*, puns on 'Niflung'. The dead children are also of Niflung stock like their mother and dead uncles.

36 *sharer-out of swords*: this type of construction, where a noun group is split up by another phrase, is very frequent in skaldic poetry, but rare in eddic verse, suggesting possible influence from the skaldic style.

THE GREENLANDIC LAY OF ATLI

3 *lady of the house*: Gudrun.

6 *both*: here, as in the *Nibelungenlied*, two messengers are sent, but the second man swiftly fades from view.

9 *The couple*: i.e. Hogni and Kostbera.

15 *burnt up*: Hogni points to some old clothes ready for burning and suggests that this domestic concern is the subject of Kostbera's dream. Her other dreams are equally interpreted as domestic in reference, while Glaumvor's seem to be understood more symbolically.

18 *white bear*: that Hogni should automatically assume that the bear is white seems to confirm the connection with Greenland.

21 *Gunnar undertook*: something is missing in the manuscript. I follow Ursula Dronke's suggestion here.

28 *disir*: female spirits who watch over a lineage and often appear in connection with a death. Such figures are often found in the sagas where they presage the death of the hero, notably in *Gisla saga*, where a good and a bad dream-woman do battle over Gisli.

30 *this was ill-advised*: the brothers decide to take just their kinsmen—Hogni's sons and brother-in-law—on the journey. The rather small number of other men who might have gone with them points to a scaled-down setting in comparison with the *Poem of Atli*.

34 *Bera*: i.e. Kostbera, Hogni's wife.

37 *didn't tie up*: thus the boat would drift away and the party be unable to return. The detail shows the resolution of Gunnar and Hogni in the face of the knowledge of their death. Similarly in the *Nibelungenlied*, Hagen rows very violently and does not tie up the boats after Gunther and his men have crossed the Rhine on their fatal journey to visit Etzel, the equivalent of Atli in that poem.

43 *struck down one*: i.e. Vingi.

54 *the brave man*: i.e. Atli.

55 *five of us brothers*: *Volsunga saga*, ch. 36, gives four brothers here. In v. 97 Gudrun refers to an earlier battle between Atli's brothers in which 'half your line were sent off to Hel'; thus two of Atli's four brothers died in the previous fraternal conflict while the final pair have been killed in battle by Gudrun. None of these brothers are mentioned elsewhere in the poetic sources.

56 *sister off to hell*: Atli, with some justification, blames the Giukungs for the death of Brynhild.

57 *wise cousin*: this detail, and the suggestion that Atli was responsible for Grimhild's death, is unknown from any other texts. Some German sources, however, recount that Atli met his death in a cave where the treasure was hidden.

59 *gallows*: in fact the gallows are never used, but the detail here, and in Vingi's remarks in v. 39, seems to be necessary to fulfil Glaumvor's dream in v. 22.

61 *fated for death*: the implication is that a coward, always fearing death, is halfway dead already. Hialli will not be missed.

65 *sons of day*: this meaning of this phrase is unclear. It must refer to Atli's household here, although Sigrdrifa uses a similar expression to invoke the gods in *Lay of Sigrdrifa*, v. 3.

66 *foot-twigs*: i.e. toes. Presumably his hands were bound.

78 *when you find out what results*: i.e. you will be furious with yourself if you commit this deed.

80 *over*: since the battle Atli and Gudrun must have kept to different sides of the hall.

82 *skulls*: this detail is probably borrowed from the *Poem of Volund*—Gudrun herself is no smith.

87 *journey to another light*: travel to the next world, to die.

88 *Hniflung*: the son of Hogni, left behind, who has now come to seek revenge for his father.

98 *captained*: Gudrun lays claim to a martial past, explaining her courageous fighting on her brothers' side in the earlier battle.

103 *coffin*: Gudrun promises a mixture of pagan and Christian rites for Atli's funeral.

THE WHETTING OF GUDRUN

Erp: it is essential to the *Lay of Hamdir* that Erp should not be Gudrun's son. That he should bear the same name as her murdered son by Atli must be coincidence.

told the king this: in *Volsunga saga*, ch. 42, a Tristan and Isolde-like theme seems to be about to emerge. Randver is sent on a wooing journey and returns with Svanhild. Bikki suggests that the two young people are better suited to one another, and Randver agrees; they spend much of the journey in conversation together. Bikki falsely tells Iormunrekk that Randver and Svanhild are lovers. Randver is hanged, although Iormunrekk, realizing that the loss of his heir is a serious matter, tries but fails to avert the execution at the last minute. Svanhild is trampled to death by horses on her husband's orders.

1 *I*: i.e. the poet.

5 *all*: Hamdir points out, ironically enough given what is to follow in the *Lay of Hamdir*, that the expedition of revenge would have been easier if the murdered Erp and Eitil had been able to join them.

8 *to visit his mother*: Hamdir foretells that he will die on the mission of revenge; that he will visit his mother again only as a corpse, and she will have to perform the funeral rites both for her daughter and for her two sons.

11 *nor did they know of such*: that is, Gudrun's brothers.

21 *oak-wood pyre*: Gudrun intends to die now; the motif of the funeral pyre is clearly drawn from that of Brynhild in the *Short Poem about Sigurd*. Our last glimpse of Gudrun here, and in the parallel passage in the *Lay of Hamdir*, is of the bereaved mother, sister, and wife lamenting the terrible story which has unfolded in the last eleven poems.

THE LAY OF HAMDIR

1 *elves weep*: if the elves (*alfar*) are ancestral spirits, as has been suggested, they would weep when they knew disaster to be imminent for the family they protect.

5 *branch-breaker comes*: this could be a kenning for a storm-wind, or (since the phrase is feminine in Norse) it may, as Ursula Dronke suggests, refer to a girl collecting dry firewood in the summertime.

6 *Hamdir*: this response must be to a verse contrasting the two brothers with Gunnar and Hogni, probably much like the *Whetting of Gudrun*, v. 3, rather than the preceding verse in this poem.

12 *son of a different mother*: this is Erp, half-brother to Hamdir and Sorli by a different mother. That he shares a name with Gudrun's son by Atli is coincidental.

15 *troll-woman*: possibly Hel, goddess of death, or a malevolent *dis*.

17 *sister's son*: i.e. stepson, Randver, whom Iormunrekk had believed to be Svanhild's lover. That he is wounded as well as hanged may suggest an Odinic sacrifice. In *Sayings of the High One*, v. 138, Odin sacrifices himself to himself, by hanging himself on a tree and being pierced with a spear. The double motif of hanging and piercing reappears elsewhere in sagas where sacrifice to Odin is mentioned.

22 *Hrodglod*: the manuscript is defective here. This is either a woman's name or else an adjective meaning 'woman pleased by glory'.

25 *spears will not bite*: the brothers are apparently invulnerable. In *Volsunga saga*, ch. 44, and in Snorri, *Edda*, pp. 104–6, this is because Gudrun had given them magic mail-coats, resistant to iron. The poet retains the detail but not the explanation.

Hamdir: the manuscript gives Hamdir verse 26, but logically Sorli needs to speak it and the one which follows. I punctuate accordingly.

26 *opened up that bag*: Iormunrekk's armless and legless torso is compared to a bag; provoking him to speak is tantamount to opening the bag from which the fatal command comes. Bags may have been traditionally thought to contain hidden wisdom; cf. *Sayings of the High One*, v. 134.6, in connection with the wisdom of the aged: 'often from a wrinkled bag come judicious words'.

28 *if Erp were alive*: in *Volsunga saga*, ch. 44, the brothers stumble shortly after killing Erp and save themselves by leaning on the other hand and

foot. Thus they already understand Erp's remark and begin to regret the murder before the torture scene. In Snorri's account, it is only Sorli who stumbles, and Gudrun has already instructed each brother as to which portion of Iormunrekk he should cut off. Reserving the realization of the brothers' error until the climax of the poem, as here, is far more effective.

disir: female ancestral spirits whose influence is felt when a member of the clan is doomed.

BALDR'S DREAMS

1 *All together*: these lines are identical to three lines of *Thrym's Poem*, v. 14.

2 *Gaut*: this word appears most often as an Odin-name, as in *Grimnir's Sayings*, v. 54, though other meanings—such as 'sacrifice' or 'Got' (inhabitant of Götaland, a province of southern Sweden—have been mooted.

whelp: this may be Garm, the dog bound before Hel's doors in the *Seeress's Prophecy*.

4 *corpse-reviving spell*: Odin boasts of his knowledge of these spells in *Sayings of the High One*, v. 157.

9 *dispatch the high glory-tree*: this line is disputed; most commentators take 'glory-tree' as a metaphor for 'warrior', but it may conceivably refer to the mistletoe dart.

11 *Rind*: Saxo gives the story of how Odin uses magic to force himself on Rind in order to beget Baldr's avenger in his *History of the Danish People*, Book III, pp. 78–82.

12 *girls who weep*: since the seeress does not answer Odin's question, we have no idea of who these girls may be, though, following the pattern of other dialogues in the *Edda*, in which protagonists often ask questions about norns, it may be that they are referred to here. That the girls weep suggests a connection with Frigg's attempt to persuade all creation to weep Baldr out of hell. The riddling quality of the question points perhaps to a concealed kenning, denoting clouds, waves, or part of a sailing vessel—perhaps Baldr's funeral ship. Odin's enquiry reveals his true identity to the seeress, who refuses to give him any further information; it seems that in the mythological poetry of the *Edda*, only Odin goes about asking such questions.

14 *Doom of the Gods*: Baldr's death is one of the first premonitions of the coming of Ragnarok. See Snorri, *Edda*, p. 49.

THE LIST OF RIG

Rig: the name is derived from the Irish *rí (ríg* in other cases) meaning 'king'. The identification of Heimdall with Rig is not absolutely secure, since it is based only on the prose introduction, but the beginning of the *Seeress's Prophecy*, asking for attention from all 'the offspring of Heimdall', seems to suggest that the god did have some connection with the creation of mankind.

4 *coarse loaf*: typical peasant fare.

7 *sprinkled him with water*: this action is a kind of pagan naming ceremony, often mentioned in the sagas.

8 *long heels*: perhaps this implies 'dragging his heels', slow in walking.

17 *advice*: a gap follows here, probably comprising two verses. Presumably Rig receives hospitality typical of a well-set-up farmer.

23 *exchanged rings*: the farming couple get married properly, unlike Thrall and Thrall-girl who simply set up house together.

27 *gazing into one another's eyes*: in the more aristocratic household the couple have some leisure for romance.

43 *young Kin*: in Norse, Kin's name is Kon. When modified by *ungr* ('young') it becomes *konungr* or 'king', emphasizing the young man's future role.

45 *called Rig*: Kin establishes a claim to kingly status through his superior knowledge and relationship with the founder of the dynasty.

47 *Why . . . charming birds*: the crow, like the nuthatches of the *Lay of Fafnir* and the helpful bird in the *Poem of Helgi Hiorvardsson*, offers good advice to the young man. It is not entirely certain whether Kin is charming the birds, or shooting at them with his bird-bolts.

THE SONG OF HYNDLA

Ottar the simpleton: Ottar's epithet (*heimski*) implies that he has no knowledge of anything outside his home: he is ignorant, not stupid.

4 *She will sacrifice*: Freyia refers to herself here in the third person.

5 *wolves*: the traditional mount of giant women.

7 *made for me*: this beast may be identical with the boar made by the dwarf Brokk for Freyr, recounted by Snorri, *Edda*, pp. 96–7. 'Battle-hog' is a name for a helmet in skaldic poetry.

10 *turned to glass*: the stone has fused into glass because of the frequency of Ottar's sacrifices.

11 *Skioldungs . . . Ylfings*: Snorri, *Edda*, p. 148, gives fuller details of these clans. The Ylfings are the line of Sigmund and Sigurd.

17 *Hildigunn*: presumably Almveig's mother.

22 *plough-maker*: this by-name is very uncertain.

23 *the two Haddings*: two brothers, heroes who appear in a list of berserk warriors in *Heidreks saga*. They were the youngest of twelve brothers and it was only collectively that they had the strength of one man.

24 *Arngrim and Eyfura*: the parents of Angantyr and his eleven brothers. See *The Waking of Angantyr*.

26 *Hiordis*: Sigurd's mother and the daughter of Eylimi by most accounts.

Hraudung may be an error for a tribal name like Odling in the line which follows.

27 *not of the line of Giuki*: if Guthorm was only a half-brother of Gunnar and Hogni it would explain his rather marginal status in the Sigurd story.

28 *ring-scatterer*: generous man.

29 *Eleven*: vv. 29–44 belong to another poem which Snorri calls *Voluspa in skamma*—*The Short Prophecy of the Seeress*. It deals with some of the same material as the first poem in the Codex Regius and has nothing to do with the tally of ancestors which Hyndla is recounting.

brother's hand-killer: that is, Hod, who threw the mistletoe dart, rather than Loki, the *ráðbani* (counsel-slayer) who plotted Baldr's death.

30 *heir to Bur*: i.e. Odin.

Aurboda: these facts accord with *Skirnir's Journey*, though there we do not learn the name of Gerd's mother.

33 *seid-practisers*: the particular form of shape-changing and cross-dressing magic associated with the Vanir.

35 *nine women*: it has been thought on the basis of this detail that this cryptic allusion may be to Heimdall, since Snorri quotes an otherwise lost text called *Heimdalargaldr* (*The Spell of Heimdall*), in which Heimdall declares himself to be the son of nine mothers (*Edda*, pp. 25–6).

37 *Iarnsaxa*: the mother of Thor's son Magni.

40 *Svadilfari*: the stallion belonging to the Giant-builder who was repairing the walls of Asgard after the Æsir–Vanir war. Loki had to change himself into a mare and entice the stallion away to prevent the builder from fulfilling the terms of his contract and thus winning Freyia and the sun and moon for himself. See Snorri, *Edda*, pp. 35–6.

Byleist: Byleist's brother is Loki; nothing is otherwise known of Byleist, who only appears in kennings like this one (*Seeress's Prophecy*, v. 48.4, as also in the Hauksbók version, v. 45.4). The witch is presumably the goddess Hel, sister of Fenrir, mentioned earlier in the verse.

41 *Lopt was impregnated*: Lopt is a name for Loki. This story is otherwise unknown, although in *Loki's Quarrel*, v. 23, Loki is said to have borne children.

44 *name his name*: it is not clear to whom vv. 43 and 44 refer. If v. 35 refers to Heimdall, then v. 43 may have the same referent; v. 44 has been interpreted as referring to Christ. Cf. *Seeress's Prophecy* (Hauksbók text), v. 59.

45 *memory-ale*: the *Song of Hyndla* proper resumes. Ottar, disguised as Freyia's boar, now has the information he needs to prove his lineage and win his inheritance in the face of Angantyr's claims. As in the *Lay of Sigrdrifa*, memory-ale is a magic potion which enables a listener to recall everything he has heard.

46 *Heidrun*: the nanny-goat of the gods who gives mead from her udder. Hyndla accuses Freyia of promiscuity.

47 *Od*: Freyia's husband according to Snorri, *Edda*, p. 29, who went away on a journey; Freyia went to seek him, weeping tears of gold.

48 *fire from the troll-woman*: that is, from Hyndla (the addressee) herself.

THE SONG OF GROTTI

7 *He*: i.e. Frodi.

12 *men seized it*: ironically, in their childhood games Fenia and Menia created the millstone to which they are now chained.

16 *strife-calmer*: the millstone, which is still—though not for much longer—grinding out peace and prosperity.

22 *son and brother*: Hrolf Kraki was the son of his own half-sister Yrsa. Yrsa was the daughter of Thora, whom Hrolf's father, Helgi, had raped. The mother deliberately sent her daughter to seduce her father and trap him into incest; the product of their union turned out to be a great hero. The story is told in Saxo, *History of the Danish People*, Book II, pp. 51–4, and in the *Saga of Hrolf Kraki*. In contrast to Snorri, who relates that the otherwise unknown sea-king Mysing was responsible for the attack on Frodi, the poem implies that Hrolf is the aggressor, if the verse is not an interpolation. It is also possible that Hrolf takes vengeance for, rather than on, Frodi.

GROA'S CHANT

3 *An ugly game*: there are a number of motifs in the two poems which constitute the *Lay of Svipdag* which seem to be drawn from Celtic sources. In the Irish 'Tale of Art, son of Conn' the hero Art loses a board-game against his stepmother and is cursed never to eat in Ireland until he brings home a certain Delbchaem. He is thus sent on a wooing journey fraught with dangers of the type which Groa anticipates for her son.

4 *Skuld*: is named as one of the three fate-figures in the *Seeress's Prophecy*, v. 20, as also by Snorri, *Edda*, p. 18; here she seems to be working alongside other forces of fate.

6 *Rind . . . Rani*: Rind is the mother of Vali, Baldr's avenger, and a victim, rather than a practitioner of magic. Rani is unknown, though it is just possible that this refers to Rán, the goddess of the sea. If this is the allusion, then Groa is calling upon two significant mythological mothers.

7 *Urd*: a second fate-figure from the *Seeress's Prophecy*, v. 20.

8 *Horn and Rud*: mythological river-names.

10 *fifth one*: compare the fetter-loosening spell in *Sayings of the High One*, v. 149.

11 *mill-box*: this is the problematic word *lúðr*, meaning primarily 'box' or 'container'; see note to *Sayings of Vafthrudnir*, v. 35 above. Here Groa

seems to imagine the ocean as milling out calm seas and good sailing conditions for her son.

13 *dead Christian woman*: why a specifically Christian female corpse might pose a threat is unclear.

14 *spear-magnificent giant*: this spell, unlike the others which find no reflex in the poem which follows, looks forward to Svipdag's encounter with Fiolsvinn. The term 'spear-magnificent' is unusual; it may have been borrowed from *Song of Hyndla*, v. 35.

THE SAYINGS OF FIOLSVINN

3 *'Bereft of fitting speech . . . go on home from here!'*: it is not clear whether these lines belong to Svipdag or to Fiolsvinn. Svipdag has good reason to reproach Fiolsvinn for failing to offer a welcome, but Fiolsvinn seems more likely to order the interloper to go home. Svipdag manages finally to prove that he can wield 'fitting speech' when he reveals his name.

4 *Much-wise*: Svipdag conceals his name, like Sigurd in the *Lay of Fafnir*, fearing to give his enemy power over him. The false name delays the joyous revelation at the end of the poem.

6 *Tell me, boy*: cf. *Lay of Fafnir*, v. 1.

10 *who lifts . . . place*: the structure of the door is parallel with those mentioned in the *List of Rig*.

12 *Clay-surf's limbs*: Clay-surf (*Leirbrimir*) seems to be a giant name.

13 *. . .*: a line is missing here.

14 *Gifr . . . Geri*: Geri shares his name with one of Odin's wolves, the halldogs of Valhall.

15 *battle-brave ones*: that is, the dogs. They sleep in shifts, so, as Svipdag suggests in the next verse, the only way to get past them is to distract them with food.

18 *Vidofnir*: in v. 24 it is revealed that Vidofnir is a cockerel roosting in the tree of Mimi.

20 *wood of Mimi*: the information that no man knows where the roots of this tree run suggests a connection with the World-Tree Yggdrasill; Odin's eye is lodged in Mimir's well, situated beneath Yggdrasill, in the *Seeress's Prophecy*, v. 29. Hoddmimir's wood in *Sayings of Vafthrudnir*, v. 45, a tree which survives Ragnarok, may be the World-Tree's successor or be identical to it. Mimi's wood is also called the 'Measuring-Tree' (*miotviðr*), a term used for Yggdrasill in the *Seeress's Prophecy*, vv. 2 and 45.

22 *suffering women*: the poem has an interest in women's illness and its healing; exactly what illness can be cured by burning the tree's fruit is unclear.

24 *Sinmara*: probably a giantess, cf. 'pale giantess' in v. 29. How Vidofnir oppresses her is not clear.

28 *Aurglasir's goddess*: since Aurglasir means something like 'loam-tree', it seems likely that Sinmara lives underground, beneath the tree on which the cockerel perches, guarding there the sinister weapon, Malice-twig, uprooted by Loki, which can slay the bird.

30 *gleaming scythe . . . container*: these lines are almost impossible to interpret. The 'scythe', it has been suggested, may be the curving tail-feather of the bird; the 'container' is the mysterious term *lúðr*, and perhaps refers to the 'cauldron' mentioned in v. 26. The circularity of the quest to enter Menglod's hall by force becomes apparent here, and Svipdag changes his line of enquiry to elicit information about Menglod's hall, lying within the impassable gates.

31 *knowing, flickering flame*: Cf. *Skirnir's Journey*, vv. 8–9.

32 *quake on a spike's tip*: the magical hall is precariously balanced; this may be a Celtic detail. In the 'Tale of Art', Delbchaem's bower rests on a single pillar.

34 *completer of the lookout*: Delling is a dwarf name; it seems likely that the other names in the verse belong to dwarf-craftsmen who constructed the magic hall.

36 *if she can clamber up it*: another reference to women's illness; cf. v. 22.

38 *'Hlif . . . Aurboda'*: Menglod's maidens have largely positive-sounding names—*Hlif* means 'Protection' for example. However, Aurboda is named as Gerd's mother in *Song of Hyndla*, v. 30, suggesting that she—and perhaps Menglod herself—is a giantess.

47 *shamefully laid down*: Svipdag refers back to his stepmother's curse, now successfully overcome since he has won his fated bride.

50 *live fully out life and time*: this final triumphant line of Menglod echoes Brynhild's declaration that she and Sigurd will pass eternity together when she is reunited with him in Hel. See *Brynhild's Ride to Hell*, v. 14.

THE WAKING OF ANGANTYR

9 *dwarfs forged*: as elsewhere, powerful magical items have a dwarf-origin.

11 *Eyfura*: the mother of Angantyr and his brothers; she and Arngrim also appear in *Song of Hyndla*, v. 24.

14 *Two men living . . . owner*: Angantyr lies about his possession of the sword though his lie suggests that if two men own the sword, one will end up killing the other.

15 *may the God then leave you*: the import of this remark is not entirely clear. It appears Hervor invokes an unnamed god to preserve Angantyr if indeed, contrary to her suspicions, he is telling the truth.

17 *spirit-enclosure*: breast, heart.

19 *sky's tent*: the heavens.

21 *metal of the Goths*: Hervor is equipped with full war-gear; the kenning may refer to her sword, or to her armour in general—perhaps her shield since none is mentioned in the verse. Hervor is descended from the Goths on her mother's side.

22 *hater of mail-shirts*: sword.

28 *gulf-horses*: ships.

APPENDIX: THE SEERESS'S PROPHECY (HAUKSBÓK TEXT)

1 *Woe-father's deception*: this might refer to Loki and his role in Ragnarok; or the epithet may designate (as does the corresponding 'Father of the Slain') Odin, who may himself be deceived, or may be—as elsewhere—deceiving the seeress about his identity.

10 *They made*: here the gods, it seems, create the dwarfs.

17 *Until three ogre-girls*: this repeats v. 8.3; the girls do not seem to be connected with the creation of humans however.

20 *hall*: in R the girls emerge from water beneath the tree.

24 *know more: and what?*: the H version does not relate the occasion of the poem's utterance: the Seeress's encounter with Odin and his payment to her. Cf. *Seeress's Prophecy*, vv. 29–30. Nor is the catalogue of valkyries included here.

25–6 *In the east . . . and what?*: these two verses (vv. 25–6) describe the inimical powers which will bring about Ragnarok; they occur earlier than in R.

27 *war in the world*: the sequence of events from the burning of Gullveig to the aftermath of the war with the Vanir does not here directly generate the bargain with the Giant-builder which risks the loss of Freyia, and leads to Thor's violence, breaking the Æsir's oaths.

31 *bonds . . . Vali*: the syntax is difficult; I assume that Vali is the implied agent and that as the avenger of Baldr he fetters Loki. In the prose associated with *Loki's Quarrel* the binding occurs after Loki's showdown with the gods. Snorri, *Edda*, p. 52, gives a rationalized account of Loki's binding. This is the only, rather indirect, reference to the circumstances of Baldr's death in H.

32 *I see further . . . utter*: H does not have the alternation between first and third persons for the seeress which R shows. Moreover, in H the verbs of seeing are all in the present tense; in the equivalent verse in R (v. 43) the tense switches from past to present as the seeress stops remembering the past and begins to address the present and future.

41 *swallows that one up*: it is not clear who is swallowed by Surt's kinsman (who is probably fire).

49 *wolf . . . Vidar's kinsman*: Odin (Vidar's kinsman) has been killed by Fenrir,

and the wolf in turn has been killed by Odin's son Vidar; 'death' is not visible in the manuscript, but seems to be implied.

50 . . . : the few words visible here in the manuscript seem to refer to the serpent and also to humans (*halir*).

56 *the golden-gods are well*: H imagines Baldr and Hod living at peace together; R here (v. 59) describes Baldr and Hod as 'slaughter-gods', implying that death in battle still exists in the new world. 'Golden' (*vell*) is what H has here, although the scribe seems to have tried to alter the vowel, giving *val* (slaughter).

59 *the mighty one*: this verse is preserved only here; it may refer still to Baldr or signal that Christ coming to the Last Judgement will displace the post-Ragnarok order among the gods.

ANNOTATED INDEX OF NAMES

LIST OF ABBREVIATIONS

Note: in the index below, references within each entry follow the order of the poems in the text, and two or more characters sharing a common name are listed according to the order of their first appearance in the text. References are to verse and line number; line numbers refer to the lineation in this translation.

Ani, kinsman of Ottar: *Hynd* 24.1

Arastein, a place: *HH1* 14.2; *HH2* prose

Arngrim, kinsman of Ottar and father of Angantyr and his brothers: *Hynd* 24.2; *Wak* 11.1, 30.4

Arvak ('Early-waker'), a horse which pulls the sun: *Grim* 37.1; *Sigrd* 15.3

Asa-Thor, 'Thor of the Æsir': *Harb* 52.1

Asgard, home of the gods: *Hym* 7.2; *Thrym* 18.3

Ash (Ask), the first man: *Seer* 17.4; *Seer(H)* 17.4

Ash-nose (Arinnefia), daughter of Thrall and Thrall-girl: *Rig* 13.2

Asmund, unknown person: *Grim* 49.2

Asolf, ancestor of Ottar: *Hynd* 21.1

Asvid, a giant: *High* 143.3

Asynior, the female Æsir (pl.): *Lok* 11.1, 31.3; *Thrym* 14.2; *Baldr* 1.2

Atla, a giantess: *Hynd* 37.4

Atli (1), son of Hring: *HH1* 52.2

Atli (2), son of Idmund: *HHi* prose, 2.1, 15.1, 19.1, 20.1, 3, 22.1, 30.2

Atli (3), son of Budli, brother of Brynhild: *Frag* 5.3; *Gud1* 25.2; *Short* 32.2, 33.2, 36.1, 40.3 ff.; *Death*; *Gud2* 26.4, 37.1; *Gud3* prose, 1.1, 10.1; *Odd* prose, 2.1, 22.1, 23.3, 25.1 ff.; *Atli* prose, 1.1, 3.1, 4, 14.1, 5 ff.; *Green* 2.2, 19.3, 20.3, 42.1 ff.; *Whet* prose, 11.3; *Hamd* 8.1

Atrid, an Odinic name: *Grim* 48.2

Aud the deep-minded, ancestor of Ottar: *Hynd* 28.2, 3

Auda, sister of Agnar (3): *Sigrd* 4.5; *Bryn* 8.3

Aurboda, Gerd's mother: *Hynd* 30.3; *Fiol* 38.4

Aurgelmir, a giant: *Vaf* 29.4, 30.3

Aurglasir, probably a giant: *Fiol* 28.4

Aurnir, a giant: *Grott* 9.3

Baby (Iod), son of Lord and Erna: *Rig* 41.2

Baldr, son of Odin: *Seer* 32.1, 33.3, 34.2, 59.2, 3; *Grim* 12.1; *Lok* 27.2, 28.4; *Baldr* 1.4, 7.1, 8.3, 9.2, 10.4, 11.4; *Hynd* 29.2, 30.1; *Seer(H)* 56.2, 3

Bari, a dwarf: *Fiol* 34.1

Barri (1), a grove: *Skir* 39.1, 41.1

Barri (2), kinsman of Ottar: *Hynd* 23.1

Battle-hog (Hildisvin), the boar on which Freyia rides: *Hynd* 7.4

Bavor, a dwarf: *Seer* 11.3; *Seer(H)* 12.1

Beiti, Atli (3)'s steward: *Green* 61.1

Beli, a giant: *Seer* 51.3; *Seer(H)* 47.3

Bera, identical with Kostbera, wife of Hogni (2): *Green* 34.1

Bergelmir, a giant: *Vaf* 29.2, 35.2

Bestla, Odin's mother: *High* 140.1

Betrayer (Ginnar), a dwarf: *Seer* 16.2

Beyla, a serving-maid: *Lok* prose; 56.1

Biflindi, an Odinic name: *Grim* 49.6

Bikki, counsellor of Iormunrekk: *Short* 64.1; *Atli* 14.2 (probably in error); *Whet* prose

Bild, a dwarf: *Seer(H)* 13.4

Billing (1), possibly a giant: *High* 97.1

Billing (2), a dwarf: *Seer(H)* 13.4

Billing's girl, wife or daughter of Billing (1): *High* 97.1

Bilrost, bridge in the divine world: *Grim* 44.5; *Faf* 15.3

Bilskirnir, a hall: *Grim* 24.2

Bivor, a dwarf: *Seer* 11.3; *Seer(H)* 12.1

Blain, a giant (possibly identical to Ymir): *Seer* 9.4; *Seer(H)* 9.4

Blind 'the malicious', unknown man: *HH2* prose

Boddi, son of Farmer and Daughter-in-law: *Rig* 24.4

Bodvild, daughter of King Nidud: *Vol* prose, 17.2, 19.1, 25.4, 26.1 ff.

Bolthor, a giant, grandfather of Odin: *High* 140.1

Bolverk (Evil-doer), an Odinic name: *High* 109.3; *Grim* 47.3

Bombur, a dwarf: *Seer* 11.3; *Seer(H)* 12.1

Bondwoman (Ambat), daughter of Thrall and Thrall-girl: *Rig* 13.3

Borghild, mother of Helgi Hundingsbani: *HH1* 1.4; *HH2* prose; *DS*

Borgny, lover of Vilmund: *Odd* prose

Boundbeard (Bundinskeggi), son of Farmer and Daughter-in-law: *Rig* 24.3

Boy (Bur), son of Lord and Erna: *Rig* 41.1

Bragalund, a place: *HH2* 8.3

Bragi (1), god of poetry: *Grim* 44.5; *Lok* prose, 11.4, 12.2, 13.2, 15.2, 16.1, 18.3; *Sigrd* 16.1

Bragi (2), brother of Sigrun: *HH2* prose, 26.4

Bralund, home of Helgi Hundingsbani: *HH1* 1.4, 3.2; *HH2* prose

Brami, kinsman of Ottar: *Hynd* 23.1

Brand-island: *HH1* 22.2

Bravoll, a plain: *HH1* 42.1

Breidablik, a palace: *Grim* 12.1

Bride (Brud), daughter of Farmer and Daughter-in-law: *Rig* 25.2

Bright (Biort), one of Menglod's hand-maids: *Fiol* 38.3

Bright One (Heid), probably a form of Freyia: *Seer* 23.1; *Seer(H)* 28.1

Brimir, a giant (possibly identical to Ymir): *Seer* 9.4, 36.4; *Sigrd* 14.1; *Seer(H)* 9.4

Brisings, an unknown tribe; here = necklace of the Brisings (Brisingamen), a possession of Freyia: *Thrym* 13.3, 15.4, 19.2

Broad (Breid), son of Farmer and Daughter-in-law: *Rig* 24.3

Broadbeard (Sidskegg), *see* Odin

Broadhat (Sidhott), *see* Odin

Brodd, ancestor of Ottar: *Hynd* 20.4, 25.1

Bruna-bay: *HH2* prose, 5.3, 6.3

Bruni, a dwarf: *Seer(H)* 13.4

Brynhild, valkyrie, lover of Sigurd, wife of Gunnar: *Grip* 27.2, 35.2, 45.3; *Frag* 3.1, 8.1, 10.1, 14.1; *Gud1* 22.3, 23.1, 25.1, 27.2, prose; *Short* 3.1, 15.1, 19.2 ff.; *Bryn* prose, 4.1; *Death*; *Gud2* 27.2; *Odd* 16.1, 17.1, 18.2, 20.2

Budli, father of Brynhild and Atli (3): *Grip* 27.3; *Frag* 8.1, 14.1; *Gud1* 23.1, 25.1, 3, 27.2; *Short* 15.2, 30.1, 56.5, 70.4; *Bryn* 4.1; *Gud2* 26.3, 27.4; *Gud3* 1.2; *Atli* 42.4; *Green* 38.2, 55.1, 63.1, 76.3 ff.

Bui, kinsman of Ottar: *Hynd* 23.1
Bulgy-calves (Okkvinkalfa), daughter of Thrall and Thrall-girl: *Rig* 13.2
Bur, a giant, father of Odin and his brothers: *Seer* 4.1; *Hynd* 30.1; *Seer(H)*
    4.1
Burden-god (Farmatyr), *see* Odin
Burgundians, Gunnar's tribe: *Atli* 18.2
Buri, a dwarf: *Seer(H)* 13.4
Byggvir ('Barley'), a servant: *Lok* prose; 45.1, 46.1, 56.1
Byleist, a brother of Loki: *Seer* 48.4; *Hynd* 40.4; *Seer(H)* 45.4

Carrion-swallower (Hræsvelg), a giant who causes the wind: *Vaf* 37.1
Chieftain (Hersir), father of Erna: *Rig* 39.2
Child (Barn), son of Lord and Erna: *Rig* 41.1
Clay-surf (Leirbrimir), a giant: *Fiol* 12.2
Colour (Lit), a dwarf: *Seer* 12.2; *Seer(H)* 12.3
Corpse (Na), a dwarf: *Seer* 12.3; *Seer(H)* 11.3, 13.3
Corpse-strand (Nastrand): *Seer* 37.2; *Seer(H)* 35.2
Counsel-clever (Radsvid), a dwarf: *Seer* 12.4; *Seer(H)* 12.5
Counsel-island Sound (Radseyiarsund): *Harb* 8.2
Cowshed-boy (Fiosnir), son of Thrall and Thrall-girl: *Rig* 12.2
Crane-bank (Tronoeyri), a place: *HH1* 24.2
Crane-legs (Tronobeina), daughter of Thrall and Thrall-girl: *Rig* 12.4

Dag (1), brother of Sigrun: *HH2* prose
Dag (2), ancestor of Ottar: *Hynd* 18.1
Dain (1), an elf: *High* 143.1
Dain (2), a hart: *Grim* 33.3
Dain (3), a dwarf: *Hynd* 7.5; *Seer(H)* 11.3, 13.3
Dame (Flioth), daughter of Farmer and Daughter-in-law: *Rig* 25.3
Damsel (Sprakki), daughter of Farmer and Daughter-in-law: *Rig* 25.2
Dan, a chieftain: *Rig* 48.1
Danes: *Gud2* 19.1
Danp, a chieftain: *Rig* 48.1
Dark-of-moon (Nidi), a dwarf: *Seer* 11.1; *Seer(H)* 11.1
Dark-of-moon Hills (Nidafiall): *Seer* 62.2
Dark-of-moon Plains (Nidavellir): *Seer* 36.3
Daughter-in-law (Snor), wife of Farmer: *Rig* 23.3
Day (Dag): *Vaf* 25.1
Delling (1), a dwarf: *Seer* 11.2; *High* 160.2; *Fiol* 34.3
Delling (2), father of Day: *Vaf* 25.1
Denmark: *DS*; *Gud1* prose; *Gud2* 14.2
Descendant (Nid), son of Lord and Erna: *Rig* 41.3
Dneiper, river: *Atli* 5.3
Dolgthrasir, a dwarf: *Seer* 15.1; *Seer(H)* 15.1
Dori, a dwarf: *Fiol* 34.3
Draupnir, a dwarf: *Seer* 15.1; *Seer(H)* 15.1

Dumpy (Kumba), daughter of Thrall and Thrall-girl: *Rig* 13. 1
Duneyr, a hart: *Grim* 33.4
Durathror, a hart: *Grim* 33.4
Durin, a chief dwarf: *Seer* 10.2, 4; *Seer(H)* 10.2, 4
Dvalin (1), a chief dwarf: *Seer* 11.2, 14.1; *High* 143.2; *All* 16.2; *Faf* 13.4; *Wak* 12.3; *Seer(H)* 11.2, 14.2
Dvalin (2), a hart: *Grim* 33.3
Dweller (Bui), son of Farmer and Daughter-in-law: *Rig* 24.4

Earth (Iord), Thor's mother: *Lok* 58.1; *Thrym* 1.4
Earth-girdler (Moldthinur), the Midgard-serpent: *Seer* 55.1, 60.2
East (Austri), a dwarf: *Seer* 11.2; *Seer(H)* 11.2
Eggther, a giant herdsman: *Seer* 41.2; *Seer(H)* 33.2
Egil (1), father of Thialfi and Roskva: *Hym* 7.2
Egil (2), brother of Volund: *Vol* prose, 2.1, 4.2, 4
Eikin, a river: *Grim* 27.1
Eikthyrnir, a deer: *Grim* 26.1
Einheriar, the warrior heroes who live in Valhall: *Vaf* 41.1; *Grim* 18.4, 36.6, 51.3
Eir, one of Menglod's hand-maids: *Fiol* 38.4
Eistla, a giantess: *Hynd* 37.2
Eitil, son of Gudrun and Atli (3): *Death*; *Atli* 37.2; *Hamd* 8.2
Eldhrimnir, cooking-pot in Valhall: *Grim* 18.2
Eldir, a servant at Ægir's hall: *Lok* prose, 1.1, 5.1
Elf (Alf), a dwarf: *Seer* 16.1; *Seer(H)* 15.4
Elf-radiance (Alfrodull), the sun: *Vaf* 47.1
Elivagar, primeval chaos: *Vaf* 31.1; *Hym* 5.1
Elves, the (Alfar): *Seer* 48.1; *High* 143.1, 159.3, 160.3; *Grim* 4.2; *Faf* 13.3; *Sigrd* 18.4
Embla, the first woman: *Seer* 17.4; *Seer(H)* 17.4
Equal-high (Iafnhar), *see* Odin
Erna, wife of Lord: *Rig* 39.4
Erp (1), son of Gudrun and Atli (3): *Death*; *Atli* 37.2; *Hamd* 8.1
Erp (2), son of Ionakr, not by Gudrun according to *Lay of Hamdir*: *Whet* prose; *Hamd* 13.1, 28.1
Eyfura, kinswoman of Ottar, mother of Angantyr and his brothers: *Hynd* 24.2; *Wak* 11.3
Eyiolf, a son of Hunding: *HH1* 14.2; *HH2* prose
Eylimi, father of Svava the valkyrie and, apparently, Hiordis, Sigurd's mother: *HHi* prose, 36.2; *DS*; *Grip* prose, 9.2; *Reg* 15.2; *Hynd* 26.3
Eymod, a warrior: *Gud2* 19.2
Eymund, opponent of Ali: *Hynd* 15.1
Eyrgiafa, a giantess: *Hynd* 37.2

Fafnir, a dragon: *Grip* 11.3, 13.1, 15.4; *Reg* prose, 12.4; *Faf* prose, 1.3, 8.1, 12.1 ff. *Gud1* prose; *Bryn* 10.4; *Death*; *Odd* 17.4; *Hynd* 25.5
Farmer (Karl), son of Grandfather and Grandmother: *Rig* 21.3, 23.2

Freyia, a Vanir goddess of fertility, daughter of Niord: *Grim* 14.1; *Lok* prose,
    30.1, 32.1, 4; *Thrym* 3.1, 3, 8.4, 11.4 ff.; *Odd* 9.2; *Hynd* 6.1
Freyr, one of the Vanir, god of fertility: *Grim* 5.3, 43.3; *Skir* prose, 3.1, 19.3,
    20.3, 33.2 ff.; *Lok* prose, 37.1, 43.1, 44.2; *Hynd* 30.2
Friaut, ancestress of Ottar: *Hynd* 13.3
Fridleif, father of Frodi (1): *Grott* 1.4
Frigg, chief goddess and wife of Odin: *Seer* 34.3, 51.1, 4; *Vaf* 1.1, 2.4; *Grim*
    prose; *Lok* prose, 26.1, 28.1, 29.3; *Odd* 9.2; *Seer(H)* 47.1, 4
Frodi (1), a legendary Danish king in whose time peace and prosperity
    prevailed: *HH1* 13.3; *Grott* 1.3, 4.2, 5.1, 8.1, 16.4 ff.
Frodi (2), ancestor of Ottar, possibly identical to Frodi (1): *Hynd* 13.3, 19.3
Frost-mane (Hrimfaxi), horse which pulls the night: *Vaf* 14.1
Frosty (Frosti), a dwarf: *Seer* 16.2
Fulla, a goddess, hand-maid of Frigg: *Grim* prose

Gagnrad ('Advantage-counsel'), name of disguised Odin in *Vafthrudnir's
    Sayings*: *Vaf* 8.1, 9.1, 11.1, 13.1, 15.1, 17.1
Gallows-wood (Galgvid): *Seer* 41.3; *Seer(H)* 33.3
Garm, a monstrous hound: *Seer* 43.1, 46.1, 55.1; *Grim* 44.6; *Seer(H)* 43.1,
    48.1, 52.1
Gastropnir, a wall at Menglod's fortress: *Fiol* 12.1
Gaut, an Odinic name: *Grim* 54.4; *Baldr* 2.1, 13.2
Gefion, a goddess: *Lok* 20.1, 21.2
Geirmund, a king: *Odd* 29.2
Geirolul, a valkyrie: *Grim* 36.4
Geirrod, a king: *Grim* prose, 2.4, 49.1, 51.1, end prose
Geir-skogul, a valkyrie: *Seer* 31.4
Geirvimul, a river: *Grim* 27.6
Geitir, servant of Gripir: *Grip* prose, 3.1, 4.1, 5.4
General (Herian), *see* Odin
Gerd, giant woman: *Skir* prose, 14, 16, 19.2, 20 ff.; *Hynd* 30.2
Geri (1), one of Odin's wolves: *Grim* 19.1
Geri (2), a dog guarding Menglod's hall: *Fiol* 14.1
Giaflaug, sister of Giuki (1): *Gud1* 14.1
Giallarhorn, Heimdall's horn, blown at Ragnarok: *Seer* 45.1; *Seer(H)* 40.2
Gialp, a giantess: *Hynd* 37.1
Giant-land (Iotunheimar): *Seer* 8.4; *Skir* prose, 40.3; *Thrym* 5.3, 7.2, 9.2 ff.;
    Seer(H) 8.4
Gifr, a dog guarding Menglod's hall: *Fiol* 14.1
Gils, a horse: *Grim* 30.3
Gimle, a hall: *Seer* 61.2; *Seer(H)* 58.2
Gioll, a river: *Grim* 28.6
Gipul, a river: *Grim* 27.5
Giuki (1), father of Gunnar (1), Hogni (2), and Gudrun, *Grip* 13.4, 14.3,
    31.6, 43.2 ff.; *Faf* 40.1; *Frag* 6.1, 9.2, 11.1, prose; *Gud1* 12.1, 16.1, 17.1,
    18.1 ff.; *Short* 1.1, 2.2, 2.4, 4.4 ff.; *Bryn* 4.3, 5.3, 13.1; *Death*; *Gud2* 1.3, 2.1,

38.3; *Gud3* 2.1; *Odd* prose, 22.2, 28.2; *Atli* prose, 1.3; *Green* 1.4, 50.1, 52.2, 105.2; *Whet* 9.1; *Hamd* 2.4, 21.4; *Hynd* 27.1, 3

Giuki (2), son of Hogni (2): *Death*

Giukungs, sons of Giuki (1): *Short* 35.2; *Death*

Glad, a horse: *Grim* 30.1

Gladsheim, a palace or territory of the gods: *Grim* 8.1

Glapsvid, an Odinic name: *Grim* 47.4

Glasislund, a place: *HHi* 1.4

Glassy (Glær), a horse: *Grim* 30.1

Glaumvor, second wife of Gunnar (1): *Death*; *Green* 6.3, 21.2, 32.1

Glitnir, a palace: *Grim* 15.1

Glow (Gloi), a dwarf: *Seer* 15.2; *Seer(H)* 15.2

Gnipa-cave (Gnipahellir): *Seer* 43.1, 46.1, 55.1; *Seer(H)* 32.1, 37.1, 43.1, 48.1, 52.1

Gnipalund, a place: *HHi* 30.4, 34.4, 40.4, 50.3

Gnita-heath, home of Fafnir the dragon: *Grip* 11.2; *Reg* prose; *Faf* prose; *Atli* 5.1, 6.3

Goin, a serpent: *Grim* 34.3

Golden (Gyllir), a horse: *Grim* 30.1

Golden-comb (Gullinkambi), a cockerel: *Seer* 42.1; *Seer(H)* 34.1

Goldtuft (Gulltopp), a horse: *Grim* 30.3

Goll, a valkyrie: *Grim* 36.4

Gomul, a river: *Grim* 27.6

Gondlir, an Odinic name: *Grim* 49.7

Gondul, a valkyrie: *Seer* 31.4

Gopul, a river: *Grim* 27.5

Gothorm (1), *see* Guthorm

Gothorm (2), a Swedish prince: *Grott* 14.2

Goths, a tribe, ruled over by Gunnar (1) or by Iormunrekk: *Grip* 35.3; *Frag* 9.2; *Bryn* 8.1; *Gud2* 17.1; *Whet* 2.6, 8.4, 16.2; *Hamd* 3.4, 22.4, 23.2; *Wak* 21.3

Grabak, a serpent: *Grim* 34.3

Grad, a river: *Grim* 27.9

Grafvitnir, father of serpents: *Grim* 34.3

Grafvollud, a serpent: *Grim* 34.4

Gram, Sigurd's sword, *Reg* prose: *Sigrd* prose; *Short* 22.3

Grandfather, ancestor of the farmers (Afi): *Rig* 16.5

Grandmother, ancestress of the farmers (Amma): *Rig* 16.5, 21.2

Grani, Sigurd's horse: *Vol* 14.1; *HHi* 42.1; *Grip* 5.4, 13.3; *Reg* prose; *Faf* prose; *Sigrd* 17.3; *Gud1* 22.2; *Short* 39.2; *Bryn* 11.1; *Gud2* 4.1, 5.1, 3; *Odd* 21.4

Granmar, father of Hodbrodd: *HHi* 18.2, 46.1; *HH2* prose, 24.1, 25.4

Great-gabbler (Eikintiasna), daughter of Thrall and Thrall-girl: *Rig* 13.3

Great-grandfather (Ai) (1), a dwarf: *Seer* 11.4, 15.3; *Seer(H)* 12.2, 15.3

Great-grandfather (Ai) (2), ancestor of the thralls: *Rig* 2.5

Great-grandmother (Edda), ancestress of the thralls: *Rig* 2.5, 4.1, 7.1

Great Wolf (Thiodvitnir), Fenrir, *Vaf* 21.1

Greip, a giantess, *Hynd* 37.1

Greyhair (Har), a dwarf: *Seer* 15.2; *Seer(H)* 15.2

Greyish (Hosvir), son of Thrall and Thrall-girl: *Rig* 12.4

Grim, ancestor of Ottar: *Hynd* 22.1

Grimhild, mother of Gudrun, Gunnar (1), and Hogni (2): *Grip* 33.2, 35.1, 51.4; *Gud2* 17.1, 21.1, 29.1, 32.1; *Odd* 15.4; *Green* 72.3, 80.2, 91.1

Grimnir ('Masked One'): *Grim* prose, 47.4, 49.1

Gripir, Sigurd's uncle: *Grip* prose, 1.3, 2.4, 3.2 ff.

Groa, mother of Svipdag: *Gro* 1.1

Grotti, a millstone: *Grott* 10.1

Gudmund, brother of Hodbrodd: *HH1* 32.1; *HH2* prose, 22.1

Gudrun, daughter of Giuki (1), wife of Sigurd: *Grip* 34.2, 45.2, 51.1; *Frag* 3.3, 6.1, 11.1, prose; *Gud1* prose, 1.1, 2.3, 3.2, 5.1 ff.; *Short* 2.2, 7.3, 8.3, 24.1 ff.; *Death*; *Gud2* 10.3, 25.1, 38.4; *Gud3* prose, 2.1, 10.2, 4, 11.4; *Odd* 27.1; *Atli* prose, 29.3, 33.1, 4, 38.3, 40.2; *Green* 46.1, 58.3, 68.3, 74.3 ff.; *Whet* prose, 1.3, 7.1, 9.1, 19.4; *Hamd* 2.4, 9.4, 10.3; *Hynd* 27.2

Gullnir, probably a giant or troll: *HH1* 43.2

Gullrond, sister of Gudrun: *Gud1* 12.1, 17.1, 24.1

Gullveig ('Golden Liquor' or 'Power of Gold'), possibly a hypostasis of Freyia: *Seer* 22.2; *Seer(H)* 27.2

Gungnir, Odin's spear: *Sigrd* 17.3

Gunn, a valkyrie: *Seer* 31.4; *HH2* 7.2

Gunnar (1), son of Giuki (1), king of the Goths: *Grip* 34.1, 35.3, 37.2, 37.4, 39.1 ff.: *Frag* 11.3, 12.4, 16.1, 17.1; *Gud1* 21.3; *Short* 7.2, 10.2, 13.1, 28.2 ff.; *Death*; *Gud2* 7.1, 18.1, 31.3; *Gud3* 8.1; *Odd* prose, 12.2, 20.1, 32.2; *Atli* 1.1, 3, 3.3, 6.1 ff.; *Green* 6.3, 7.3, 21.3, 32.1 ff.; *Whet* 3.1, 17.4; *Hamd* 7.4; *Hynd* 27.1

Gunnar (2), ancestor of Ottar: *Hynd* 22.1

Gunnlod, giantess, keeper of mead of poetry and seduced by Odin: *High* 13.4, 105.1, 108.3, 110.4

Gunnthorin, a river: *Grim* 27.9

Gunnthro, a river: *Grim* 27.2

Gust, presumably a dwarf, previous owner of Andvari's hoard, *Reg* 5.1

Guthorm (Gothorm), brother of Gunnar (1) and Hogni (2): *Grip* 50.2; *Frag* 4.2; *Short* 20.1, 22.3; *Gud2* 7.4; *Hynd* 27.3

Gymir, a giant, father of Gerd: *Skir* 6.1, 11.4, 12.3, 14.4, 22.3, 24.3; *Lok* 42.1; *Hynd* 30.2

Gyrd, ancestor of Ottar: *Hynd* 18.3

Habrok, a hawk: *Grim* 44.6

Haddings, the, sea-kings (?): *HH2* end prose; *Gud2* 22.3; kinsmen of Ottar, *Hynd* 23.2

Hæming, son of Hunding: *HH2* prose, 1.1

Hænir, a god: *Seer* 18.3, 60.1; *Reg* prose; *Seer(H)* 18.3

Haft, a dwarf: *Seer* 13.2; *Seer(H)* 13.2

Hagal, foster-father of Helgi Hundingsbani: *HH2* prose, 2.1

Haki, son of Hvædna: *Hynd* 32.1

Hakon, a Dane: *Gud1* prose; *Gud2* 14.2

Half, a Dane: *Gud2* 13.2

Halfdan (1), father of Kara: *HH2* end prose

Halfdan (2), ancestor of Skioldungs: *Hynd* 14.2

Half-Danes, a tribe: *Grott* 22.2

Hall-Stone (Salar-stein), a place: *Seer* 14.3; *Seer(H)* 14.4

Hamal, son of Hagal: *HH2* 1.4, prose, 6.1

Hamdir, son of Ionakr and Gudrun: *Whet* prose, 4.1, 8.1; *Hamd* 6.1, 21.1, 24.1, 26.1, 27.1, 31.2

Hamund, son of Sigmund: *DS*

Hanar, a dwarf: *Seer* 13.2; *Seer(H)* 13.2

Happy (Blid), one of Menglod's hand-maids: *Fiol* 38.3

Harald Battletooth, ancestor of Ottar: *Hynd* 28.1

Harbard, an Odinic name: *Grim* 49.7; *Harb* 10.1 ff.

Hatafjord, fjord-home of Hati (2): *HHi* 12.1

Hati (1), a wolf who will devour the moon: *Grim* 39.3

Hati (2), a giant, father of Hrimgerd: *HHi* prose; 17.1, 24.2

Havard, a son of Hunding: *HHi* 14.3

Healing-mountain (Lyfjaberg), a mountain: *Fiol* 36.1, 49.1

Hedin, son of Hiorvard (2): *HHi* prose, 31.1, 33.2, 34.1, 41.3

Hedins-island: *HHi* 22.4

Heid, daughter of Hrimnir: *Hynd* 32.3

Heiddraupnir, unknown being: *Sigrd* 13.6

Heidrek (1), a king: *Odd* prose, 1.4

Heidrek (2), Hervor's son: *Wak* 19.3

Heidrun, goat with udders filled with mead: *Grim* 25.1; *Hynd* 46.4, 47.4

Heimdall, god who creates human society: *Seer* 1.2, 28.1, 45.3; *Grim* 13.2; *Lok* 48.1; *Thrym* 15.1; *Rig* prose; *Seer(H)* 1.2, 24.1, 40.3

Heimir, foster-father of Brynhild: *Grip* 19.1, 27.1, 4, 28.2, 29.2, 31.4, 39.4

Heir (Arfi), son of Lord and Erna: *Rig* 41.2

Hel, goddess of the dead: *Seer* 42.4; *Grim* 31.3; *Faf* 21.4; *Gud1* 8.2; *Green* 55.2, 97.4; *Baldr* 3.4; *Seer(H)* 34.4

Helgi (1) Hundingsbani, hero of two Helgi poems: *HHi* 1.3, 8.1, 18.3, 23.3 ff.; *HH2* prose, 1.1, 4.5 ff.; *DS*; *Grip* 15.2 (?)

Helgi (2) Hiorvardsson: *HHi* 6.1, 7.1, 13.1, 17.4 ff.; *HH2* prose

Helgi (3) Haddingia-damager: *HH2* end prose

Hellblind (Helblindi), *see* Odin

Helmet-Gunnar: *Sigrd* prose; *Bryn* 8.2

Helm-wearer (Hialmberi), *see* Odin

Herborg, queen of the Huns: *Gud1* 6.1

Herfiotur ('War-fetter'), a valkyrie: *Grim* 36.3

Herkia, serving-maid and mistress of Atli (3): *Gud3* prose, 2.2, 10.3, 11.4

Hermod, a protégé (or, according to Snorri, son) of Odin: *Hynd* 2.3

Hervard (1), a son of Hunding: *HH2* prose

Hervard (2), a brother of Angantyr: *Wak* 10.1

Hervor (1) (also called Alvit), a swan-maiden: *Vol* prose, 15.1

Hervor (2), warrior-woman, daughter of Angantyr: *Wak* 8.3, 9.1, 13.1, 18.1, 25.1

Hialli, a cowardly retainer of Atli (3): *Atli* 22.1, 23.2, 25.2; *Green* 61.2, 63.5

Hialmar, killed by Angantyr: *Wak* 20.5, 23.1, 29.2

Hialprek, a king, father of Sigurd's stepfather, Alf (4): *DS*; *Reg* prose

Hidden-hoof (Falhofnir), a horse: *Grim* 30.3

High (Har), *see* Odin

Highmeadow (Hatun), an estate owned by Helgi (1): *HHi* 8.3, 25.2

High One (Havi), *see* Odin

Hild ('Battle'), a valkyrie: *Seer* 31.4; *Grim* 36.3

Hildigunn, ancestor of Ottar: *Hynd* 17.1

Hildolf, unknown person: *Harb* 8.1

Himinbiorg, a palace: *Grim* 13.1

Himinfell, a mountain: *HHi* 1.2

Himinvangi, an estate owned by Helgi (1): *HHi* 8.3, 15.3

Hindarfell, mountain where Sigrdrifa lies: *Faf* 42.1; *Sigrd* prose

Hiordis, wife of Sigmund (1), mother of Sigurd: *DS*; *Grip* prose, 3.4; *Hynd* 26.2

Hiorleif, a lieutenant of Helgi Hundingsbani: *HHi* 23.3

Hiorvard (1), a son of Hunding: *HHi* 14.3; *HH2* prose

Hiorvard (2), father of Helgi Hiorvardsson: *HHi* prose, 1.3, 3.1, 10.1, 38.1, 43.3

Hiorvard (3), son of Hvædna: *Hynd* 32.2

Hiorvard (4), a berserk, brother of Angantyr: *Wak* 3.4, 10.1

Hladgud (also known as Swanwhite), a swan-maiden: *Vol* prose, 15.1

Hlebard, a giant: *Harb* 20.3

Hlebiorg, a place: *HH2* 27.2

Hledis, grandmother of Ottar: *Hynd* 13.2

Hlesey (modern Læssø), an island: *Harb* 37.1; *HH2* 6.2; *Odd* 30.1

Hlidskialf, Odin's high-seat: *Skir* prose

Hlif, one of Menglod's hand-maids: *Fiol* 38.1

Hlifthrasir, one of Menglod's hand-maids: *Fiol* 38.1

Hlodvard, father of Hrimgerd's victims: *HHi* 19.4

Hlodver, a king: *Grim* prose; *Vol* prose, 10.3, 15.1; *Gud2* 25.4

Hlodyn, a name for Earth, Thor's mother: *Seer* 53.1

Hlokk, a valkyrie: *Grim* 36.3

Hlorridi, a name for Thor: *Hym* 4.3, 16.2, 27.1, 37.1; *Thrym* 8.1, 14.4, 31.1

Hlymdales, Brynhild's home: *Bryn* 7.1

Hniflung, son and avenger of Hogni (2): *Green* 88.3

Hniflungs (*see also* Niflungs), sons of Gudrun and Atli (3): *Whet* 12.3

Hnikar, an Odinic name: *Grim* 47.2; *Reg* 18.1, 19.1

Hnikud, an Odinic name: *Grim* 48.1

Hod, a blind god: *Seer* 33.2, 59.3; *Baldr* 9.1, 10.3; *Seer(H)* 56.3

Hodbrodd, son of Granmar, unsuccessful suitor of Sigrun: *HHi* 18.3, 35.1, 48.3; *HH2* prose, 16.1, 20.1, 21.3, 25.1

Hoddmimir, possibly a giant: *Vaf* 45.2

Hoddrofnir, unknown being: *Sigrd* 13.7

Hogni (1), father of Sigrun: *HH1* 17.1, 52.1, 56.4; *HH2* 4.6, prose, 17.1, 18.1 ff.

Hogni (2), brother of Gunnar (1) and Gudrun: *Grip* 37.2, 50.1; *Frag* 7.1;
    Short 14.4, 17.1, 44.1, 45.1; *Death*; *Gud2* 7.1, 9.1, 10.1, 18.1 ff.; *Gud3* 8.1, 3;
    Odd 8.2, 28.3; *Atli* 6.1, 12.3, 19.1, 4, 21.1 ff.; *Green* 6.1, 7.1, 3, 4, 10.1, 11.1,
    13.1 ff.; *Whet* 3.2, 4.2; *Hamd* 6.2; *Hynd* 27.1

Holl, a river: *Grim* 27.8

Horn, a river: *Gro* 8.3

Hornborer (Hornbori), a dwarf: *Seer* 13.3

Horsefly (Kleggi), son of Thrall and Thrall-girl: *Rig* 12.3

Horse-thief (Hrossthiof), son of Hrimnir: *Hynd* 32.3

Horvi, ancestor of Ottar: *Hynd* 20.4, 25.1

Hrani, a brother of Angantyr: *Wak* 10.1

Hraudung (1), a king, father of Geirrod: *Grim* prose

Hraudung (2), father of Hiordis (only here): *Hynd* 26.2

Hreid-Goths, a northern tribe: *Vaf* 12.3

Hreidmar, father of Regin (2) and Fafnir: *Reg* prose, 9.1, 11.1

Hrid, a river: *Grim* 28.4

Hrimgerd, a troll-woman: *HHi* 14.1, 17.1, 21.4, 24.1, 27.1, 29.1, 30.1

Hrimgrimnir, a frost-giant: *Skir* 35.1

Hrimnir, a frost-giant: *Skir* 28.2; *Hynd* 32.3

Hring, father of allies of Hodbrodd: *HH1* 52.1

Hringstadir, an estate owned by Helgi (1): *HH1* 8.1, 56.4

Hringstod, an estate owned by Helgi (1): *HH1* 8.3

Hrist, a valkyrie: *Grim* 36.1

Hrod, a giant?: *Hym* 11.4

Hrodmar, suitor of Sigrlinn: *HHi* prose, 11.1

Hrodrglod (?), woman at Iormunrekk's court: *Hamd* 22.1

Hrodvitnir, father of the wolf Hati (1): *Grim* 39.3

Hrærek, father of Harald Battletooth: *Hynd* 28.1

Hrolf the old, a hero: *Hynd* 25.2

Hrollaug, father of Hodbrodd's allies: *HH2* 27.2

Hronn, a river: *Grim* 28.3

Hropt, an Odinic name, perhaps meaning 'Sage': *Seer* 59.3; *Sigrd* 13.3;
    Seer(H) 56.3

Hroptatyr, an Odinic name, perhaps meaning 'Sage-god': *High* 160.4; *Grim*
    54.3

Hrotti, a sword: *Faf* prose

Hrungnir, a giant, killed by Thor, *also* Rungnir: *Harb* 14.2, 15.1; *Hym* 16.1;
    Lok 61.3, 63.3; *Sigrd* 15.4; *Grott* 9.1

Hrym, a frost-giant: *Seer* 47.1; *Seer(H)* 44.1

Hugin ('Thought'), one of Odin's ravens: *Grim* 20.1, 3; *HH1* 54.4

Humlung, a son of Hiorvard (2): *HHi* prose

Hunding, a king, enemy of Helgi Hundingsbani: *HH1* 10.3, 11.2, 14.3, 53.3;
    HH2 prose, 1.4, 10.2, 39.1; *DS*; *Grip* 9.3; *Reg* 15.1, prose

Hundland, Hunding's kingdom: *HH2* prose
Huns: *Gud1* 6.1; *Gud2* 15.3; *Odd* 4.2; *Atli* 2.2, 4.2, 7.6, 15.4 ff.; *Whet* 3.5, 6.1
Hvædna, daughter of Hiorvard (3): *Hynd* 32.1, 2
Hvergelmir, a source of rivers: *Grim* 26.3
Hymir, a giant: *Hym* 5.2, 7.4 ff.; *Lok* 34.3
Hymling, a son of Hiorvard (2): *HHi* prose
Hyndla, a giantess: *Hynd* prose, 1.2, 7.1

Ialk, an Odinic name: *Grim* 49.2, 54.4
Iari, a dwarf: *Seer* 13.4; *Fiol* 34.1; *Seer(H)* 14.1
Iarizleif, probably a Slav prince: *Gud2* 19.1
Iarizskar, probably a Slav prince: *Gud2* 19.2
Iarnsaxa, a giantess: *Hynd* 37.4
Idavoll, a plain: *Seer* 7.1, 57.1; *Seer(H)* 7.1, 54.1
Idi, a giant: *Grott* 9.3
Idmund, father of Atli (2): *HHi* prose, 2.2
Idunn, goddess who possesses the apples of youthfulness: *Lok* prose, 17.1
Ifing, a river: *Vaf* 16.1
Im, a giant, son of Vafthrudnir: *Vaf* 5.3
Imd, a giantess: *HH1* 43.3; *Hynd* 37.4
Innstein, father of Ottar: *Hynd* 6.4, 12.1, 12.2
Ionakr, third husband of Gudrun: *Short* 62.4, 63.1; *Whet* prose, 14.4; *Hamd* 25.4
Iormunrekk, emperor of the Goths and husband of Svanhild: *Short* 64.2; *Whet* prose, 2.3, 5.3; *Hamd* 3.2, 19.1, 20.1, 24.2, 5; *Hynd* 25.3
Iorovellir, a plain: *Seer* 14.4; *Seer(H)* 14.5
Iosurmar, ancestor of Ottar: *Hynd* 18.4
Iri, a dwarf: *Fiol* 34.1
Iron-wood (Iarnvid): *Seer* 39.1; *Seer(H)* 25.1
Isolf, ancestor of Ottar: *Hynd* 19.3
Isung, unknown victim of Hodbrodd: *HH1* 20.1
Ivaldi, a dwarf: *Grim* 43.1
Ivar, father of Aud the deep-minded: *Hynd* 28.3

Kara, a valkyrie: *HH2* end prose
Kari, ancestor of Ottar: *Hynd* 19.3
Kerlaugar, two rivers: *Grim* 29.1
Ketil, ancestor of Ottar: *Hynd* 19.1
Kialar, an Odinic name: *Grim* 49.3
Kiar, king of Valland: *Vol* prose, 15.2
Kili, a dwarf: *Seer* 13.1; *Seer(H)* 13.1
Kin (Kon), son of Lord and Erna: *Rig* 41.5, 43.1, 46.1, 47.2
Kinsman (Kund), son of Lord and Erna: *Rig* 41.5
Klypp, ancestor of Ottar: *Hynd* 19.1
Knefrod, messenger of Atli (3): *Death*; *Atli* 1.2, 2.3
Known (Thekk) (1), a dwarf: *Seer* 12.2.

Known (Thekk) (2), *see* Odin
Knui, a Swedish warrior: *Grott* 14.3
Kolga, personification of wave, daughter of Ægir: *HH1* 28.2
Kormt, a river: *Grim* 29.1
Kostbera, wife of Hogni (2): *Death*; *Green* 6.1, 9.2, 53.5

Lærad, a tree: *Grim* 25.2, 26.2
Lad (Svein), son of Lord and Erna: *Rig* 41.4
Lady (Svanni), daughter of Farmer and Daughter-in-law: *Rig* 25.2
Landlord (Hold), son of Farmer and Daughter-in-law: *Rig* 24.2
Langobards, a tribe: *Gud2* 19.4
Lass (Snot), daughter of Farmer and Daughter-in-law: *Rig* 25.2
Laufey, mother of Loki: *Lok* 52.1; *Thrym* 18.1, 20.1
Lee-plain (Hlevang), a dwarf: *Seer* 15.2
Lee-wolf (Hlevarg), a dwarf: *Seer(H)* 15.2
Leipt (Leift), a river: *Grim* 28.6; *HH2* 31.3
Lejre, chief settlement of Denmark, Frodi (1)'s capital: *Grott* 20.1
Life (Lif), human survivor of Ragnarok: *Vaf* 45.1
Lifthrasir (?'Life-persister'), human survivor of Ragnarok: *Vaf* 45.1
Lightfoot (Lettfeti), a horse: *Grim* 30.3
Limfjord, a fjord in Denmark: *Green* 4.4
Liquor (Veig), a dwarf: *Seer* 12.1; *Seer(H)* 11.4
Loam-field (Aurvang), a dwarf: *Seer* 13.4, 14.4; *Seer(H)* 14.1, 5
Loddfafnir, initiand into wisdom: *High* 112.1, 113.1, 115.1 ff., 162.3
Lodur, a god: *Seer* 18.4; *Seer(H)* 18.4
Lofar, a dwarf: *Seer* 14.2, 16.4; *Seer(H)* 14.3, 16.4
Lofnheid, daughter of Hreidmar: *Reg* 10.1
Logafell, mountains: *HH1* 13.2, 15.2
Loki, half god, half giant, friend and enemy of the gods: *Seer* 35.2, 48.2, 52.3,
    54.7; *Lok* prose, 6.2 ff.; *Thrym* 2.2, 5.1; *Reg* prose, 3.1, 6.1; *Baldr* 14.3;
    Hynd 40.1, 41.1
Longlegs (Leggialdi), son of Thrall and Thrall-girl: *Rig* 12.5
Look (Blik), one of Menglod's hand-maids: *Fiol* 38.3
Lopt, a name for Loki: *Hynd* 41.3
Lord (Iarl), son of Father and Mother: *Rig* 34.2, 35.1, 40.2, 42.1
Lowbent (Lur), son of Thrall and Thrall-girl: *Rig* 12.5
Lyngheid, daughter of Hreidmar: *Reg* prose, 10.1
Lyngvi, a son of Hunding: *Reg* prose
Lyr, a hall within Menglod's fortress: *Fiol* 32.1

Magni, son of Thor: *Vaf* 51.3; *Harb* 9.3, 53.2
Maiden (Svarri), daughter of Farmer and Daughter-in-law: *Rig* 25.2
Man (Hal), son of Farmer and Daughter-in-law: *Rig* 24.2
Mask (Grim), *see* Odin
Masked One (Grimnir), *see* Odin
Master-thief (Althiof), a dwarf: *Seer* 11.2; *Seer(H)* 11.2

Mead-wolf (Miodvitnir), a dwarf: *Seer* 11.4; *Seer(H)* 12.2

Measuring-Tree (Miotvid), probably identical with Yggdrasill: *Seer* 2.4, 45.1; *Fiol* 22.4; *Seer(H)* 2.4, 40.1

Meili, Thor's brother: *Harb* 9.3

Melnir, a horse: *HH1* 51.3

Menia, a giantess: *Short* 52.3; *Grott* 1.2, 4.3

Menglod, Svipdag's beloved: *Gro* 3.4; *Fiol* 8.1, 37.4, 41.4, 42.4, 43.4, 44.1, prose

Midgard, the earth as inhabited by humans: *Seer* 4.2; 53.3; *Grim* 41.2; *Harb* 23.4; *Seer(H)* 4.2

Midgard's-protector, a term for the Midgard-serpent: *Seer* 53.3

Midvidnir, a giant?: *Grim* 50.3

Mighty One, Jesus Christ?: *Seer(H)* 59.1

Mighty Winter (Fimbulvetr): *Vaf* 44.4

Mild One (Svasud), father of Summer: *Vaf* 27.2

Mim, identical with Mimir: *Seer* 45.1, 45.4; *Sigrd* 14.3; *Seer(H)* 40.1, 40.4

Mimi, probably identical with Mimir: *Fiol* 20.1 24.2

Mimir, mythological being: *Seer* 29.5, 6

Miollnir, Thor's hammer: *Vaf* 51.3; *Hym* 36.2; *Lok* 57.2, 59.2, 61.2, 63.2; *Thrym* 30.3

Mismade (Oskopnir), battle-place at Ragnarok: *Faf* 15.1

Miss (Sprund), daughter of Farmer and Daughter-in-law: *Rig* 25.3

Mist, a valkyrie: *Grim* 36.1

Mist-hell (Niflhel), part of the kingdom of the dead: *Vaf* 43.4; *Baldr* 2.3

Mistress (Vif), daughter of Farmer and Daughter-in-law: *Rig* 25.3

Modi, a son of Thor: *Vaf* 51.3; *Hym* 34.1

Mogthrasir, unknown person: *Vaf* 49.1

Moin, a serpent: *Grim* 34.3

Moinsheim, a place: *HH1* 46.3; *HH2* 24.3

Moon (Mani): *Vaf* 23.1

Mornaland, a place: *Odd* 1.2

Mother (Mothir), ancestress of the race of nobles: *Rig* 27.3, 31.1, 34.1

Motsognir, a dwarf: *Seer* 10.1; *Seer(H)* 10.1

Mound-river (Haugspori), a dwarf: *Seer* 15.2; *Seer(H)* 15.2

Much-wise (Fiolsvinn) (1): *see* Odin

Much-wise (Fiolsvinn) (2), giant opponent of Svipdag: *Fiol* 4.1, 7.1, 9.1 ff.

Munar-bay, a place: *Wak* 1.1, 11.4

Munarheim, a place: *HHi* 1.2, 42.1

Mundilfæri, father of the moon and sun: *Vaf* 23.1

Munin ('Memory'), one of Odin's ravens: *Grim* 20.1, 4

Muspell, a fire-giant: *Seer* 48.1; *Lok* 42.3; *Seer(H)* 45.1

Mylnir, a horse: *HH1* 51.3

Myrkheim, site of snake-pit: *Atli* 42.2

Myrkwood (1), forest separating the gods and giants: *Lok* 42.3; *Vol* 1.1

Myrkwood (2), a forest somewhere in central Europe: *HH1* 51.3; *Atli* 3.2, 5.4, 13.2

Odinic Names: All-Father (Alfodur), *Grim* 48.2; *HH1* 38.2; Broadbeard
   (Sidskegg), *Grim* 48.1; Broadhat (Sidhott), *Grim* 48.1; Burden-god
   (Farmatyr), *Grim* 48.2; Equal-high (Iafnhar), *Grim* 49.6; Father of Hosts
   (Herfodur), *Seer* 30.1, 42.2; *Vaf* 2.1; *Grim* 19.2, 25.1, 26.1; *Seer(H)* 34.2;
   Father of Men (Aldafodur), *Vaf* 4.3, 53.1; Father of the Slain (Valfodur),
   Seer 1.3, 28.4, 29.7; *Grim* 48.2; Flame-eyed (Baleyg), *Grim* 47.3; General
   (Herian), *Seer* 31.5, *Grim* 46.2; Hellblind (Helblindi), *Grim* 46.4; Helm-
   wearer (Hialmberi), *Grim* 46.2; High (Har), *Seer* 22.3; *Grim* 47.2; *Seer(H)*
   27.3; High One (Havi), *High* 109.2, 111.6, 164.1; Known (Thekk), *Grim*
   46.3; Mask (Grim), *Grim* 46.1, 47.4; Masked One (Grimnir), *Grim* 47.4;
   Much-wise (Fiolsvid), *Grim* 47.4; Terrible One (Ygg), *Seer* 29.2; *Grim*
   53.1, 54.1; Third (Thridi), *Grim* 46.3; Victory-father (Sigfodur), *Seer* 52.1;
   Grim 48.1; Victory-god (Sigtyr), *Atli* 30.3; Wanderer (Gangleri), *Grim*
   46.1; *Grim* 48.1; War-merry (Herteit), *Grim* 47.2; Way-tame (Vegtam),
   Baldr 6.1, 13.1; Weak-eyed (Bileyg), *Grim* 47.3; Woe-father(?) (Vafodur):
   Seer(H) 1.3
Odlings, a clan: *Hynd* 11.4, 16.2, 26.3
Odrerir, a name for the mead of poetry or its container: *High* 107.3, 140.4
Offspring (Mog), son of Lord and Erna: *Rig* 41.2
Ofnir (1), a serpent: *Grim* 34.5
Ofnir (2), an Odinic name: *Grim* 54.5
Oin, father of Andvari: *Reg* 2.1
Olrun, a swan-maiden: *Vol* prose, 4.4, 15.2
Omi (1), an Odinic name: *Grim* 49.6
Omi (2), kinsman of Ottar: *Hynd* 24.2
Ori, a dwarf: *Fiol* 34.3
Orkning, Hogni (2)'s brother-in-law: *Green* 30.6
Ormt, a river: *Grim* 29.1
Orvasund, a place: *HH1* 24.4
Oski, an Odinic name: *Grim* 49.6
Ottar, protégé of Freyia: *Hynd* prose, 6.4, 9.2, 10.4, 12.1, 16.5 ff.
Otter (Otr), brother of Regin (2) and Fafnir: *Reg* prose

Peaceful (Frid), one of Menglod's hand-maids: *Fiol* 38.3

Rackety (Ysia), daughter of Thrall and Thrall-girl: *Rig* 13.3
Radbard, ancestor of Ottar: *Hynd* 28.4
Radgrid, a valkyrie: *Grim* 36.5
Raggedy-clothes (Totrughypia), daughter of Thrall and Thrall-girl: *Rig* 13.4
Ragnarok, the end of the world: *HH2* 40.2
Ran, goddess of the sea: *HH1* 30.4; *HHi* 18.3; *Reg* prose 3; (possibly) *Gro* 6.2
Randgrid, a valkyrie: *Grim* 36.5
Randver (1), son of Iormunrekk, hanged by him: *Whet* prose
Randver (2), ancestor of Ottar: *Hynd* 28.4
Rani, unknown figure, if not Ran: *Gro* 6.2
Ratatosk, a squirrel: *Grim* 32.1

Regin (1), a dwarf (same as (2)?): *Seer* 12.4; *Seer(H)* 12.5

Regin (2), foster-father of Sigurd: *Grip* 11.3; *Reg* prose; *Faf* prose, 22.1, 33.1 37.3, 39.1

Reginleif, a valkyrie: *Grim* 36.5

Reifnir, kinsman of Ottar: *Hynd* 23.1

Relative (Nithiung), son of Lord and Erna: *Rig* 41.3

Rennandi, a river: *Grim* 27.4

Rhine, river: *Vol* 14.2; *Grim* 27.4; *Reg* prose; *Frag* 5.1; *Short* 16.2; *Atli* 17.3, 27.3

Ridil, a sword: *Faf* prose

Rig, Heimdall's name while creating human society: *Rig* prose, 1.3, 3.1, 5.1, 14.1 ff.

Rin (the Rhine), a river: *Grim* 27.4

Rind, mother of Vali (2), avenger of Baldr: *Baldr* 11.1; *Gro* 6.3

Rodulsfiall, a place: *HHi* 43.2

Rodulsvellir, a place: *HHi* 6.2

Rogheim, a place *HHi* 43.2

Rud, a river: *Gro* 8.3

Sæfari, an ancestor of Ottar: *Hynd* 12.4, 5

Sæhrimnir, a boar: *Grim* 18.1

Sækin, a river: *Grim* 27.1

Sæmorn, a river: *HHi* 5.3

Særid, a wife of Hiorvard (2): *HHi* prose

Sævarstadir, island on which Volund is imprisoned: *Vol* 17.5, 20.4

Saga (1), a sea-goddess or possibly another name for Frigg: *Grim* 7.3

Saga (2), a headland: *HH1* 39.1

Salgofnir, a cock: *HH2* 49.4

Samsey, an island (modern Samsø): *Lok* 24.1

Sanngetal, an Odinic name: *Grim* 47.1

Saxi, a prince: *Gud3* 6.1

Sea-pool (Loni), a dwarf: *Seer* 13.3; *Seer(H)* 13.4

Sefafell, home of Sigrun in *HH2*: *HH2* 25.1, 36.1, 42.1, 45.1

Segjarn, unknown being: *Fiol* 26.3

Shagger (Kefsir), a son of Thrall and Thrall-girl, *Rig* 12.3

Shaggy (Lodin), a giant: *HH1* 25.1

Shining-mane (Skinfaxi), horse who pulls the day: *Vaf* 12.1

Shy-girl (Feima), daughter of Farmer and Daughter-in-law: *Rig* 25.3

Sid, a river: *Grim* 27.1

Sidgrani, an Odinic name: *All* 6.2

Sif, Thor's wife: *Harb* 48.1; *Hym* 3.3, 15.3, 34.3; *Lok* prose; *Thrym* 24.5

Sigar (1), messenger of Helgi Hiorvardsson: *HHi* 36.1

Sigar (2), brother of Hogni (1): *HH2* 4.6

Sigar (3), companion of Siggeir: *Gud2* 16.4

Sigarsholm, an island: *HHi* 8.1

Sigarsvoll, an estate owned by Helgi (1): *HH1* 8.2; *HH1* prose, 35.4

Sleipnir, Odin's eight-legged horse, born from Loki: *Grim* 44.4; *Sigrd* 15.4; *Baldr* 2.2; *Hynd* 40.2

Slid, a river: *Grim* 28.4

Sluggard (Drot), son of Thrall and Thrall-girl: *Rig* 12.4

Smelly (Fulnir), son of Thrall and Thrall-girl: *Rig* 12.3

Smith, son of Farmer and Daughter-in-law: *Rig* 24.2

Smoothbeard (Brattskegg), son of Farmer and Daughter-in-law: *Rig* 24.4

Snævar, son of Hogni (2): *Death*; *Green* 30.5

Snowfell (Snæfiall), an estate owned by Helgi (1): *HH1* 8.2

Sogn, a region of Norway: *HH1* 50.2

Sokkmimir, unknown person: *Grim* 50.1

Sokkvabekk, a palace: *Grim* 7.1

Solar, son of Hogni (2): *Death*; *Green* 30.5

Solheim, a place: *HH1* 47.2

Sonny (Son), son of Lord and Erna: *Rig* 41.4

Sorli, son of Gudrun and Ionakr, brother of Hamdir: *Whet* prose; *Hamd* 9.1, 21.2, 31.1

South (Sudri), a dwarf: *Seer* 11.1; *Seer(H)* 11.1

Sparins-heath: *HH1* 51.2

Sparky-girl (Ristil), daughter of Farmer and Daughter-in-law: *Rig* 25.3

Spear-Skogul (Geirskogul), a valkyrie: *Seer* 31.4

Spring-cold (Varkald), supposed name of Svipdag's father: *Fiol* 6.3

Spurwolf (Sporvitnir), a horse: *HH1* 51.2

Staff-elf (Gandalf), a dwarf: *Seer* 12.1; *Seer(H)* 11.4

Stafnsness, a place: *HH1* 23.1

Starkad, a son of Granmar: *HH2* prose, 27.1

Steady (Sad), an Odinic name: *Grim* 47.1

Stout (Klur), son of Thrall and Thrall-girl: *Rig* 12.3

Strange-Creature (Alvit), a swan-maiden (identical with Hervor): *Vol* prose

Strond, a river: *Grim* 28.5

Stumper (Drumb), son of Thrall and Thrall-girl: *Rig* 12.4

Stumpy (Drumba), daughter of Thrall and Thrall-girl: *Rig* 13.1

Styr-cleft, a place: *HH2* 27.1

Summer (Sumar): *Vaf* 27.2

Sun (Sol): *Seer* 5.1, 5.3; *Vaf* 23.2; *All* 16.1; *Seer(H)* 5.1, 5.3

Sun-blind (Solblindi)'s sons, makers of Menglod's fortress gate: *Fiol* 10.2

Sunbright (Solbjart), Svipdag's father: *Fiol* 47.1

Sunfell (Solfiall), an estate owned by Helgi (1): *HH1* 8.2

Surt, a fire-giant: *Seer* 50.1, 51.3; *Vaf* 17.4, 18.2, 50.4, 51.2; *Faf* 14.3; *Seer(H)* 41.4, 46.1, 47.3,

Suttung, a giant, possessor of mead of poetry: *High* 104.5, 109.4, 110.3; *Skir* 34.2; *All* 34.4

Svadilfari, stallion, father of Sleipnir: *Hynd* 40.2

Svafa, Hervor's mother: *Wak* 9.2

Svafnir (1), a serpent: *Grim* 34.5

Svafnir (2), an Odinic name: *Grim* 54.5

Svafnir (3), father of Sigrlinn: *HHi* prose, 1.1, 5.4

Svafrlami, previous owner of the sword Tyrfing: *Wak* 9.4

Svafrthorin, Menglod's paternal grandfather: *Fiol* 8.2

Svalin, shield in front of the sun: *Grim* 38.1

Svan, ancestor of Ottar: *Hynd* 12.4

Svanhild, daughter of Gudrun and Sigurd: *Short* 55.3, 63.2; *Death*; *Whet* prose, 8.5, 15.1, 3, 16.4; *Hamd* 2.5, 3.1

Svarang, unknown person: *Harb* 29.2

Svarinshaug, a place: *HH1* 31.3; *HH2* prose

Svarthofdi, ancestor of witches: *Hynd* 33.3

Svava (1), valkyrie lover of Helgi Hiorvardsson: *HH1* prose, 37.2, 40.1, 41.1, 43.1; *HH2* prose

Svava (2), ancestor of Ottar: *Hynd* 17.2

Svavaland, land of Svafnir (3), Sigrlinn's father: *HHi* prose

Sveggiud, a horse: *HH1* 47.2

Svid, a dwarf: *Seer(H)* 13.2

Svidrir, an Odinic name: *Grim* 50.1

Svidur, an Odinic name: *Grim* 50.1

Svipal, an Odinic name: *Grim* 47.1

Svipdag, beloved of Menglod: *Fiol* 42.2, 43.2, 44.2, 47.1

Svipud, a horse: *HH1* 47.2

Sviur, a dwarf: *Seer* 13.2

Svol, a river: *Grim* 27.2

Swanwhite (Svanhvit, also known as Hladgud), a swan-maiden: *Vol* 2.3, 4.5

Sweden: *Vol* prose; *Grott* 13.1

Sylg, a river: *Grim* 28.4

Terrible One (Ygg), *see* Odin

Thakkrad, a thrall: *Vol* 39.1

Thane (Thegn), son of Farmer and Daughter-in-law: *Rig* 24.2

Thialfi, Thor's servant: *Harb* 39.3

Thiazi, a giant, father of Skadi: *Grim* 11.1; *Harb* 19.1; *Lok* 50.4, 51.2; *Hynd* 30.4; *Grott* 9.2

Thiodmar, father of Thiodrek: *Gud3* 3.3

Thiodnuma, a river: *Grim* 28.2

Thiodrek, king captured by Atli (3): *Death*; *Gud3* prose, 2.3, 5.1

Thiodrerir, a dwarf: *High* 160.1

Thiodvar, one of Menglod's hand-maids: *Fiol* 38.2

Third (Thridi), *see* Odin

Tholl, a river: *Grim* 27.8

Tholley, an island: *HHi* 25.2

Thor, a god: *Seer* 27.1; *Grim* 4.3, 29.2; *Skir* 33.1; *Harb* prose, 9.4, 22.3, 26.3 ff.; *Hym* 16.2, 17.1, 21.4 ff.; *Lok* prose, 54.3, 55.1, 58.2, 60.4; *Thrym* 1.1, 7.4, 8.1, 9.4 ff.; *Hynd* 4.1; *Seer(H)* 23.1

Thora (1), a Dane: *Gud1* end prose; *Gud2* 14.1

Thora (2), ancestor of Ottar: *Hynd* 18.1

Wanderer, *see* Odin

War-merry (Herteitr), *see* Odin

Way-tame (Vegtam), *see* Odin

Weak-eyed (Bileyg), *see* Odin

Weatherglass (Vedrglasir), part of Mimi's tree: *Fiol* 24.1

West (Vestri), a dwarf: *Seer* 11.2; *Seer(H)* 11.2

Wind-cold (Vindkald), assumed name of Svipdag: *Fiol* 6.3

Wind-cool (Vindsval), father of Winter: *Vaf* 27.1

Wind-elf (Vindalf), a dwarf: *Seer* 12.1; *Seer(H)* 11.4

Winter (Vetr): *Vaf* 27.1

Wise (Vit), a dwarf: *Seer* 12.2; *Seer(H)* 12.3

Woe-father, either Odin or Loki: *Seer(H)* 1.3

Wolfdale (Ulfdalir): *Vol* prose, 5.1, 6.2, 13.3

Wolf-lake (Ulfsiar): *Vol* prose

Yeoman (Bondi), son of Farmer and Daughter-in-law: *Rig* 24.3

Yewdale (Ydalir), home of Ull: *Grim* 5.1

Yggdrasill ('Steed of the Terrible One' (Odin)), the World Ash: *Seer* 19.1,
    45.1; *Grim* 29.4, 30.6, 31.2, 32.2, 34.1, 35.1, 44.1; *Seer(H)* 19.1, 41.1

Ylfings, a dynasty, here = kinsman of Ylfings, Sigmund (1): *HH1* 5.1, 34.3,
    494; *HH2* prose, 4.7, 8.1, 47.2; *Hynd* 11.4

Ylg, a river: *Grim* 28.4

Ymir, primeval giant: *Seer* 3.1; *Vaf* 21.1, 28.3; *Grim* 40.1; *Hynd* 3.3; *Seer(H)*
    3.1

Ynglings, a Swedish dynasty: *Hynd* 16.2

Yngvi (1), a dwarf: *Seer* 16.1; *Seer(H)* 15.4

Yngvi (2), an ally of Hodbrodd: *HH1* 52.2

Yngvi (3), ancestor of Helgi (1) and Sigurd's clan (possibly identical with
    Freyr): *HH1* 55.2; *Reg* 14.2

Yrsa, mother and sister of Hrolf Kraki ('Crow'), legendary king of Denmark:
    Grott 22.1

Thorin, a dwarf: *Seer* 12.2; *Seer(H)* 11.4

Thorir, ancestor of Ottar: *Hynd* 22.2

Thorsness, a headland: *HH1* 40.4

Thrain, a dwarf: *Seer* 12.1; *Seer(H)* 12.3

Thrall, son of Great-grandfather and Great-grandmother: *Rig* 7.2, 11.4

Thrall-girl (Thir): *Rig* 10.3, 11.4

Thrar, a dwarf: *Seer(H)* 12.3

Thror (1), a dwarf: *Seer* 12.2; *Seer(H)* 12.3

Thror (2), an Odinic name: *Grim* 49.4

Thrud, a valkyrie: *Grim* 36.3

Thrudgelmir, a giant: *Vaf* 29.3

Thrudheim, a palace: *Grim* 4.3

Thrym, a giant: *Thrym* 6.1, 11.2, 22.1, 25.1, 30.1, 31.3

Thrymheim, a palace: *Grim* 11.1

Thund (1), an Odinic name: *High* 145.4; *Grim* 46.3, 54.2

Thund (2), a river (?): *Grim* 21.1

Thyn, a river: *Grim* 27.8

Tind, kinsman of Ottar: *Hynd* 23.2

Tough-Guy (Dreng), son of Farmer and Daughter-in-law: *Rig* 24.2

Tyr, one-handed god of oaths: *Hym* 4.3, 33.3; *Lok* prose, 38.1, 40.1;
   Sigrd 6.4

Tyrfing (1), kinsman of Ottar: *Hynd* 23.2

Tyrfing (2), a sword: *Wak* 14.2, 15.3, 18.3, 19.2, 27.3

Ud, an Odinic name: *Grim* 46.3

Ulf, ancestor of Ottar: *Hynd* 12.3, 22.2

Ulfrun, a giantess: *Hynd* 37.3

Ull, god of the bow: *Grim* 5.1, 42.1; *Atli* 30.4

Una-bay (perhaps identical with Muna-bay): *HH1* 31.1

Uni, a dwarf: *Fiol* 34.1

Unn, a well or the name of a wave: *HH2* 31.4

Urd (Fated), a fate or norn: *Seer* 19.4, 20.3; *High* 111.1; *Gro* 7.3; *Fiol* 47.3;
   Seer(H) 19.4, 20.3

Vadgelmir, a river: *Reg* 4.2

Vafthrudnir, a wise giant: *Vaf* 1.2, 2.4, 3.4, 6.1 ff.

Vafud, an Odinic name: *Grim* 54.3

Vak, an Odinic name: *Grim* 54.3

Valaskialf, a palace: *Grim* 6.3

Valbiorg, a fortress: *Gud2* 33.3

Valdar, a warrior: *Gud2* 19.1

Valgrind, a gate: *Grim* 22.1

Valhall (Hall of the Slain—Valhalla), home of heroes after death: *Seer* 34.4;
   Grim 8.1, 23.2; *HH2* prose; *Hynd* 1.4, 6.3, 7.2

Vali, son of Odin and Rind, born to avenge Baldr: *Vaf* 51.1; *Baldr* 11.1; *Hynd*
   29.3: *Seer(H)* 31.1

Valland, land of foreigners, often a designation for what is now France: *Harb*
    24.1; *Vol* prose
Van, a river: *Grim* 28.5
Vanaheim, home of the Vanir: *Vaf* 39.1
Vandilsve, a place: *HH2* 35.2
Vanir, one of the tribes of gods: *Seer* 25.4; *Vaf* 39.4; *Skir* 17.2, 18.2, 37.4;
    Thrym 15.2; *All* 10.2, 12.2 ff.; *Sigrd* 18.5; *Seer(H)* 30.4
Var (1), goddess of promises, invoked at marriage: *Thrym* 30.4
Var (2), a dwarf: *Fiol* 34.2
Varins-bay: *HHi* 22.2
Varinsfjord: *HH1* 26.5
Varins-island: *HH1* 37.1
Ve, brother of Odin: *Lok* 26.3
Vegdrasill, a dwarf: *Fiol* 34.2
Vegsvinn, a river: *Grim* 28.1
Veor, a name of Thor: *Hym* 11.5
Verdandi (Becoming), a fate or norn: *Seer* 20.3; *Seer(H)* 20.3
Verland, a place: *Harb* 56.3
Very-cold (Fiolkald), supposed name of Svipdag's grandfather: *Fiol* 6.4
Victory-god, *see* Odin
Vid, a river: *Grim* 27.1, 28.5
Vidar, son of Odin: *Seer* 52.3, 55.7; *Vaf* 51.1, 53.2; *Grim* 17.2; *Lok* prose, 10.1;
    Seer(H) 49.4
Vidofnir, a cockerel: *Fiol* 18.1, 24.1, 25.3, 30.2
Vidolf, ancestor of seeresses: *Hynd* 33.1
Vidrir, an Odinic name: *Lok* 26.3; *HH1* 13.4
Vidur, an Odinic name: *Grim* 49.5
Vigblaer, Helgi (1)'s horse: *HH2* 36.4
Vigdal, a place: *HH2* 35.2
Vigrid, a plain: *Vaf* 18.1
Vili (1), a dwarf: *Seer* 13.2; *Seer(H)* 13.2
Vili (2), Odin's brother: *Lok* 26.3
Vilmeid, ancestor of wizards: *Hynd* 33.2
Vilmund, lover of Borgny, killer of Hogni (2): *Odd* prose, 6.1
Vin, a river: *Grim* 27.8
Vina (the Dvina), a river: *Grim* 28.1
Vinbiorg, a fortress: *Gud2* 33.3
Vingi, Atli (3)'s messenger: *Death*; *Green* 4.1, 32.2, 33.1, 39.1, 41.1
Vingskornir, a horse: *Faf* 44.2
Ving-Thor, name for Thor: *All* 6.1
Virvir, a dwarf: *Seer* 15.3; *Seer(H)* 15.3
Volsungs, family line of Sigmund (1) and Sigurd: *HH1* 52.4; *HH2* prose; *DS*;
    Reg 18.1; *Short* 1.2, 3.3, 13.6; *Hynd* 26.1
Volund, a smith: *Vol* prose, 2.5, 5.1, 6.2 ff.
Vond, a river: *Grim* 28.5